VINLAND VOYAGE

J. R. L. ANDERSON

Vinland Voyage

Come, my friends,
'Tis not too late to seek a newer world.
TENNYSON, *Ulysses*

Funk & Wagnalls   New York

First published in Great Britain 1967
© 1967 J. R. L. Anderson
Library of Congress Catalog Card Number: 67-27234

Contents

INTRODUCTION by George D. Painter   *page* 11
AUTHOR'S PREFACE   15
1 Wellington Dock   19
2 The Vinland Story   22
3 An Expedition Forms   33
4 Dover to Scarborough   49
5 On Our Own   61
6 To the Faeroes   76
7 A Rough Passage to Iceland   89
8 An Ambassador Comes to Tea   104
9 Beards and Other Matters   113
10 'Ice now dominates our thoughts'   126
11 Greenland   144
12 Navigational Detective Work   157
13 Trapped in the Ice   179
14 Off Labrador and Newfoundland   195
15 A Week of Fog   218
16 To Vinland   240
17 A Footnote in History   253

APPENDICES
i *Griffin*   263
ii Time and Distance Run   263
iii Entrance to Nantucket Sound – Extract from Log   267
iv Radio   268
v Medical Supplies   271
vi Stores   272
vii Bibliography   275

Illustrations

Between pages 144–5
1 The Vinland Map
2 J. R. L. Anderson, Peter Haward, T. R. Lee
3 Peter Comber, R. A. Garrod, Allister McIntosh
4 Checking stores
5 Painting the topsides
6 Five thousand miles to go
7 Allister McIntosh and Reg Garrod
8 Keeping the journal
9 Peter Comber and Peter Haward
10 Heavy weather
11 Repairing a sail
12 Statue of Leif Eiriksson at Reykjavik
13 Moment of calm
14 a *Weather Adviser*
   b Dangerous ice
15 Iceberg and fog
16 a The *Griffins*
   b Under way

ACKNOWLEDGMENTS

Acknowledgments are due for permission to reproduce the following pictures: to the author for nos 7(a), 8(b), 9, 13, 14, 15; to J. R. Freeman & Co. for no. 1; to the *Guardian* for nos. 2, 3, 4, 5, 6, 7(b), 8(a), 11, 16; to Peter Haward for no. 10; and to Mats Wibe Lund Jr. for no. 12.

Introduction

by GEORGE D. PAINTER

In May and June 1966 John Anderson and his five companions sailed in a small but apparently unsinkable ocean-yacht, the *Griffin*, on the *Guardian* newspaper's Vinland Expedition, following the old Norsemen's route via the Faeroes, Iceland and Greenland to the north-east coast of America. Their leader, as it turns out, is not only a brave man and efficient sailor like his comrades, but an instinctive scholar and a born writer. The *Vinland Voyage* is an important contribution through direct action to the still unsolved problems of the tenth- and eleventh-century Norse discovery of America; but the reader will probably feel as I do that it is also a literary classic of twentieth-century adventure at sea.

I suppose John Anderson did me the unmerited honour of inviting me to introduce his fine book partly because we share an interest in the mystery of Vinland, and partly because I was concerned in the publication of Yale University's Vinland map, which was the unpredictable cause or pretext for his journey. During seven years of working on and living with the Vinland map the three co-authors had foreseen most of the consequences, both logical and illogical, of its publication. However, our crystal balls never showed us that there would be anyone sensible and crazy enough, practical and reckless enough, to decide to sail to Vinland himself. Historians or biographers and their readers know that the past is permanently alive, that people and their actions never die. But here was a totally unexpected proof that a piece of parchment is as violent as a bomb, as compelling as a dream, that Leif Eiriksson can speak directly to a modern man across the gulf of a thousand years, and change his life.

So I first met John Anderson on October 8, 1965, at the London launching-party given by Yale University Press for *The Vinland Map and the Tartar Relation.* Tom Marston of Yale who dealt with the palaeography and physical nature of the map, and R. A. (Peter) Skelton of the British Museum who elucidated its cartography, were both out of England, and only I, their junior co-author, was able to be present, with my wife, in this benevolent but alarming jamboree of Scandinavian diplomats, of geographers, historians, radiomen and journalists. 'Here is Iceland, here is Greenland,' I said, pointing to a huge replica of our map propped on an easel, 'and here, drawn about A.D. 1440 from a model made about a century earlier, is the first and only pre-Columban outline of the coast of North America, divided into the three landfalls of the Norsemen, Helluland, Markland and Vinland.' The man standing near, whose lounge-suit seemed a disguise for oilskins, had the look on his spectacled, harassed still-young face of a gentler Captain Ahab who has just received his first news of a white whale.

Three months later John Anderson told me he had decided to sail a small boat – 'like the Norsemen' – to Vinland. 'Land changes, but it still looks the same from the sea. The sea doesn't change. We shall have their winds, and their currents, and their fogs, we shall see what they saw, and we'll go and find what happens, as they did.' The North Atlantic, with its storms, pack-ice and fogs, is the most savage sea in the world, an ultimate challenge as terrifying and tempting for the yachtsman as the Eiger North Wall for the climber. 'What will you do if you find yourselves off the coast of Labrador in an easterly gale?' 'It's quite simple,' he replied, 'in a situation like that there are certain things that you have to do and know how to do, so you do them and wait for it. And you feel better off, or no worse, than if you were sitting at home trying to cope with the children's school bills.'

They left from Scarborough, after urban civilisation had done its best for them – ICI, Exide, Shell and others were absolute trumps. The boat and radio were superb, but the rudder (which they providentially got mended at the Faeroes), the auxiliary engine (which always conked out after an hour's chugging), and the mainsail (which split again and again in different gales) were not fit to set out with. It was a horrible late spring, and the streets and gardens of southern England felt the tail-ends of the Force 9 storms that battered the *Griffin* many hundreds of miles to the northwest. I kept repeating by way of a charm the fifteenth-century poem about Englishmen who sailed

> *. . . without peril*
> *Gon and come, as men were wont of old*
> *From Scarborough unto the costes cold.*

and never thought they would escape with their lives, until they arrived. In Vinland?

There is no doubt whatever, and no serious scholar has ever doubted, that the northeast coast of America was discovered, visited and temporarily colonised by Norsemen from Greenland during the years from A.D. 985 until about twenty years later. The vivid and detailed account in the sagas of the physical appearance, climate, vegetation and native inhabitants of these lands is far too accurate to have been dreamed up by a story-teller in Greenland. It must derive ultimately from the first-hand experience of Norsemen who actually went there. Archaeological evidence is beginning to turn up: excavators in Greenland have found on Norse sites a flint arrowhead probably from Labrador, boxwork identified as American larch, a lump of anthracite coal perhaps from Rhode Island. Since 1960 Helge Ingstad has uncovered an apparently Norse settlement in northern Newfoundland, though it does not necessarily follow that this was Leif Eiriksson's Vinland. The Vinland map gives a Norse cartographer's idea (some three hundred years after the discovery and without any direct link with geographical experience) of what the Vinland coasts ought to have looked like. But all this evidence still leaves the exact location of Vinland doubtful. Doubtful, that is, unless we pick out the two features which the sagas emphasise most strongly, and which are true of one tract of coast and fit no other. According to the sagas Vinland was on or near a long stretch of sands that the astonished Norsemen called Furdustrands, or Wonder-sands, and wild grapes grew there. Furdustrands suits the enormous and unique sandspit of Cape Cod and the New England coast southward, but nowhere else; and wild grapes grow there to this day. I am sure that John Anderson was right in deciding to make for Martha's Vineyard: Vinland was either there or near there, on that same coast.

Had his journey any scientific value? Of course it had: it represented the very testing of documentary evidence by practical experiment which armchair scholars need, but do not always realise that they need. John Anderson has shown, paradoxically, that these stay-at-home Vinland-seekers have looked too closely at the land on their maps, whereas the Norsemen sailed without maps on the everchanging, neverchanging ocean, driven by wind, fog and seamanship. The voyagers on the *Griffin* had Bjarni's fog, Bjarni's and Leif's northeaster. The modern map shows how Labrador (Helluland) and Newfoundland (Markland) trend southeast, until a sharp right-angled turn leads southwest to Nova Scotia and New England. Until now I could never understand, though I was sure it happened, how or why the Norsemen turned this bend. Now it is clear that Bjarni, fogbound in a northeaster from Iceland, missed it altogether and drove straight upon Nova Scotia; while for Leif, in a northeaster from Greenland, this very bend was a welcome release from the dangerous leeshores of Labrador and Newfoundland: once he had turned it, he could sail safely before the same northeaster to Cape Cod and Vinland. That is what happened to the *Griffin*, and I am now convinced that it is what happened, a thousand years ago, to Leif Eiriksson.

John Anderson has travelled through time as well as place – through the lost time of the past and the borrowed time of the present. He has brought new life and truth to a moment in history, and sailed the round trip from urban civilisation to the edge of the world and back again. Perhaps it is no less an achievement to have communicated these experiences in a superb book. The *Vinland Voyage* is wildly funny, extremely frightening, humane and kind and moving, beautifully written and constructed. Perhaps it will be a bestseller, and perhaps people will still read in fifty or a hundred years' time the story of Anderson, Reg Garrod, Peter Haward, Tim Lee, Peter Comber and Allister McIntosh, those six good men and true. There is also a seventh hero, or heroine: the wife who encouraged Anderson to go, as he had to, and waited for him to return alive.

Preface

In this book I have tried to do two things: to present a straight-forward record of our voyage in *Griffin*, nearly five thousand miles under sail to the Faeroes, Iceland, Greenland and North America, and to add a little to the accumulating store of knowledge of the Norse discovery of America close on a thousand years ago. This is one of the forgotten chapters of history – we know more of Egypt three thousand years ago than of North America at the time of the Norman Conquest of England. But facts are coming to light, and to the next generation of schoolchildren, perhaps, the story of Leif Eiriksson will be as familiar as that of Christopher Columbus. It is a fascinating story, not all of which is yet known. But enough is known to make it clear that men and women of European stock settled in America, and tried to establish a homeland there, some five centuries before Columbus sailed.

There would have been no Vinland Expedition without the *Guardian*. Newspapers are accused, sometimes justly, of many sins, but they do more than is often realised to further knowledge. The *Guardian* let me plan and carry out the Vinland Expedition with absolute freedom to do what I thought fit. I had the idea of going to look for Vinland, and the *Guardian* gave me the means to pursue it. You can't ask more than that. If we have added anything to history, we owe it primarily to two men, Laurence Scott, chairman of the company that owns the *Guardian*, and Alastair Hetherington, the editor.

An expedition, however, needs many kinds of help, and we were given much. Lists of acknowledgments often seem written merely from a sense of duty: I wish I could convey the sense not alone of gratitude but of pride with which I compile mine. Why should a great industrial company go to endless trouble to provide equipment for individuals who want to cross an ocean, or a desert, or a range of mountains in search of something or other? The cynic may say, 'Oh, they do it for publicity.' In fact, there is seldom much publicity, and it would be vastly easier to spend money on more normal forms of advertising. The truth is that industry, for all its commercial aspects, has a warm humanity for which it is seldom given credit. Marconi International Marine, Exide, ICI, Shell Mex and BP, Henri-Lloyd, Vacuum-Reflex, Aladdin Industries, Edward Lumley and Sons (Insurance), Smith and Nephew, and many others, helped us generously.

I have dedicated this book to the companions who sailed with me. Expressions of gratitude are so overworked that at best they sound conventional and fulsome. Words cannot repay loyalty and courage. I cannot envisage a grander ship's company than *Griffin's*. I will leave it at that. It remains for me to add that where I have drawn on other men's scholarship, notably the work of Captain J. Kr. Tornoe, Mr George Painter, Mr R. A. Skelton and Professor Gordon Manley, I have acknowledged it, and that the views and opinions in this book are solely my own responsibility.

                                          J. R. L. ANDERSON

for the *Griffins*
Reg Garrod
Peter Haward
T. R. Lee
Peter Comber
Allister McIntosh

I

Wellington Dock

I am sitting in Wellington Dock, Dover, on the third fine day we have had – only three days without rain or snow since we started. And it is clouding over now and looks like rain. Disaster during the night when a wretched boat came alongside *Griffin* about 1 a.m. and the crew wrecked our hardly-acquired deck paint by clambering all over it. Tim Lee, Peter Comber and I were loading stores until 12.15 a.m. This morning, shopping – the hydrometer most important, and other oddments. Peter Comber is now dealing with bonded stores. Tim Lee is looking after bosun's stores, making twenty-four fathom warps, etc. There was a slight crisis when Whitbread's liquor came unexpectedly with a Customs officer at noon – they were expected at 3 p.m. tomorrow. The Customs were nice and trusted me with bonded liqour until 3.30 p.m. this afternoon, when they are coming back. Goodness knows where we are going to stow it for sealing. The BBC wants me to go over to Canterbury for an interview at 4 p.m. This is a desperate nuisance, but I don't want to let them down. I went up the masthead in a bosun's chair to grease blocks and shrouds. Made a fearful mess of my trousers and pullover.

That was written on Monday, April 25, 1966, a couple of days before we sailed from Dover in the 44-ft cutter *Griffin* to try to rediscover America by the old Norse route, via Iceland and Greenland, of about one thousand years ago. Those last days of preparation at Dover were, I suppose, a beginning; but they were not really the start. Why try to rediscover America? Why set out in an overcrowded small boat for some months of at least intense discomfort, and possibly danger? I find these questions not easy to answer, even for myself. From my childhood in the West Indies I have loved boats, and this was a chance of a fine small-boat voyage. But not exactly a yachting voyage; the seas off Greenland, Labrador and Newfoundland are inclined to be rough, and hazardous with ice and fog. With my fifty-fifth birthday only two months away, I ought, perhaps, to have grown out of falling for the bright eyes of adventure. Unsettlement in middle-age is not uncommon; but was I unsettled? I had a good job with the *Guardian*, a pleasant home in a Berkshire village in the Vale of the White Horse, a family who apparently like me, and to whom I am deeply attached.

Yet I had to sail in *Griffin* – had planned the whole voyage so that I could sail in her. Some six months before this, one autumn afternoon in 1965, a parcel from Manchester had brought me a book to review, called *The Vinland Map and the Tartar Relation*, published by Yale University Press. It was heavy, and large chunks of it seemed to be in medieval Latin. I turned over some pages, and suddenly I found that tingling at the end of one's fingers that comes only once or twice in a lifetime on opening a book. This was not just another book: it was a document of the first historical importance, for it recorded the discovery, by Yale University Library, of a map showing an unquestionably authentic outline of the coast of North America – *drawn (or copied) at least fifty years before Columbus sailed*. It was as exciting as the late Michael Ventris's decipherment of the Cretan inscriptions – more exciting, because Minoan Crete, although vastly important in the development of early Greek civilisation, was not in itself a new world. The Yale map showed the New World as known in Europe long before it is commonly supposed to have been discovered. It seemed (and seems) to me that much of the history of Northern Europe at the end of the Middle Ages, and the whole of the pre-Columban history of America, need rewriting in the light of the discovery of the Yale map.

The map absorbed my thoughts. I wrote about it for the *Guardian*, took it home, and lived with it. I knew something of the old Icelandic sagas recording the discovery of a legendary land called Vinland, because I have always been interested in the history of navigation. The Yale map proves beyond doubt that Vinland was on the eastern seaboard of North America. But where? As I thought more

and more about the Vinland map, I began to want more and more
to go to look for Vinland. For although the map confirms the saga-
stories of old Norse settlements in North America, cartographically
it is not in anything like enough detail to show where Vinland was.
Vinland may have been anywhere from Labrador to Virginia.

2

The Vinland Story

Where was Vinland, and what is known of it? The main historical sources are in the old Icelandic sagas, notably two, *The Grænlendinga Saga* and *Eirik's Saga*. These have been known, at least to a limited field of scholarship, for centuries. They record the emigration from Iceland to Greenland in the tenth century of a man known as Eirik the Red, and later voyages from Greenland to Vinland by Eirik's son Leif and various relations and relations by marriage of Eirik's clan. But the sagas are unsatisfactory history. They began as family records composed by Icelandic storytellers, and were handed down from generation to generation by word of mouth. They were not put into writing until some centuries after they were composed. To some professional historians oral history is not good history – clearly it cannot be checked by reference and cross-reference as written documents can be checked, and in the course of time errors and embellishments of one sort and another can creep in. But although it may not be history in a strictly academic sense, oral history is not necessarily to be dismissed as fairy-tale.

Most personal family history is oral history: a mother tells her daughter of interesting things that her own grandparents did, and so family records and traditions are created and survive. They do tend to get a bit mixed up: one human lifetime is a short span of years and even in one century a man is liable to be confused with his father.

Moreover, the Icelandic sagas were composed primarily to record genealogies and the doings of ancestors – we like our ancestors to be a little larger than life because their greatness tends to glorify us, so inevitably some of the actions of Icelandic ancestors now seem exaggerated. They also tend to become mixed with myth and magic. Nevertheless, the record of the Icelandic sagas is credible and coherent, and even before the discovery of the Vinland map most people who went into them at all believed that they embodied historical truth.

As far as Vinland is concerned they begin with a voyage by a man called Bjarni Herjolfsson, who about the year 986 of our calendar discovered America by accident. Bjarni seems to me to be in one sense one of the saddest and in another one of the most maddening figures in history, for he discovered America, but forfeited all claim to be regarded as its discoverer because he did not bother to land there. He was an Icelandic merchant shipowner, who traded between Iceland and Norway. The round voyage and the collection and sale of cargoes used to take about a year and at the end of one trip, when he returned to Iceland, he discovered that his father had gone off to Greenland with Eirik the Red. So he decided to go to Greenland to look for him. This was not an easy decision for, in tenth-century Iceland, Greenland was about as remote and mysterious as, perhaps, Tierra del Fuego seems to us. Its very existence had been discovered only a year or two before by Eirik the Red, and in Bjarni's time hardly anyone in Iceland knew how to get there. The saga account is moving. Bjarni asked his crew whether they were prepared to go off with him to Greenland, observing candidly that the voyage would probably be considered foolhardy because none of them knew the way. However, Bjarni's reputation as a seaman obviously stood high, for his crew all agreed to sail with him. It was not a happy voyage. They knew that Greenland lay vaguely west of Iceland, so they set off in that general direction. But after three days at sea a northerly gale sprang up and they were driven fast and far to the south. They had worse luck still, for they ran into fog and for what the sagas describe as 'many days' they did not see the sun. This was a disaster to them, for the sun was all-important to Norse seamen. They had no navigational instruments as we know them, no accurate timepieces and no means whatever of reckoning longitude. They navigated by latitude and the sun, and without the sun they did not know where they were. All that Bjarni and his crew did know was that they were being driven far off their course for Greenland. After an unspecified time of 'many days' they were blown out of the fog

and saw not only the sun but a strange coastline. The sun told them
that they could not be anywhere near Greenland, but must be very
far to the south. The coast, which they described as 'not mountainous but well wooded and with low hills', seemed attractive.
Bjarni's crew wanted to go ashore and have a look at it, but Bjarni
himself did not want to. He sailed fairly close inshore, but would
not allow anybody to land. If this seems miserably unenterprising
now, one must try to look at things from Bjarni's point of view. His
ship and his cargo were his sole possessions, he was not exploring,
and he wanted to get to his father in Greenland. Obviously this
coast was not Greenland – he had no idea whether it was a friendly
land, or whether the local inhabitants might be fierce and hostile.
The Norsemen were accustomed to getting a rough reception when
they put into somebody else's country – not surprisingly for, although by Bjarni's time the Norse were more interested in trading
and settlement than piracy, the record of the Vikings as pirates and
sea raiders is among the bloodiest in history. Bjarni took bearings of
the sun and knew that he had to get a long way north. Since the
wind was apparently favourable by this time, he went north, leaving
the land to port. Clearly, this was some part of the North American
coastline – just where it probably was I shall discuss later. Bjarni went
on sailing northward and after a few more days he sighted land once
more. This land is described in the saga as 'flat and wooded', and the
crew were even more impatient to go ashore. The saga here is very
human – the crew complained that they needed fresh water and
firewood, and that they would have to go ashore to get them. One
can see and sense the incidents on Bjarni's ship through the mists of
a thousand years. 'Look, Skipper,' one can hear the mate saying, 'it's
no good telling the men that they have got to sail on. They're
pretty fed up with this voyage and a run ashore would do everybody good.' And from the foredeck one can hear the grumbles –
'We don't know where we are or where the hell we're going –
why can't the old man put in and at least let us top up the water
casks?' But Bjarni was adamant. He told the crew roundly that they
had enough water and firewood on board, and that he was damned
if he was putting in. He was still a long way from Greenland and he
was determined not to hazard his ship and his cargo before he got

there. He was helped at this point by the coming of a good south-westerly wind which was a fair wind for the northing and easting that they had to make to get to Greenland. So they sailed on. After a few more days they sighted land again – 'high and mountainous and topped by a glacier'. By this time they were getting pretty far north up the Labrador coast and the shore was far from attractive. Men who had been cramped up in the ship, perhaps for more than a month, were still anxious to get ashore but Bjarni's view that the place seemed to be worthless was apparently accepted without much argument. Again they sailed on, and four days later they came to yet another coast. I quote from the translation of the *Grænlendinga Saga* by Magnus Magnusson and Hermann Palsson: 'The men asked Bjarni if he thought this would be Greenland or not. "This tallies most closely with what I have been told about Greenland," replied Bjarni, "and here we shall go into land." They did so and made land, as dusk was falling, at a promontory which had a boat hauled up on it. This was where Bjarni's father, Herjolf, lived and it has been called Herjolf's Ness for that reason ever since. Bjarni now gave up trading and stayed with his father and carried on farming there after his father's death.'

It was one of the luckiest landfalls in the history of navigation – to strike Greenland at precisely the right spot after being hopelessly lost and wandering over thousands of square miles of the North Atlantic, the Labrador Sea and the Davis Strait seems almost beyond credibility. This is the kind of thing that casts doubt on the sagas, because although it just could have happened, it is all but beyond belief. But one must remember what the sagas were: Bjarni was an important ancestor and his descendants would want to credit him either with super-human skill in navigation, or with semi-magical powers. I have no doubt that in the end he made Greenland safely and found his father – there is plenty of evidence for this – and if he had to search the west Greenland coast for some hundreds of miles before doing so I think it is understandable that the composer of his saga preferred to omit what may have seemed to him to be tedious and unnecessary detail. One can understand the exasperation that the sagas bring to those who try to work out precisely what is their real historical content, for they *are* exasperating, but I am sure that it is utterly wrong to dismiss them as a whole because of incidents that sometimes border on the miraculous or magical. In the long Greenland or Icelandic nights men and women needed a bit of magic.

To understand the next bit of the story, it is necessary again to go back a little in time. Eirik the Red was the son of a Norwegian called Thorvald, and he and his father left their home in Norway for Iceland 'because', as the saga puts it tersely, 'of some killings'. On account of this Eirik is sometimes regarded as a sort of blood-thirsty old pirate, but this is unfair. In the days before there was much central authority in Scandinavia men had to be a law to themselves, and family feuds inevitably led to fighting. In such fighting men get killed – it is not murder as we understand it. Viking feuds were long-lasting affairs, liable to be carried on from generation to genera-tion, and if you happened to kill a member of a powerful clan it was the course of wisdom to go off and live somewhere else. This hap-pened to Eirik and his father, so they departed for Iceland which, in the past century, had been settled by their Norwegian kinsfolk, and were able to take possession of some land there. The remoteness of Iceland then must be understood – in modern times to go there would be like emigrating to Australia or New Zealand: but even that is an unreal comparison because modern communications have shrunk the whole world. In Eirik's time, Iceland was at the rim of the known world. He and his father made their home first at a place called Drangar, where Thorvald died. After this, Eirik made rather a good marriage to a woman called Thjodhild, whose family had better land in the district known as Haukadale. On his marriage Eirik moved there and established a patriarchal home, for himself and his family, which became known as Eirikstead. But things did not go altogether well for him. He had trouble with his neighbours, and again there were incidents that led to killings. Iceland at that time was run by its leading families on a patriarchal system, but in accordance with Norse tradition the leading men came together periodically in a parliament which was recognised as having general authority. As a result of his troubles Eirik was banished from Haukadale by the assembly and driven off to a district of small islands in Breidaford. I have seen these islets, and even in the tenth century when men were content with rougher lives than anything we can now imagine they could not have provided much of a living. The enemies Eirik had made in the various vendettas in which he had become involved pursued him. So he took to the sea with such kinsmen and dependants as could be persuaded to follow him, and sailed off westwards, where there were vague rumours of new land. He did not have much choice. He could not go back to Norway because of the old feuds there, and he had made Iceland too hot to hold him. A century or so earlier he could have raided England, but this was the tenth century and England was becoming better organised against piratical Viking raids. So Eirik sailed off to the west. His ship might easily have foundered and he would have disappeared from history, but as things turned out he made the east coast of Greenland – one of the most desolate and icebound coasts in the world. He sailed round it to the south, weathering Cape Farewell, and put in at a fjord in the southwest at a place that is now called Julianehaab. Here he established a homestead, which naturally became known as Eiriksfjord. After three winters he decided to make his home there permanently, and went back to Iceland to try to attract a few more settlers. He called his new land 'Greenland' because, as the saga puts it, 'he said that people would be more tempted to go there if it had an attractive name'. It was a notable bit of real estate promotion.

The fjords on the west Greenland coast are just capable of settlement, but nowadays they can scarcely be regarded as good agricultural country. There is some evidence that the climate has worsened slightly since Eirik's time, but even in his day the life that Greenland offered must have been hard and poor. But it offered independence, and to men as tough as the Norsemen it offered a home. To Iceland, Eirik's discovery of Greenland came as a godsend, for Iceland was becoming over-populated, and enterprising Icelanders needed new land if they could find it. So Eirik's account of the new land in Greenland attracted a great deal of interest, and enough people to fill twenty-five ships agreed to emigrate there with him. It must have been an appalling voyage, for the sagas record that of the fleet of twenty-five vessels that sailed with Eirik, only fourteen made Greenland. These fourteen ships, however, carried enough people to start a colony, and they settled around Eiriksfjord (modern

Julianehaab), recognising Eirik as their leader. The Norse colony in Greenland gradually extended northwards, forming separate and more or less independent settlements along the coast. Eirik's own settlement, and the farms grouped around it, became known as the Eastern Settlement. Farther north, around Godthaab, a group of families established what was called the Western Settlement. Between Godthaab and Julianehaab, around Ivigtut, some fifty miles south of Frederikshaab, grew up what was called the Middle Settlement. Less is known of this than of the Eastern and Western Settlements. Archaeologists have done much work around Julianehaab, and traces of Eirik's homestead and of a church built by his wife have been found. Thjodhild's church is one of the oldest in North European Christendom, and there is a moving little story attached to it. She herself became a convert to Christianity, but Eirik clung to his old Norse paganism, worshipping the old Norse gods. He is recorded as telling his wife that he was prepared to accept that her religion was really better than his, but that he was too old to change. This seems to have annoyed his wife, for although they apparently remained on reasonably good terms, she refused to go on living with him.

This was the situation in Greenland when Bjarni Herjolfsson rejoined his father, who was one of those who had emigrated with Eirik. Bjarni reported on the new lands he had seen far to the south and west, and he was much criticised for not having gone ashore to explore them. Among those who were most interested in his story was Eirik's son Leif, known to later history as Leif Eiriksson, or by his nickname of Leif the Lucky. Leif was a man of great ability, and he seems also to have been a man of exceptional integrity. When he met Bjarni, Eirik was ageing, and Leif knew that he was about to succeed him as leader of the Greenland colonies. He took this leadership with a high sense of responsibility. The colonies were growing, and the fjords and thin valleys of the west Greenland coast were not capable of supporting much more in the way of population. So Leif, knowing that he must find new land or new resources somewhere for his people, was deeply interested in Bjarni's story. In the end he bought Bjarni's ship from him and set off himself to try to sail back along the route of Bjarni's voyage, to explore the lands that Bjarni had seen. Leif, like his mother, was a Christian and through-out his life he held his faith with deep conviction. This is important to a later understanding of the Vinland colonies.

Leif set off on his voyage of discovery about the year 1001. Dutifully he had asked his father Eirik to lead the expedition and at first Eirik had consented. But on the way to the ship Eirik fell from his horse. Regarding this accident as an ill omen, he handed over the leadership of the expedition to his son, saying that in any case he felt too old to be involved in it. It was a wise decision, for Leif turned out to be a superb leader. Where did he go?

Since the rest of this book is mainly about trying to work out Leif Eiriksson's landfalls in the New World I shall content myself here with saying briefly where I believe he went: the evidence and the explanations will come later. He crossed the Davis Strait, making his first landfall somewhere on the northern coast of Labrador or per-haps even as far north as Baffin Island. He agreed with Bjarni that this was worthless land. He did, however, give it a name – he called it 'Helluland', which means literally 'Land of Flat Stones'. That is as good a description as one could want of this icy and rockbound coast. It must be remembered that Leif was looking for land that could be settled, and clearly Helluland could not. He sailed on southwards and came to Bjarni's second land, a coast densely wooded but with not much else in its favour for settlement. Leif called this Markland, which means 'Land of Forests'. It was not worthless to the Green-landers, for they needed timber almost as much as food – timber for building ships and houses. Greenland and Iceland had no timber, and its importance in the economy of the eleventh-century Norsemen can scarcely be over-stressed.

Markland was clearly a useful source of timber, but southern Labrador was scarcely an enticing area for settlement. Here, I think, one must consider carefully all that is known of Bjarni's own voyage, and also what sailing directions Leif might have been able to get from him. The saga records definitely that when Bjarni had been blown out of the fog and saw his first coast, he also saw the sun 'and got his bearings'. Not much is known of the details of early Norse navigation, but it is certain that these Norse seamen knew a great deal about latitude and were able to take, and to record, observations on the sun. Bjarni would certainly have given Leif whatever navigational details he had, and his sun sights would have been the most important of them. Leif was an outstanding seaman and from his own observations at the Markland stage of his voyage he would have known that he was not yet nearly sufficiently far south to have reached Bjarni's first landfall. Moreover, he would also have known, from Norse experience in Europe, that the best lands for settlement tended to lie to the south. So I am sure that he went on sailing southwards, coasting past Newfoundland which, since he knew nothing of the St Lawrence River, he would have taken to be an extension of southern Labrador. The saga record of Leif's voyage states precisely that on leaving Markland 'they sailed away to sea in a northeast wind'. This would have taken them quickly along the Newfoundland coast, and it would also have made that coast a lee shore, on which Leif, as a prudent seaman, would have had no wish to try to land. On passing Cape Race at the southern tip of Newfoundland I think that Leif would have continued to sail south, but that he would also have followed the trend of the coast as well as he could – Norse seamen were accustomed to making coastal voyages, and on an exploring voyage it would obviously have been a comfort to know that land was not very far away. If Leif's northeasterly held – and there is nothing to suggest that it did not – he would have sailed southwest on weathering Cape Race, bringing him towards Nova Scotia. I think that he went on in this general direction as long as his fair wind held and that he made his final landfall on Cape Cod, sailing on into Nantucket Sound and landing on the island off the Massachusetts coast that is now called Martha's Vineyard. The evidence for this I shall produce in detail later. For the moment I shall say simply that I believe Leif's Vinland to have been in the area of the United States that is now called New England.

Much of this could have been worked out or at least deduced in a speculative way from the sagas alone, before the Yale map was ever heard of. The discovery of the map was like finding a missing piece in a jigsaw puzzle – suddenly oddly-shaped bits fall into place, and what was speculation becomes history. In some ways even more interesting than the map itself is a Latin inscription on it recording a visit to the Vinland colonies by a Papal Legate in the year 1117. The inscription says this:

Henricus, Bishop Legate of the Apostolic See in Greenland and the neighbouring regions, entered this extensive and most wealthy country (Vinland) in the last year of our most Holy Father Pascal, in the name of God Almighty; he remained for a long time both in summer and in winter, and then returned northeast to Greenland, whence in most humble obedience to superior command he proceeded. . . .

'Henricus' here is the Latinised version of the name Eirik and the bishop referred to is a known historical figure, Bishop Eirik Gnupson. George Painter, of the British Museum, one of the scholars who worked on the Yale map, and one of the co-authors of the Yale University's book, has this to say about the inscription on the map and Bishop Eirik's visit:

This sober and weighty statement both as a whole and in detail seems hardly open to adverse criticism. It could be dismissed as a fabrication only by an act of arbitrary incredulity and we may take it *ex hypothesi* as authentic. When seen in its historical context it is both confirmed and illuminated. Bishop Eirik's mission falls precisely within the period when Pope Pascal II (1099–1118) was spreading and reorganising the papal control of Scandinavia and the north colonies. In 1106 Pascal had appointed John the first Bishop of Holar, the northern see of Iceland, and the establishment of a Greenland bishopric was the natural next step. The motives of Rome, as shown by the emphasis on the proper collection of Peter's pence in the thirteenth-century bulls relating to Greenland, were in part hierarchical and financial; but the obligation to improve the pastoral ministrations of the Church among the little-tended Greenland flock was no doubt paramount. Similarly, the motives of the Greenlanders in requiring a bishop must have been not only religious but also political and commercial.

Bishop Eirik's visit to Vinland is of the first importance in trying to lift the screen of centuries that hides the Norse colonies in North

America. A Papal Legate was not a missionary, setting off to explore
and to convert the heathen; he was an important Church official, an
ecclesiastical diplomat, concerned with Church administration and
with ensuring that the proper share of ecclesiastical revenues went to
Rome. A Papal Legate would not have been visiting Vinland in the
twelfth century unless there was something quite extensive in the
way of a colony for him to visit. The date – 1117 – is in itself of great
significance. It is an accurate date because it is not recorded in figures,
which could easily be copied wrongly in a medieval text, but given
precisely as 'in the last year' of the reign of Pope Pascal II. Since
Pascal died in 1118, Bishop Eirik's Vinland journey must have taken
place in 1117–8. This was rather more than one hundred years *after*
Leif Eiriksson's voyage, and is conclusive evidence that the settlement established by Leif became a colony in the true sense, and that
the Norsemen who settled in Vinland intended to make it their
permanent homeland. I believe that these early Norse colonies in
North America were both more extensive and much longer-lasting
than has hitherto been conjectured: and that they lasted for some
350 years, until well into the fifteenth century. This casts a whole
new light on North American history.

3

An Expedition Forms

Having got so far in my thinking about Vinland in November and December 1965, I became obsessed by the conviction that I must go to look for the place. The one certain link between our world of the twentieth century and that forgotten period of nearly one thousand years ago is the sea; the sea took Leif Eiriksson to Vinland and the sea could also take me.

I studied maps and charts. The climate of southwest Greenland may have changed slightly over one thousand years, but the sea has not changed, and the winds that blow today are the same winds that have been blowing over the ocean not for one thousand, but for tens of thousands of years. The main ocean currents must also be unchanged, because these are not a matter of surface climate but are formed by the spinning globe itself, and by the sweep of the ocean under the Arctic ice-cap coming up against the Greenland continental shelf far below the surface. It seemed to me that if I could work out from the sagas roughly where Bjarni Herjolfsson was carried when he was blown off-course, and the route that Leif Eiriksson must have followed, a small sailing boat with me on board would be carried by the forces of wind and sea to much the same landfalls that they made. I began to consider how this might be done practically.

At first, I thought that I might try to sail to Greenland and on to North America single-handed in my own small $2\frac{1}{2}$-tonner, *Mary Lane*. She would be a tiny boat for such a voyage, but small boats have crossed oceans many times in the history of the sea and I thought it might be done. In another part of my life I had been deeply involved with Francis Chichester and his fellows in the Single-handed Transatlantic Race, and although none of their boats had been quite as small as mine, I had little doubt but that my boat could make it. But then I took a hard look at myself and came reluctantly to the conclusion that, although my boat could make the voyage, I myself almost certainly could not. I am not really a very expert seaman: most of my sailing has been weekend sailing in coastal waters, and a long ocean passage through some of the stormiest seas in the world would be a very different kind of sailing. The accurate navigation required would be quite beyond me. I was ready to have a go, but I saw a real possibility – indeed a probability – that my great voyage might end ignominiously with my being wrecked on the coast of Scotland, a few days after setting out. Moreover, there was the all-important question of finance. In my involvement with the Single-handed Transatlantic Race I had contrived with Francis Chichester, with the Marconi Marine Company, and with radio experts of the Post Office, a workable system of communicating with London by radio telephone over what had formerly seemed impossible distances for radio communication from small boats. My pen or pencil have always been my livelihood, and in wondering how I could finance the voyage I naturally thought that I would have to write about it. Francis Chichester had written daily for the *Guardian*, while sailing single-handed across the Atlantic and coped alone with the radio and all the problems that it brings. But I am not Francis Chichester, nor was my boat anything like as big as his yacht. Even if I could have made the voyage I doubted whether there would have been room for the radio and the weight of its batteries.

At this point in time, when I wanted more and more to make the voyage, and the whole thing seemed more and more impossible, an old sailing friend of mine, Reg Garrod, paid a weekend visit to our cottage in the village of Charney Bassett. We went for a drink to Charney's one pub – the 'Chequers' – and in the bar I suddenly turned to Reg and said, 'Will you come to Greenland with me?' Reg said, 'Yes.' From that moment I knew that the voyage was on – I had not the least idea how to do it, but I knew that it could be done.

I took the idea of the voyage and of the attempt to reconstruct the Vinland history to Alastair Hetherington, the editor of the *Guardian*. The nice thing about newspapers is that the men who work for

them have quick imaginations, so that ideas do not need long explanations. Alastair Hetherington understood at once what I wanted
to do and said simply, 'If you think you can do it, John, go ahead.'
This made the whole thing practicable, at least to the extent that
the *Guardian* was with me, and was prepared to trust me and to
underwrite the voyage. I had Reg Garrod – but I had no other crew
and no boat. The next step was to set about obtaining both. There
was not much time. It was now Christmas 1965 and if the voyage was
to be made at all it would have to start not later than the end of April
1966. You may ask, 'Why?' In planning a historical expedition is
there any need for hurry? The world had waited the best part of a
thousand years without any great show of impatience for an attempt
to reconstruct Leif Eiriksson's voyage: would it make any difference
if my voyage was made in 1967 or 1968?

For me, the voyage would have to be made in 1966 or not at all.
My reasons for this were compelling. My whole career has been with
newspapers and the time scale in newspaper work is that things must
be done at once. The Yale map had been published in the autumn of
1965 and the first possibility of making the voyage was the late
spring of 1966 – it could not be done in winter because of the weather
and the long Arctic darkness. I could have sailed later in the year; in
many ways the voyage would have been easier in August and Septem-
ber than in May and June, because ice conditions off Greenland would
have been easier. But there is evidence in the sagas that suggests that
Leif Eiriksson sailed around midsummer, and I wanted particularly
the long hours of daylight that midsummer brings to the Davis
Strait. Around midsummer in those latitudes there is all but no
darkness, and since my greatest anxiety was ice it seemed imperative
to make the voyage when there would be light enough to see over
almost the whole twenty-four hours in the area of greatest danger.
So there was never any question in my mind but that the voyage
would have to be made in the late spring of 1966.

I set out to find a navigator. Reg Garrod, like me, is a weekend
sailor and although we might between us have struggled across an
ocean navigating by guess and by God, my responsibility to the
Guardian made it important that not too much be left to chance.
Moreover, I also felt responsible for Reg – I had involved him in this

adventure and it was my job to see that his personal safety was secured as far as possible.

In the summer of 1965 I had been involved in some international trials to select a new one-man sailing dinghy. These had taken place at Weymouth and I had met there, and liked greatly, a young naval officer, Lieutenant Commander Tim Line, who had acted as Race Officer for the trials. So I wrote to Tim Line and asked (a) whether he would like to sail to Greenland and on to some unspecified part of North America with me, and (b) whether there was any chance that the Navy might give him leave for the voyage. He responded quickly and came up to London to discuss things. But the prospects as far as he was concerned were not hopeful: although he is a fine small-boat sailor, by profession he is a computer expert, and in his special branch of the Navy there was not much likelihood of getting leave to go adventuring in the Greenland seas. So Tim Line said that there was next to no chance that he would be able to come, but that he would scout around among his naval friends and see whether there was anybody else who might like the idea of the voyage. He was as good as his word. A few days later I got a letter from Lieutenant Timothy Richard Lee, saying that Tim Line had told him about the trip and that he was game to come, if the Navy would let him. Tim Lee is a specialist in navigation, and for a navigating officer the voyage offered useful professional experience. He was, at that time, serving in a submarine, got leave for a week-end and came down to see us at Charney. We discussed things as far as we could and he agreed to sign on if the Navy would give him leave. It did.

An expedition seemed to be forming itself. I had a friend and personal mate in Reg Garrod, who I asked to be deputy leader of the expedition, and I had a navigator in Tim Lee. That was a start, at any rate. But it was now January and I still had no boat. I asked various friends and acquaintances whether they knew of any boats that might be obtainable at short notice, but nobody seemed to have any practical ideas. Then Reg came to the rescue. Another friend of his, Ernest Large, who is a school-master at Dover, suggested that a 44-ft cutter called *Griffin*, then lying at Wellington Dock, in Dover, might be both suitable and available. *Griffin* is a famous boat, and she had had a distinguished career as the club yacht of the Royal

Ocean Racing Club. But she had been built in 1938 and had been sold by the club to her present owners, the Iverson family of Dover, who had used her for fairly gentle cruising. Both Reg Garrod and Ernest Large knew Bernard Iverson and they asked him whether I could charter her for the voyage. Bernard Iverson was willing to do this, so I went to see him and to look over *Griffin*.

All boats look miserable when they are laid up in winter. *Griffin* was lying in the dock, without her mast, and with her deck stripped, unpainted, and looking as unhappy as a human being waiting on a windswept railway platform on a vile January day. I went on board her and had a look round – and I knew at once that if she could be got ready in time she was the boat I wanted. She was elderly, but so was I – we seemed to go together, and if it is not over-sentimental to say so, I felt that she was trying to tell me that she wanted to come. She had been built near Ipswich, and she is a superb example of traditional east coast boatbuilding. Everything about her is solid and heavy – built to stand up to the sea. On that first visit I could see her only laid up in the dock, but I looked at her powerful shoulders and I could see them taking gallantly whatever the sea might fling at her.

Bernard Iverson and I discussed things: he runs a yacht yard at Dover, which made things easier for getting work done on her quickly, and he thought that she could be made ready in time. He agreed to charter her to me for a year (later the *Guardian* bought her) and I went home from Dover knowing that at last I had a boat.

I still had not got a crew. In her ocean racing days *Griffin* would have been sailed by a crew of eight or nine, but that was far too many for my voyage: *Griffin*'s races – the Fastnet, the race to Santander, and others in the RORC's programme – cover only a matter of days, and I would have to store her for at least two months. It is possible to pack in crew for a race in a way that is quite impossible on an ocean voyage.

In many ways a total crew of four would have been about right: four could live in relative comfort on *Griffin*, and four men could certainly work her. But a voyage to Greenland and the ice was a fairly formidable undertaking and watch-keeping over a long period, shared only among four, would also be formidable: a tired crew is always a potential danger. I had also to consider the possibility of illness or injury. Four of us could have worked *Griffin* well enough, but one man sick or injured would have produced an immediate crisis: not only because he would reduce the working strength of the crew, but those who were left would also have to look after him. And this would be a heavy responsibility if he were badly injured. So I came to the conclusion that we ought to be six. Six of us could just manage to live on *Griffin* for a long period, and six would be a relatively strong crew: we could afford an injury, put an injured man ashore, and still have enough crew left to continue the voyage. This logistical approach may seem somewhat cold-blooded, but it is imperative when planning an expedition.

There was no lack of candidates. Months later, when we finally landed in America, I was asked by a television reporter why we had made the trip. We had just sailed in after an arduous struggle through fog, and were desperately tired. I could think of nothing to reply except by saying, 'Well, the English are well known to be mad.' Readiness to endure the discomfort of small boats is, perhaps, a form of lunacy, but it is a good form of lunacy, and I thank God for it.

As soon as it began to be known that I was planning my voyage, I was deluged with requests from people who wanted to join me. Selection was difficult and distasteful, but the process was helped greatly by the time that the expedition would take: however eager a man may be in principle to sail off to Greenland, it is not easy to take time off from the problems of earning a living. Two more members of the crew more or less selected themselves. One was Peter Comber, a housemaster at Wellington College, who managed to persuade his school to let him go for a term. The other was a young Scotsman, Allister McIntosh, whom I had known as a boat-builder and who offered to come in the capacity of ship's carpenter. I felt that I was lucky to have him – a ship's carpenter is invaluable on any sailing boat.

That made five of us, but I was still unhappy about our general capacity to work *Griffin* safely on an arduous ocean voyage. Tim Lee was a professional sailor, but the rest of us were weekend amateurs – game enough, but sadly lacking in experience of meeting an ocean in its angriest moods. I felt badly the need to have someone of long experience who could act generally as *Griffin's* sailing master or skipper while we were at sea.

I turned to another friend of mine, Alasdair Garrett, who edits the *Journal* of the Royal Cruising Club, and who has done a great deal of small-boat sailing. Alasdair liked the idea of the voyage but had so many commitments in England that he was unable to come. The selection of this last – and in many ways the most important – member of the crew was the most difficult of all; I was looking not merely for a man, but for a particular man with very special qualities. By what seems the intervention of providence, I found him.

During February, in the middle of preparations, I complicated things by going down with an attack of influenza, and I had to spend some days in bed. While in bed I read a book about sailing by a man called Peter Haward. Peter is a remarkable person – in so far as anybody can merit the term, he is unique. As a boy he learnt to sail on the Broads and when he came out of the Army after the war he had no particular job. He saw an advertisement by a man who wanted a crew to deliver a yacht from one place to another, replied to it, and was duly accepted. When he got on board, he found that the man who was to have been skipper had not turned up, and that he was expected to take charge. He contrived to deliver the yacht safely, and it then occurred to him that perhaps other yacht owners might need to have their boats delivered about the place. His idea was a good one, and he created a profession for himself as a yacht deliverer. It is an arduous profession – Peter is ready to go anywhere, and for the past fifteen years he has spent about nine months of every year at sea, sailing every conceivable kind of boat through every conceivable variety of weather. On the spur of the moment I wrote to him and asked whether he would like to join *Griffin*. I did not then know Peter Haward but a colleague of mine on the *Guardian*, David Fairhall, the paper's Shipping Correspondent, had once sailed with him when he took a large yacht from the United States to Greece. So I had at least a sort of introduction to Peter Haward: what is more, David Fairhall thought the world of him and said he thought that we would be able to get on together. This last was an important consideration, for personal relations among men living cramped together for months make all the difference between success and failure. But I got no reply to my letter, and I had almost stopped thinking about Peter Haward when one evening he rang me up out of the blue. He had only just received my letter, because he had been at sea when I wrote, and he had telephoned as soon as he came ashore. He was fascinated by the idea of the expedition and he was keen to come, but doubtful whether he could spare the time. He, too, came down to Charney – an extraordinary starting point for the re-discovery of America, but so it was; almost all the planning of the expedition was done in a cottage in this tiny Berkshire village. In the end, Peter Haward and I devised a way of making time for him to sail with me, and the expedition was then complete.

What might have been a rather difficult relationship between us worked out well, partly, I think, because we were both honest with each other, and partly because Peter is a gentle and tolerant person. I wanted Peter to take on the job of sailing *Griffin* but at the same time I could not abdicate from my own position as leader. There could have been a dangerous division of command in certain cir-stances, but we worked out things between us before we started. I was leader of the expedition and for a number of reasons, partly concerned with paperwork and port authorities, I was legally *Griffin*'s master. But I appointed Peter as *Griffin*'s sailing master and explained to the other members of the crew that Peter would have all the traditional authority of a skipper while we were at sea. This meant that I was responsible for the strategical planning of the voyage, while Peter took on responsibility for the tactical handling of the vessel. I worked out an imaginary set of circumstances to illustrate things. 'Suppose,' I said, 'I want to anchor in a particular bay in order to take a close look at a particular stretch of coastline. Suppose an onshore wind gets up and you consider that the anchorage is not safe. In such circumstances, if your judgment considers this, then I shall accept your judgment without question, and we shall up anchor and put out to sea. But if I feel that our work in that particular bay is not done and I want to go back when the weather moderates, then you must accept my decision about what I want to do.' At any rate to ourselves, this seemed to explain things perfectly and it was on this principle that we lived and sailed together. No leader of any expedition could have hoped for a better and more understanding companion than Peter Haward.

I repeated this pattern of distinct areas of responsibility in arranging the second-in-command. Reg Garrod was deputy leader, and if I had gone overboard or died he would have taken command of the expedition as a whole. But if Peter Haward were also to be put out of action, sailing responsibility would have devolved on Tim Lee. I gave much thought to these questions of pattern of command – in any human activity it is imperative that command should be clear and understood by all; men's lives may depend on this. At first sight it may seem that a system of spheres of responsibility is rather complicated, but in practice it is the only system that can really be made to work. The leader of any expedition is liable to be so bedevilled by many different things – often utterly unexpected – that it is right for him to delegate clearly defined areas of responsibility as much as possible, particularly where technical skills are concerned. And having delegated, he must not interfere.

With Peter Haward's signing on the expedition was complete – I had a ship and a crew in whom I had every confidence. I continued to get applications by almost every post from people who wanted to join, and some were from such outstanding people that it was horrible to have to say no. One thing puzzled me a little: of all the many applications to join the expedition, only one was from a woman. She wrote to me, from the United States, a rather moving letter offering to serve as cook. In a postscript to her letter she wrote, 'Do please take me seriously.' I know nothing whatever about her except that her christian name was Cherry and that she was twenty-two years old. A little regretfully I had to write declining her offer. People have asked me since why I would not take any women on the expedition. The answer is straightforward – I do not think that it would have worked. Women can be splendid sailors – my wife Helen is certainly a better helmsman than I am – but I am sure that a small expedition is best kept to one sex. Physical conditions on a small boat at sea make privacy impossible and the presence of a woman would have made much difficulty both for her and for the rest of us. Even so, I remain a little puzzled that only one woman wanted to sail with us.

Although the crew was complete by the end of February, we were far from being ready to sail. Rashly, I accepted a kindly invitation from the Mayor and Corporation of Scarborough to take our departure from there – Scarborough was celebrating the thousandth anniversary of its foundation by an Icelander called Skardi, who landed there in 966 and established a fort called Skardborg, from which the modern Scarborough gets its name. Since we were concerned with another aspect of Norse expansion from Iceland, Scarborough was a fitting place from which to sail. But civic functions have to be arranged in advance – and small sailing boats are subject always to the whims of the sea, to say nothing of the inevitable delays in making ready. Accepting the invitation from Scarborough meant getting there by April 30 and sailing on May 2 – a rash, almost a foolhardy commitment to have entered into when *Griffin*, at Dover, had not even had her mast stepped. But I did, and as things turned out, we made our sailing dates. The cost was even greyer hair than I had already. I would not embark on any such undertaking again.

I would not, indeed, embark on any other expedition of any sort in the conditions I made for myself in planning this. Perhaps it was simply faith that somehow things would be all right, but I undertook all the planning of the expedition as a spare-time job, while continuing to carry on with my normal work of the paper, up to a week before we sailed. It was an appalling time, made worse by the savage vagaries of the English climate. Instead of having a pleasant early spring, March and April brought harder weather than at any time during the winter, and when *Griffin* was ready for painting there was three inches of snow on her deck. It speaks highly for Bernard Iverson's yacht yard that things got done at all. I was able to help materially by recruiting Allister McIntosh a month before we sailed and sending him to Dover to work on *Griffin*.

It is always a miracle that any ship is ever ready for sea – in fact, I think, no vessel ever is ready. There simply comes a point when she has all her essential gear and *can* sail, and in sheer desperation you set off. The attitude of some parts of British industry did not help. Months beforehand – before I came on the scene – Bernard Iverson had decided to fit *Griffin* with roller reefing, but the metalwork was not done in time, and we had to sail with the old and laborious system of reef points. A life raft was essential equipment, and one manufacturer of inflatable rubber rafts had undertaken to supply one. At the end of March I was getting bothered by its non-arrival and a telephone call suddenly informed me that I could not have a life raft for at least another ten weeks: new regulations about the carrying of inflatable rafts by merchant ships had come into force recently and apparently there was a critical shortage of manufacturing capacity. I was angered at being told casually that I could not have a life raft within a few weeks of my sailing date, but it was no use feeling angry. The only thing was to move heaven and earth to get hold of a life raft somehow. The Beaufort people, and Captain Watts, the yacht chandler of Albemarle Street, came to the rescue and Beaufort put a raft for me on a passenger train from their factory near Liverpool. The railways then lost it, and it was another ten days before it was run to earth. Reg Garrod finally collected it personally a day or two before we sailed. But if some things went wrong, other aspects of British industry made one feel proud to be British. ICI were splendid. Not only did they present us with nylon and Terylene rope, but they also arranged with the firm of Henri-Lloyd in Manchester to equip us with the highest grade of nylon sea clothing. On the most critical parts of our voyage these garments were our salvation. Then there was the Marconi Company.

To anyone concerned with wireless or the sea the Marconi Marine Company at Chelmsford needs no introduction. But my own relations with the company have helped in a small way to make maritime history. They began in 1962, when Francis Chichester set out to beat his own time when he won the first Single-handed Transatlantic Race in 1960. He wanted to see if it was possible to report the voyage from day to day by radio telephone, a thing that had never been attempted before, and we of the *Guardian* were keen to help. The Marconi Company equipped Chichester's yacht *Gipsy Moth III* with one of its Kestrel R/T sets and the Exide Company provided batteries. The Kestrel is a beautiful little set, but the power it uses is only 50 watts, roughly half the power of an ordinary electric light bulb. Its normal use is for radio communication over relatively short distances to coastal stations – from trawlers and the like. We wanted to try to use it over ocean distances, across the whole Atlantic. Nobody really thought that it could be done, but Chichester and I were eager to try. I knew next to nothing about radio. This was a real advantage, for when experts produced all sorts of reasons to explain why this or that was impossible, I was in the strong position of being able to say, 'Well, why not try?' I got in touch with Graham Wilson, who was then Assistant Controller of Wireless Telegraphy for the Post Office, and concerned with marine wireless communications with all ships. He and his colleagues were sceptical but splendid: they thought that what I wanted to do was probably impossible, but they were ready to experiment in any way I cared to suggest. The Marconi people were the same and a small band of us – William Maconachie and George Gardiner of Marconi, Graham Wilson and his colleagues of the Post Office and I – got together in a sort of informal partnership to see just how far we could maintain direct radio contact from London with *Gipsy Moth III* at sea. I had one stroke of genius – like most strokes of genius it was, in fact, making use of the obvious. Most radio telephone calls at sea are either short messages which can be sent more or less like telegrams, or telephone calls which can be put through to ordinary telephones via the ordinary telephone system. But the Post Office itself has a great international telephone exchange at a place called Brent, in North London. Here, there is always a staff of R/T experts on duty. I asked whether, instead of trying to have calls from *Gipsy Moth III* put through on the ordinary telephone exchange, we could take them directly at Brent, and the Post Office generously agreed to this. The people at Brent set aside a small room equipped with everything possible in the way of radio telephone controls, where we could try to talk to Chichester at sea. The Marconi people, accustomed to installing wireless sets in big ships (compared with the 39-ft *Gipsy Moth III* a trawler is a big ship), went to work to devise ways and means of installing high-grade marine wireless equipment on a small wooden sailing boat. The problem seemed limitless – aerials had in some way to be fixed to the mast, but how could they be installed without interfering with all the working gear of a sailing boat, and what would happen if they were blanketed by wet sails? Insulation was another tricky matter. In the end, all these problems were solved and with the help of the engineers at Brent we remained in direct contact with Chichester right across the Atlantic to New York. Our last conversation with him on that voyage was from New York Harbour. The next year – 1963 – the partnership went to work again, this time bringing in the Muirhead Company to see whether it might be possible to transmit pictures from a small sailing boat at sea, again using the Marconi Kestrel R/T set. Dr David Lewis, who was fitting out his catamaran *Rehu Moana* for a voyage to Iceland, agreed to carry the equipment and we succeeded in transmitting the first pictures ever sent by radio telephone from a vessel at sea. By this time, the partnership had acquired so much experience that we were prepared to tackle anything in the way of long-distance communications with yachts, and in the second Single-handed Transatlantic Race in 1964 no fewer than four yachts were reporting daily via Brent.

So when it came to planning my own voyage I again turned to the Marconi Company and to the partnership. George Gardiner and his mates went to Dover to fit *Griffin* with a Kestrel, and the Post Office people and I worked out a schedule of communications. Nothing is ever as easy as it sounds: we had plenty of experience of the Kestrel and infinite confidence in it, but radio is kittle stuff, akin to magic, and requires a kindly conjunction of the planets, sunspots, and electromagnetic performance in the upper atmosphere to work happily. In the Greenland seas to which we were bound there are various magnetic hazards, and the aurora borealis seemed likely to be a nuisance. However, we made our plans in the belief that they could be carried out, and in the event there was no period of twenty-four hours in which we failed to make direct contact with London from *Griffin* – my last call was from Nantucket Sound.

As well as bristling with technical problems, international marine radio has a bureaucracy of its own which cannot be dodged. A ship, even the smallest yacht, equipped with radio, is given a call sign of her own which will be honoured by any radio station in the world in accepting calls from her. But before she is allowed to make calls she must be licensed, and she must carry a licensed wireless operator. For big ships the exams for wireless operators are a professional affair, and professional radio officers must be men of the highest skill. For yachts, the demands are tempered, but an examination has still to be passed. Reg Garrod undertook to go to Chelmsford and study the Kestrel and to take the Post Office examination required. So he became our official radio officer. What I did not know at the time was that Tim Lee, in addition to being a navigating officer in the Navy, was also a considerable expert in radio, so not only did we have Reg Garrod as our licensed operator, but we had in Tim an immensely competent naval signals officer.

In spite of the dreadful weather that early spring, the expedition took shape. Peter Haward could not join us until the day we sailed, but he managed a hurried visit to Dover to discuss gear and equipment in *Griffin*'s fitting out. Tim was still serving in his submarine and had to make a voyage to Denmark, but he too got away for a weekend between duties, and paid a visit to Dover. Reg Garrod looked after the radio side, and Peter Comber took on the vital job of acting as quartermaster and looking after stores. With the end of the Lent term at Wellington, Peter Comber was free to go to live at Dover. He slept on *Griffin*. I was still carrying on my newspaper job in London as far as I could, but I was practically commuting to Dover. A week before we sailed I joined *Griffin* there. A couple of days later Tim Lee and Reg Garrod arrived. Allister McIntosh, who was working on *Griffin* in the yacht yard, was already there. For the last few days Helen came to join me. In our own sailing she has always looked after all sorts of things on our boat, and I felt an almost childlike need for her to be around in the storing and making ready of *Griffin*. Our three young children, David (9), Timothy (7) and Ricarda (2), had to come too, because there was no one with whom they could be left.

Looking back on those horrible last days, I have no clear recollection of anything. They were not individual days, separated by sleep and night; the whole period was one time span that went on. McIntosh had to go back to his home in Scotland and we arranged that he should rejoin us at Scarborough. Everybody who was left – Reg Garrod, Tim Lee, Peter Comber, Helen and I, even the children – seemed to be at work for about twenty hours out of each twenty-four. Peter Comber had collected a mountain of provisions – they filled a whole store room. There were hundreds of tins, packets, boxes of eggs. The getting together of all these stores, a task formidable enough in itself, was only a starting point. Tins have labels on them, and paper labels do not take kindly to being stored in a small boat's bilges where they are liable to swill around in water. Nor do the outlets from bilges take kindly to being blocked by masses of sodden paper – in an emergency this can interfere dangerously with the working of the pumps. So every label had to be removed from every tin, and a code sign painted on it to identify its contents. Every egg had to be painted with a sort of egg varnish to persuade it to keep. Almost all this work was done by Peter Comber, with some help from Helen in the final stages. Then the provisions had all to be transported from the chandler's store to the quay at Wellington Dock and loaded on to the boat. It seemed impossible that they could ever be fitted in. We spent hours on our knees with *Griffin*'s floorboards up, stowing tins in every cubic inch of space that we could find. Somehow everything got done.

Then there were what seemed like miles of rope to be reeved into halliards, sheets and warps of one sort and another, sails to be bent on, checked and stored, instruments and charts to be dealt with. In her earlier years, *Griffin* had been rigged as a gaff cutter, but Bernard Iverson had decided to re-rig her as a Bermudan cutter. This meant lengthening the mast by some seven feet and getting her old mainsail recut. In my own earlier planning, I had hoped that *Griffin* would be ready for sailing trials by about the middle of April, so that we could have a week or two of shaking down and of making sure that everything worked. The dreadful weather held up work so much that there was no time for sailing trials at all – we were not ready to sail until the day we left for Scarborough. *Griffin*'s recut mainsail arrived at almost the last moment.

But we kept our sailing date of April 27. Peter Haward joined us at lunchtime, and we planned to sail in the late afternoon. My colleague, David Fairhall, also joined us for the passage to Scarborough, and Bernard Iverson, who was the only one around who had ever actually sailed *Griffin*, agreed to come to Scarborough too. When Peter Haward got on board that miserable Wednesday afternoon, he was appalled by the general mess – bits of rope everywhere, electricians still working down below and *Griffin*'s saloon looking like the worst sort of slum. 'I don't see how we can possibly sail today,' he said.

But I was determined to sail. In fact, I had left myself a day in hand for getting to Scarborough, but a sailing date postponed is a savage blow to everybody's morale. The mess on *Griffin* was mostly superficial and all the serious work of stowing had been done. Helen and the children had gone home, but Jenny, a friend of Peter's, gallantly agreed to tackle the housekeeping side. I told everybody else to clear out while she and I went below, and in half an hour the whole situation was transformed. I do not know why women have a special gift in this way, but they have. I can work hard for an hour in trying to dust and tidy up a room, and at the end of the hour it will still look a shambles. Jenny was superb. All the slum appearance in the cabin vanished, and by the time that we were through below, the deck was also beginning to look shipshape. We left the dock on the tide and spent the next hour in the outer harbour at Dover while the compass adjuster swung our compasses. The rest of us went on frantically tidying up. When the compass cards had been made out we went back to the quay in the outer harbour to put ashore Jenny, the compass adjuster and those of Bernard Iverson's yacht yard people who were working on board up to the last moment. Then we sailed.

It should have been a moving moment. If I report honestly, I must say that I was so drained of emotion that I felt absolutely nothing at all. We had sailed on our sailing date, and that was that.

4

Dover to Scarborough

Griffin was badly overcrowded. She has berths for six, but two of them are merely pipe cots – canvas stretched on iron piping – in the forepeak, where people must fit themselves in as best they can among sailbags, coils of spare rope, and masses of bosun's stores. There are two berths in what is called, politely, her main cabin, roughly amidships, and one good settee berth in her saloon. The saloon (aft), cabin, a grim little space occupied by lavatory and hanging locker for wet oilskins, and forepeak all open into one another. A pipe cot can be let down over the settee berth in the saloon to make another sleeping place, and it is possible to fit in another body by removing her saloon table. I had the cabin bunk to starboard, probably the best berth in the ship, given to me by virtue of my leadership of the expedition and (perhaps rather selfishly) accepted. Reg Garrod had the port berth in the cabin – superficially a rather better berth than mine because it is really a double berth, but in actual conditions at sea, far less desirable because it is too wide for comfort: Reg could never wedge himself in as well as I could. Peter Haward had the settee berth in the saloon, the most convenient berth for getting quickly to the cockpit. Tim Lee had the pipe cot over Peter Haward. Peter Comber and Allister McIntosh had the two berths forward. We changed things a good deal later, but that is how we started off.

On the passage to Scarborough, Allister McIntosh was not on board, but we had David Fairhall and Bernard Iverson to fit in. David took what would have been Allister's berth forward and I made Bernard take mine: he was rather nicely reluctant to do this, but I was so restless that I knew that there was no possibility of getting much sleep, and I thought that Bernard (who must have been

D

nearly as harassed as I was) should have at least the chance of a fair night's rest. I decided to curl up, if I felt able to go to sleep, on one of the seats alongside the saloon table.

Soon after we got under way we had a meal – rather a scratch meal of cold meat and bread and cheese, but it did everybody good. The log reads:

1843 hoisted main
1902 passed eastern breakwater
1914 streamed log
2036 Goodwin fork buoy abeam
2059 Goodwin (fl. 5 sec.) abeam
2310 raised Kentish Knock light vessel, bearing 028 . . .

That was the opening of a log that would not close until *Griffin* had sailed all but five thousand miles.

During the evening I put through our first call on the radio telephone, getting through to the *Guardian* office via North Foreland Radio. The paper next day carried a brief message headed '*Griffin* on first stage of voyage', and saying, 'On board *Griffin* at sea. This is mainly a test call to check our radio. We are at sea, making about three knots before a gentle southwesterly wind, on our way to Scarborough on the first stage of our Vinland expedition.'

With seven on board, we took only one-hour watches. Mine was from 2200–2300, and around midnight, when apart from the man on watch, the others were trying to get some sleep, I settled down to write my journal:

Wednesday, April 27
Well, we are at sea. A harrowing day in all. I am writing having just come off my first watch on *Griffin* – a gentle, easy one, but I don't like her wheel and still find it pretty confusing.

There was a slight crisis on our departure, when on raising our yankee [a big, high-cut jib], we found that it had no jib-sheets! This was soon overcome, though. Reg Garrod and I shackled on the staysail upside down, but mercifully we noticed before anybody else did. I took the helm for a little and made rather a mess of it, finding the backwards-facing wheel rather odd. At 2000 we made our first attempt to get North Foreland Radio – it was a great thrill to hear them call back to 'Yacht *Griffin*'. They told us we were 'four' – we thought they meant 'use channel 4', and told them that we had only channels 1 and 2. It turned out that they meant that *our turn* was fourth – there were three other ships ahead of us for the station to work first. They told us to stand by, and called us up about 2020. Since we were so near the coast I had my telephone call put through to the *Guardian* instead of to Brent. There was slight trouble at first because the operator on our *Guardian* switch-board did not realise that we had only Simplex, but this difficulty was soon overcome and I sent a short message. ['Simplex' is a telephone system by which only one voice can be transmitted at a time. With a normal telephone, people can both hear one another and talk. That is called Duplex. With the Simplex system one person can talk while the other listens: when you want the other person to talk you have to press a small switch on your receiver, say 'Over', and keep the switch pressed while you listen to the other person's voice. It is a little tricky at first, but you soon get used to it.]

I wrote about my first watch:

It was rather harrowing steering – our course at first 022°, then 020°. But as our old compass is not marked in degrees, and has only the traditional compass points, it is difficult to be accurate. I had to pass a green wreck buoy to starboard. The wind freshened a bit in my watch and *Griffin* was doing about 6½ knots under mainsail, yankee and staysail. The wind was about Force 3, westerly, the sea calm and it was a rather lovely night.

Griffin's wheel bothered me a good bit in the early stages of our voyage, and indeed, I never liked it much. It is a traditional form of steering for the larger east-coast boats, a wheel working through a double-worm gear to turn the rudder. It is simple and immensely strong, and the gearing enables the helmsman in normal circumstances to leave the wheel for a moment or two without going off course – the gearing tends to hold the rudder. But the wheel is at the back of the cockpit, so that the helmsman has either to stand or sit beside it, or stand in front of it and hold the wheel behind his back. Unlike a tiller, by which you move the helm to port to go to starboard, a geared wheel works like the wheel of a motor car – the vessel's head turns in the direction you turn the wheel. I was used to steering with a tiller, and had never before steered a yacht as big as *Griffin*.

I did not realise this at the time, but the layout of *Griffin's* cockpit also proved to have serious disadvantages. It is an open cockpit, and since we were bound for extremely cold seas I had a canvas and Perspex dodger fixed over the cabin top, to cover the entrance to the companionway, and to provide some extra protection for the helmsman. This worked well from the point of view of giving protection, but interfered badly with forward vision from the cockpit. Our six-footers – Peter Haward, Reg Garrod, Peter Comber and Tim Lee – did not do so badly, but Allister McIntosh and I, who are 5 ft 9 in, found it difficult to see over the top. We lowered it a bit later, but it was always rather a nuisance. Another difficulty was that *Griffin's* wheel is not dead centre in the cockpit – there was room to sit to port of it, but not to starboard. However, every arrangement on a small boat has to be in some sense a compromise, and although *Griffin* had faults – some rather serious faults – she made up for everything by being a magnificent sea boat.

Thursday, April 28

Last night was a good one, with a fair wind giving us about seven knots across the Thames Estuary. I came on watch again at 0500, with dawn just broken – a calm sea and very lovely early sun, though it was miserably cold. Breakfast (cooked by Peter Comber) was of bacon and eggs *and fried bread*: how he does it, I don't know. The wind headed us later, and we crept past Yarmouth in a series of short tacks. We had one scare when David Fairhall read the depth sounder at eight feet, which meant that we should be aground at any moment. Peter Haward went quickly about! Tim Lee discovered, however, that the reading should have been *sixty-eight* feet! The sounder has an occasional trick of reading round twice, so all was well.

Having spent the night sitting up, I kipped for a couple of hours in the morning. Lunch (Peter Comber again) was ham, salad and apples. I am still bothered by *Griffin's* wheel and was rather ham-handed on my 1200–1300 watch, messing her up twice by getting the jib aback. There was some excuse, for the wind was fluky, but I was angry with myself. Practically everybody slept again in the afternoon, including me (because I have to sit up again tonight). My evening watch was 1900–2000, running with the jib boomed out. It was rather scary, and I am afraid there was a bit of running by the lee, but all was well. Tim Lee has started sending meteorological reports, and transmitted his first message to Humber Radio. We are certainly crowded – *Griffin* can just take six all right but stores for so long a voyage do present difficulties. As of now, if I were planning this voyage over again I think that I should prefer four – but the old arguments against four are very strong. So on balance (not that anything in life ever *is* balanced!) six is probably right. We shall see when we meet ice. I am sleeping on the short settee by the cabin table again tonight to give Bernard Iverson my berth. I got some rest this afternoon, so I am not so badly off for sleep. In a way, I am being rather silly to do things like this, because the cabin table *can* let down to form a bunk. But I think it would be a great nuisance, and people coming on or off watch do find the table useful for a cup of coffee, etc. My next watch is 0200 – not the best of times. And there is new job to-night, to get the 0200 forecast for shipping on the B E M E radio – I have just asked Tim Lee to show me how to work it. It seems odd that I have done so much with radio while remaining quite ham-handed about it for myself. Peter Haward and Tim Lee are washing up – they really are a grand pair, both professional sailors but nicely gentle with us amateurs. It is a nice night so far, but wickedly cold. I am wearing the trouser half of Helen's track suit under my sailcloth trousers, like long pants. It is comfortable, but a great nuisance in having no water place (as the children would say). I shall wear the top half over two pullovers when I go on watch. The wind is at present S S E, about Force 2. When I finish writing this I shall settle down on the short settee again for a couple of hours before going on watch. How relative space is! *Griffin* has far less space than our Charney cottage, yet six of us are living in it – seven at the moment, with Bernard Iverson. And I still look on *Griffin* as a *big* boat, whereas the cottage always seems incredibly small. I suppose this is because *Griffin* is so much bigger than our own *Mary Lane* – if we had been living in a caravan no doubt the cottage would seem big.

April 29, 0400
I came off watch half an hour late, because just at the change of watch the spinnaker pole had to come in. This was done by Reg Garrod and Peter Haward. The wind, which had been S S E, went round to S and then to S W, justifying the forecast. This made it a beam wind instead of our previous run. It was a beautiful night but damned cold. I have just got out of my watch clothes – that is, the top ones. I am wearing vest, short pants, shirt, thin pullover, thick pullover, track suit, nylon oily trousers, nylon oily top, two pairs of socks, rubber boots. Oily trousers, track suit top, and oily top, come off in the cabin.

We lighted the Aladdin stove tonight, and very comforting it is. The Aladdin vacuum flasks are a godsend; I have just had a welcome cup of coffee and so have Peter Haward and Reg Garrod.

The rest of that day – our third day out by the reckoning of nights, though in fact we had been sailing only for about forty hours – was quite lovely. It was a beautiful sunny morning, with the wind generally southwesterly, blowing at about Force 2–3. *Griffin* soared along at around six knots. I was still too much a landsman, however, not to feel the chill of the sea: my journal is full of references to the cold. Compared with what was to come, the North Sea at the end of April was relatively warm, but in relation to the warmth of houses, shops, cars and buses and all the comforts of land, the sea is always cold. I reckon that there is at least one thick pullover's difference between whatever the weather is doing on land and the chill of the sea. At breakfast that morning Bernard Iverson observed that the butter seemed as if it had just come out of a refrigerator: I felt as if I had come out of a refrigerator when I came off watch. We were due to make Scarborough some time that afternoon, and Peter Haward did a good job in scrubbing out the ship. Our brief shakedown since leaving Dover had transformed *Griffin*: we had tidied up everything and her working gear was all efficient and in place. None of us had ever sailed into Scarborough before, and Tim Lee pored over the charts and tide-tables, working out how best to enter. It is a drying harbour and we discovered that if we could not enter by about 1500 hours we should have to anchor off until about 2200.

The last hour or two of our passage was a glorious sail. The wind freshened to Force 3–4, coming from more west than south, which gave us a very close reach. I had the last watch before we made Scarborough and for the first time I really enjoyed handling *Griffin*. On a reach there was no risk of gybing, the sheets were iron hard and she answered the lightest touch on her helm. It was tricky work, too, for there were hundreds of buoyed fishing pots – lobster or crab – to be avoided: it was rather like picking one's way through a maze. But it was picking one's way through a maze in the marine equivalent of a high-performance car, with a grand feeling of *Griffin*'s power and breeding as she drove along.

We arrived a little before 1800 hours and made ready to anchor off about two cables south of the east breakwater. As we were getting ready to let go the anchor, a man came out in a motor boat and said, 'Are you for Greenland?' We said, 'Yes,' and he explained that there would not be enough water for us in the harbour until some time after 2100. This we knew, but it was a kindly thought by the harbourmaster to send out a message to us. As *Griffin* rode gently to her anchor we stowed our sails and made everything shipshape. We had been at sea for just over forty-seven hours, covering the 233 nautical miles from Dover to Scarborough at an average speed of 4·95 knots: this was good going. As things turned out, it would have been better for us had we met rougher weather and strong headwinds on that trip to Scarborough, for we should then have experienced troubles that were unguessed until they came upon us harshly in far worse conditions later. We had kept to our schedule and made our arrival at Scarborough just as I had promised so rashly nearly two months before. For the first time, I felt almost at peace and happy as we lay safely in the evening light, waiting for the tide to enter harbour. We had been at sea only a short time but I think that everybody shared in the general feeling, partly of lassitude, partly of relief. I wanted to let the *Guardian* know of our arrival, and waited rather hopefully for somebody to come off to visit us in a boat, so that I could go ashore and telephone. We ran up our Q flag because we were carrying bonded stores, but nobody came near us. We could have launched the dinghy, but it was securely lashed on deck and I did not feel like going to the trouble of launching it. I remembered suddenly that we had a high-grade radio telephone. Radio is in-clined not to work happily close in-shore, but we had a go and in a few minutes I got through to the office quite well. We had a meal, and then idled or dozed as we felt inclined.

About 2200 we got up the anchor and, using *Griffin's* elderly engine, motored slowly into harbour. We made fast to one wall of the quay, when a man came and told us that a berth had been reserved for us on the other side. I stayed on shore while the others worked her round. I was bothered about not seeing any Customs – I had never before been legally master of a vessel carrying stores in bond, and I was anxious not to blot my copybook. The only place we could find for our few bottles of whisky, brandy and gin that seemed to the Customs officers at Dover to be suitable for sealing was a small hanging locker at the head of my bunk. It was a nuisance not to be able to use it for clothes, but I felt oddly proud of the fact that the seals were all solemnly intact. We were, of course, entitled to unseal our stores as soon as we were more than three miles off the British coast, but since we had put in to another British port our stores would have had to be sealed again. To save bother and explanations I had decided not to break our stores. Perhaps because I felt virtuous, I was a bit nettled that no Customs officer appeared. However, nobody else seemed bothered about Customs and when we made fast in our berth we were all invited into Scarborough Yacht Club – a pleasant clubhouse at the end of the breakwater – to have a drink. It was a welcome interlude. But we were all rather tired and did not stay long. We went back to *Griffin* and turned in.

Our berth was rather a horrible one – not Scarborough's fault, but because it is a drying harbour and we had to go aground when the tide fell. This meant that we had to secure *Griffin* to a wall, leaning towards the wall, so that she would not fall over as the water left her. This is always worrying, for you can never be sure that a vessel may not shift as she settles, and perhaps get into a dangerous position. In fact *Griffin* did shift a little, and one of the spreaders of her mast nearly got caught underneath an iron railing at the top of the wall: had this happened, it would have snapped off as the tide came back and the mast righted itself. Fortunately, we noticed it in time.

I never find it comfortable to sleep aboard a boat aground: everything seems to feel wrong, and I have a constant sense of unease. A vessel afloat is never wholly still, and even if she seems motionless there is always a sense of being cradled in her proper element. I slept badly that night, and about 0630 was glad to get up and make myself a cup of coffee. We had a heavy day in front of us, with commitments to various press and television people, and we had a good deal of very careful shopping to do, making up a few deficiencies in our stores, and getting what we had forgotten to buy before leaving Dover: for this would be our last chance to shop for goodness knew how long. So just before 0700 I made coffee for everybody. They got up dutifully at this, the first of our ports, and demanded baths. I had no clear idea what to do about baths, but Scarborough has good hotels, and I asked the man on duty at the coastguard office on the breakwater if he could tell me where we might get a taxi. He telephoned for one, and a few minutes later we all set off in the cab for the Royal Hotel. Although it was so early in the morning, we were given a courteous reception and no one blinked an eyelid when I asked whether we might have seven baths before breakfast. Fresh towels and soap were handed round, and we disappeared to our various bathrooms, to meet again at the breakfast table. One thing puzzled me, we were taken for Americans. Whether it seemed to the hotel staff more likely that a bunch of Americans would want early morning baths than a bunch of Englishmen I do not know, but it hurt my national pride a little. I pointed out that the English have been known to wash, too.

After breakfast we went our separate ways shopping. Reg Garrod and I did the domestic chores, hunting for plastic buckets, floor cloths, scrubbing brushes, etc., which we had rather forgotten about at Dover, but of which our few days at sea had proved a crying need. I had lunch with a *Guardian* colleague, Gerry Knight, who had come to see us off, and after lunch went back to *Griffin* to try to get a little sleep. But it was no good. The local paper had written us up and there was a constant stream of visitors to see the little boat that was about to set off for Greenland and America. There were also people to see on ship's business. A Marconi representative came, bringing us an additional crystal for a frequency used by some coastal stations, and installed this in our Kestrel at the expense of losing the crystal that would enable us to call the frequency of Boston. At that time, Boston seemed a long way away, and the exchange did not really matter, for we could always put back the Boston crystal if we needed it.

I turned in about 2300 and again slept hardly at all, waking out of a doze at 0430 with a violent tummy pain. This was inconvenient, for the tide was out and *Griffin* was aground, which meant that I could not use her lavatory. We were at the foot of the harbour wall, with a long climb up a vertical iron ladder to get ashore. I scrambled up the ladder and ran to the town end of the breakwater where there was a public lavatory, hoping that it would be open at that early hour of the morning. Mercifully, it was. I went back to *Griffin* feeling a little better, but no sooner had I climbed down the ladder to reach her than I had another spasm of pain and had to rush back to the lavatory again. This went on for three or four hours, but gradually the diarrhoea worked itself off. It was just nervous strain, I suppose.

My journal for Sunday, May 1, consists of one scrawled sentence: Today has been indescribable – hordes of my own trade and endless photographers.

Having been a working journalist all my life, it was perhaps rather good for me to be at the receiving end of press attention. I did my best to be as helpful as I could be, having a fellow feeling for the men who had been sent out on a Sunday to interview me. But I now have a clear understanding of the ordeal that journalists and broadcasters (inevitably) ask people to endure.

That Sunday evening the Bethel Mission in the harbour at Scarborough gave a service of benediction for us. It was conducted by the Rev Tom Johnson and the Rev A. S. Craig, assisted by members of the Scarborough Fishermen's Choir. Such a service could have seemed artificial and rather embarassing, but it turned out to be extraordinarily moving. The little mission hall was full and the Fishermen's Choir was superb. I was invited to read the First Lesson and Tim Lee the Second. Mine was verses 23–32 of Psalm 107, that lovely passage about 'They that go down to the sea in ships, that do business in great waters.' Tim's was from Chapter IV of St Paul's Epistle to the Philippians, the verses beginning 'Rejoice in the Lord always, and again I say Rejoice'. The men and women in that little mission hall on the edge of the North Sea mostly served the sea in one way or another, and they understood its bitterness as well as its beauty. Their faith to them had real meaning as they sang their hymn, 'Will your anchor hold in the storms of life?' and the chorus, 'I have an anchor to keep my soul'. I am not ashamed to write that my eyes were wet and there was a lump in my throat when there was a special prayer for us, 'For those who sail in the *Griffin* on this Vinland Voyage.' It went:

'Oh eternal Lord God, who alone spreadest out the heavens and rules the raging of the sea, be pleased to receive into Thy protection these Thy servants. Make Thou their voyage to be safe to their persons, and fruitful in their discoveries, and joyful in the fulfilment of their aims. Through Jesus Christ Our Lord. Amen.'

After the service we marched in procession from the mission hall to *Griffin* for her blessing by the ministers. This, too, was very moving. The fishermen's choir sang the hymn, 'Eternal Father strong to save', their rich unaccompanied voices giving deep meaning to the words. I shall always be grateful to the ministers and men and women of that little Scarborough mission.

After our blessing we all, I think, felt a slight sense of anti-climax. We also felt hungry, and set off to see what we could find in the way of a meal. On a late Sunday evening even the best of English holiday resorts is not over-populated with places willing to give you something to eat. We tried various cafés, but they were all shut. Finally, we found a place offering fish and chips and fell upon it hungrily. Allister McIntosh had joined us that afternoon, so as we sat down to tuck into our fish and chips the crew was complete.

The morning of our sailing day was a frantic rush. We started early with a final bath at an hotel and then split up for all the last-minute

things that had to be done. I asked Peter Haward to see to the
watering of *Griffin*, and arranged with the harbourmaster to run a
waterpipe to her. A Shell lorry arrived, with the few gallons of
petrol and paraffin that we needed. I went off on my own to try to
do something about my glasses. These were to torture me con-
tinually. I cannot read a chart, or even see a compass card properly
without glasses. But I cannot see across a room or look at anything
farther away *with* glasses. This means that my glasses are constantly
being taken on and off, and constantly lost. I was also far from happy
about the ability of the frames of my glasses to stand up to the conditions in which they would have to be worn on *Griffin* at sea. I had
metal frames (rather expensive ones) but they didn't seem to be
much good. Since a fair number of people who have to wear glasses
climb mountains, sail small boats or engage in other forms of out-
door activity, I do not understand why it is apparently so difficult
to obtain really strong frames which will stay on. I decided that the
only thing to do about mine was to get a piece of elastic which I
could tie from earpiece to earpiece behind my head. The arrangement
was never satisfactory: when the glasses were tied on, they were hard
to take off quickly, and I found that if the elastic was tight enough
to be of any use, it gave me a headache. But it was the best that I
could do.

We had one further engagement to meet on land – a reception by
the Mayor of Scarborough at lunchtime. Things had to be timed
carefully, for I was determined to sail on the afternoon tide, and this
meant that we had to stick to a rather ruthless timetable. Somehow
we managed it. The Mayor sent cars for us, and we just succeeded in
getting out of our working clothes and making ourselves respectable without keeping the cars waiting. Many personal friends came
to Scarborough to see us off. A lot more people sent telegrams: those
messages meant a great deal, for they seemed to enfold us in a
warmth of human sympathy and goodwill that was wonderfully
comforting.

5

On Our Own

Said we'd sail at 1500 and we did.

That is the opening of my journal for the first day of our voyage proper. I remember writing it with a sense of combined triumph and exhaustion. It was the end of all planning and the coming months would show what had been done well, and what had been done badly. Nothing more could be done: *Griffin* and her crew were one entity, committed to the North Atlantic and whatever it might bring.

Several small motor boats accompanied us out of the harbour and crowds of people stood waving on the pierhead. The commercial shipping in the harbour all sounded sirens as we sailed out – big ships saluting a little ship in the generous tradition of the sea. Soon the little boats fell away, and we were alone. We started a routine of two-hour watches, which we stuck to for the whole of the voyage. Reg Garrod took the first watch from 1500–1700. I followed him from 1700–1900, Peter Haward followed me, and then came Allister McIntosh, Tim Lee and Peter Comber. We kept to this order from then on.

Our system of working *Griffin* was slightly eccentric but it worked well. It is more normal for the crew of a vessel at sea to be divided into two watches, who are on or off duty together. This has some advantages in companionship, but on a long voyage with a small crew it means four hours on and four off continuously. Peter Haward suggested that we should work single watches, which would give people more time for sleep. I was a little dubious at first, but ready to try it. Now I would recommend it for the crew of a small boat on any ocean passage. It has disadvantages, but they are all outweighed by the reduction in fatigue. Human exhaustion is the deadliest of all enemies at sea and there are times when the crew of a small boat come near exhaustion, whatever you do to try to prevent it. If people can get a fair amount of sleep at non-critical times, they are infinitely better placed to meet emergencies. Our system gave us two hours on watch, followed by ten hours off duty. Of course, this did not mean that people did nothing for ten hours – there were sails to be set and changed, cooking and galley work to be done; all the housekeeping and seafaring activities that are needed to work a ship. But it did mean that when you came off watch you were free from further watchkeeping for ten hours, so that when you had done whatever job needed doing on deck or below, you could arrange your time for sleeping, reading or writing to suit yourself.

Our system also provided flexibility. We kept meticulously to punctual reliefs – there is probably nothing that engenders more bad feeling in a small community than a sense of grievance that you are doing more than your fair share of the work. No such grievance ever touched us on *Griffin*. But obviously it was not always possible for reliefs to be carried out on the normal rota. People had other jobs to do, which sometimes had to have priority. I had daily messages to write and to transmit to the *Guardian*, and these had to be transmitted on radio schedules that varied from time to time in accordance with radio conditions, and might be at any hour of the twenty-four. Tim Lee had to navigate, and he had also undertaken to make regular meteorological observations and to send daily reports to the Meteorological Office at Bracknell in England. Peter Haward was responsible for sailing – at any moment he might be needed on deck to trim or alter sails, to take in or to let out a reef. Awake or asleep Peter Haward seemed to know by instinct when a sail needed trimming. When somebody was needed for a job other than watchkeeping, our system enabled a turn to be switched, without seriously upsetting other people's time below. Thus I normally relieved Reg Garrod, and Peter Haward normally relieved me, but if there was some radio work or ship work that required any of us at a particular time Reg and I, or Peter Haward and I, could swap our turns. So with Tim Lee and the rest of us.

We were also a bit eccentric in arranging galley work. The question of who was to be ship's cook had bothered me in planning the

voyage. I have done a fair bit of cooking at sea, and it is an arduous
and sometimes horrible job. It is also a vitally important job, for
unless people get regular meals, morale disintegrates. I did not want
to ask anybody to take on the job of ship's cook, nor did I want to
commit myself to the galley as a regular thing. So, rather weakly, I
did nothing. This was the best thing that I could have done. I still
cannot explain precisely how things worked, and all I can say is that
they *did* work. We never had any formal system of galley duty but
we were never without a man in the galley when the time came for
a meal. Peter Comber, who was our supplies officer, more or less
supervised the galley, because he knew better than any of us where
things were, and just what we had on board. But we never expected
Comber to act as regular cook. What happened was that there was
always somebody, who had either come off watch and was not
feeling particularly sleepy, or who was up and waiting to go on
watch, who seemed to take on the galley as part of the natural order
of things. Sometimes we would most of us be awake and discuss a
meal before we cooked it, but for the most part whoever decided to
go into the galley used his own ideas of what a meal should be. So
with the chores of washing up. Without any formal arrangement,
the man who had done the cooking regarded himself as responsible
for washing up and seeing that the galley was left tidy for the next
person to use it, but there was a general feeling that whoever had
done the cooking ought not to be left to deal with the washing up.
Volunteers for washing up always came forward and, without
asking or suggesting, the work always got done. That this system
worked for two months, happily and without friction, seems to
me about the highest tribute that can be paid to the men who sailed
with me.

We were well stocked with food. Basically, we relied on ordinary
food in tins, cooked and prepared in the normal domestic way.
Griffin's galley had a gas stove, worked by bottled gas and, although
it was often extremely hard to keep pots and pans on the stove, the
preparation of meals was a normal domestic process. As far as we
could, we combined tinned meats and preserves with fresh vegetables: potatoes, carrots and onions keep fairly well at sea, and fresh
vegetables make an enormous difference to well-being. Greenstuff is

more difficult, but hard white cabbage can be made to last at least for several days. Mr Cunnington, our chandler at Dover, had supplied us with apples with remarkable keeping qualities, and we found that grapefruit kept well. Peter Comber took on the job of devising lists and quantities, and we were never short of anything that mattered. I was considerably worried about scurvy; people tend to think that scurvy is a disease of the past, and, with modern methods of food preservation, of no great concern nowadays. But I had met scurvy, on land during the war, and I believe that it can come far more quickly than is commonly realised, from even a brief deficiency in diet. I believe, too, that the beginnings of scurvy are insidious, and may be unrecognised: you can suffer from scurvy, manifested by a general feeling of lassitude and malaise, long before your gums start bleeding, or your teeth start falling out, and the beginnings of scurvy can be felt after even a few days of inadequate Vitamin C. I always begin to feel ill by about the fourth day of living wholly on food out of tins, and nothing can wholly make up for the absence of fresh vegetables. We managed enough in the way of vegetables to keep everybody fit. I had a good supply of Vitamin C tablets but, apart from Allister McIntosh who thought them of some slight help in treating seasickness, nobody ever used them. I am sure that we kept well mainly because we were never without raw vegetables, uncanned and unpreserved.

We had also emergency rations of one sort and another, notably those excellent packets of highly-concentrated and easily-prepared food manufactured by Horlicks. The two main varieties of these rations are curried meat and rice, and minced beef and potatoes. Their special virtue is that a substantial meal can be cooked in one pan in a few minutes, with the addition only of water. I have used them at various times in my life, and have the highest respect for them – when my daughter Ricarda was born and we had a domestic crisis in which I had to carry on with my job and do all the housekeeping as well, I kept the family going on Horlicks emergency rations. They were invaluable on *Griffin*. I called them our Stage I emergency rations, and we turned to them whenever rough weather made cooking an ordeal or whenever, for any reason, people were too tired for elaborate cooking. We had Stage II emergency rations as well – highly concentrated food to keep us alive if we had to take to our life raft.

We streamed the log at 1505 and the land fell away. Compared with any other form of modern transport, even a bicycle, a sailing boat moves at crawling speed, but like the tortoise in the fable she keeps going minute after minute, hour after hour, day after day. It always surprises me how quickly the land falls away when you leave harbour or an anchorage: at one moment you are still living in a world of houses and roads and people walking; the next, the land world becomes a blur of coastline and you are alone in a private world at sea. The weather over our weekend at Scarborough had been a magic spell of early summer, cloudless skies and warm sun – the fresh warmth of an early summer sun with no touch of the tired heat that later summer brings with a hot day. The English climate can be compared only with the most tiresome and damnable sort of woman: you have to live with her and time and time again her behaviour is so vile that you make up your mind to emigrate and leave her: then suddenly she turns on such bewitching charm that you are enthralled again. Having treated us vilely at Dover, the English weather seemed anxious to make amends on our passage to Scarborough, and over our weekend there. In fact, it was another sort of treachery, for which we were soon to pay.

Shortly after we streamed our log, we streamed our fishing line, with high hopes of fish for breakfast next morning. This line had been bought by Tim Lee at Dover, and it was his pride and joy – a beautiful line with a breaking strain of 200 lb. Just what he hoped to catch with it is still unclear to me: what we did catch, almost at once, was our patent log: log line and fishing line made a horrible tangle which took the best part of an hour to sort out. When we were able to stream the log again, we reckoned that we had sailed four miles, and we reset the log to allow for this.

May 3 It is not easy to write on *Griffin* at the moment – she is heeling her gunwale under before a Force 4 from the N W, sailing beautifully, hard over, but kicking about. We lost our old Yankee about 1015 this morning: it just blew out in not much more than a

E

Force 3. It was a very ancient sail, but I was sorry to see it go because it set beautifully. It was much patched, and I doubt it is worth doing anything with the remains.

I turned in last night soon after 2100, and slept well, for the first time since joining *Griffin*, until 0315. Reg Garrod, turning out for his watch at 0300, didn't even wake me. I was on watch at 0500 this morning, so I didn't go to sleep again, but got up about 0345 and had a cup of coffee, pre-made by Reg, from the Aladdin flask. Got into heavy clothes in leisurely fashion and went on watch at 0500. It was a misty morning, which soon became thick, with visibility down to about one hundred yards. Reg suggested that we ought to send up the radar reflector, so we did – he did the work while I kept *Griffin* on course. We had much trouble through having no small shackles – the holes in the radar reflector are pinholes, ridiculous tiny things. Reg managed to find one small dinghy shackle, which came out of a box of bits and pieces that I brought from *Mary Lane*. I suggested a wire ring for the downhaul shackle, so we made one and the reflector went up at 0650. It was a worrying watch in the fog, but fog is inevitable and I must learn to live with it. The ship moves in a small circle of the visible world – it seems to be the whole world. One is terrified the whole time of the bows of a big ship suddenly appearing on your quarter. But all was well – no ships, nothing.

Breakfast (Peter Comber again, bless him) was bacon and tomatoes, and after breakfast I wrote the first piece for our scheduled call to Brent. We had been warned by Humber Radio at 0700, when Tim put through his weather report, that there might be 'turns', so we started our call at 0850 (BST). We got through almost dead on time at 0900 (BST) and Brent, as usual, was very efficient. Anne Bradbury was there, and the call was quite good. I turned in for a bit more sleep with some feeling of triumph – shortlived.

Anne, in a way, is the heroine of this story, indeed about the only female character in it (apart from *Griffin* herself who, like all ships, is, of course, female). Anne was a member of the *Guardian* staff in Manchester, the daughter of a sailing father, and a sailor herself.

She had been detailed to take our daily calls at Brent and as time went on we came to regard her as our sole link with the rest of the world. In a curious way, she became an integral part of the expedition, and when conditions were bad I think she suffered with us. I have been through the same sort of experience myself, in talking to Francis Chichester from Brent when we made our first experiments with long-distance radio. It is terrible to be in a warm room in a comfortable chair, talking by telephone to a man who is going through hell in really rough weather at sea. He breaks off suddenly, and you can almost hear him being flung across the boat – and you can do nothing whatever about it. So Anne lived and suffered with us, and across hundreds and later thousands of miles of ocean she was always a cheerful companion.

That morning brought the first of our serious troubles. As we made our way northwards up the east coast of Britain the weather freshened, bringing that vicious tumble of short waves for which the North Sea is famous (or infamous). It was not really much in the way of hard weather, but it was the hardest we had met so far, and it brought out a grave deficiency in *Griffin*'s rudder. There was far too much play in the steering, and every time a short sea struck her, the rudder made a worrying 'clonk', a dull menacing sound as if it was loose on its pintles. As the day wore on, the 'clonking' from the rudder became more frequent. We hung over the transom and peered down into the water round the rudder, but we could see nothing to account for the trouble. I talked things over with the others, and we agreed that *Griffin* ought to be slipped and the rudder examined before we went much farther. I decided to put into Aberdeen, and wrote in my journal, 'It is a horrible nuisance, but we can't go off to Greenland and points west with any avoidable doubt about our rudder, so there is nothing to be done about it except to say, "Oh well".'

Putting in anywhere within a day or two of leaving Scarborough seemed like running home with our tails between our legs. I was also worried about the cost of what might be major repairs. But whatever my own feelings, the safety of *Griffin* and her crew had to come first. We looked up the charts for the entrance to Aberdeen.

Early next morning (May 4), Peter Haward, Tim Lee, Reg Garrod and I had another conference about the rudder. We had come through the night without any noticeable deterioration in the steering and although the 'clonking' went on intermittently, it did not seem to be creating any immediate danger. None of us wanted to put in to Aberdeen if it could be avoided, but I was also determined not to let our reluctance to put in stand in the way of prudent seamanship. After discussing things this way and that, we decided that the rudder would probably hold all right for a bit longer, and that we could continue to make for Reykjavik in Iceland. There were the Shetlands and the Faeroes we could run to if necessary, and although I didn't want to put in anywhere, I preferred the idea of the Shetlands or the Faeroes to Aberdeen – at least we should have got away from the mainland of Britain. So for the moment we held our course for Reykjavik, and tried to forget about the rudder. My journal turns to thoughts of dinner:

I was lucky tonight; my watch was 1700–1900, but we have made this the dog watch so I only did one hour (1700–1800) and Peter Haward did one hour (1800–1900). This shifts the watches, so that we get fair shares of all the hours of the day and night. After my short watch I cooked dinner.

Menu: Asparagus soup
Fried liver, boiled potatoes, carrots and gravy
Dessert. Fresh apples, oranges
Liqueur. Brandy

I peeled the potatoes and carrots on deck – quite a pleasant job. I cooked in the pressure cooker for the first time – hate it. It was very slow – boils only on the starboard tack. They say nothing in the leaflet of instructions about pressure cookers that they boil only on the starboard tack. The only thing to be said for it is that it does save water. Tim Lee (who, with me, likes salt) put a bit of seawater with the freshwater in the pressure cooker to cook the potatoes and carrots. Nobody noticed it! The liver took ages to cook and I don't like liver much, but everybody else said that it was a very good dinner. The making of it was the gravy – people were surprised to have gravy. But it was really very simple – some Oxo cubes in a teacup of water!

After dinner we wanted to put some charge in the battery but had trouble with the engine – a blocked petrol pipe. Peter Haward struggled for ages – but I think he rather *likes* engines! I got on with the washing up, and caused some mystification by getting things beautifully clean in what I called the *Griffin* washing-up machine. It is really the *Mary Lane* washing-up machine, and consists of putting things in a bucket, and towing them through the water. All you need then is a roll of kitchen paper to get off the worst of the grease, and, after drying, all the crockery is sparkling.

My journal, however, soon records more troubles:

Damned radar reflector taking up far too much room astern. And fouling mainsheet. So relashed in bows.

Had a nasty shock – found the shackle that holds the life rail running round the deck very loose. Tightened it. Don't like to think what happens if no one notices these things.

Deck leak over Tim's berth – a great mystery because there is no water on deck.

Living on a small boat is rather like living in the corridor of a train – a leaning train. Nobody's sleeping quarters are in the least private, and everybody has to walk through Reg's and my cabin to get to the fo'c'sle or go to the lavatory. I hate this lavatory and can't make it work properly. I get a bucket of seawater and send that down – it seems the only way to deal with the thing. Peter Haward calls my bunk my 'den'. With the canvas leeboard up it is a sort of den. All our kit has to live on our bunks and to be taken off when we want to lie down.

Fog kept coming and going, and late that afternoon we made a dramatic landfall at Buchan Ness. I was on watch in a murk of fog and drizzle, and suddenly I saw rocks and lighthouse close to port. I yelled out 'land ahead' and Peter Haward and Tim Lee came rushing up.

I said, 'Damned good navigation, Tim.' He said, 'Well, I didn't mean to bring us quite as close as this.' It was really a pretty close shave, for we were no more than a quarter mile offshore when the rocks and lighthouse suddenly appeared out of the murk. I stayed at the helm while Peter and Tim slacked off and brought the sails round, and then we paid off on a new course, standing safely out to sea. The land soon disappeared in the mist. Apart from the nerve-racking experience of our over-dramatic landfall, it was grand sailing. In the two hours of my watch, *Griffin* covered seventeen miles, giving her an average speed of 8½ knots. In Peter Comber's watch later, she averaged 8·7 knots.

We discussed the possibility of going through the Pentland Firth, but Tim Lee wisely decided against it, and we set a course to go well outside, via the Orkneys. The weather steadily worsened.

May 5 What a night! Not much, I suppose, to a real seaman but even Tim Lee recorded it as 'rough'. It was. Wind ESE, Force 7, and a wicked steep sea. *Griffin* crashed through it, lee deck buried, with thousands of gallons of water hurled up by her weather shoulder and sent over the helmsman. We carried our full main until 2100 hours and then took in two reefs – Peter Haward, Tim Lee, Allister McIntosh and I. I, being a fool, put on oily top but no oily trousers, and no gloves – result, soaked through in a moment and hands frozen. Peter Haward and Tim Lee showed what magnificent seamen they are, lying out along the boom to gather in the hellishly-flapping sail. Allister and I were not much real use, but we lent weight where we could. We were all shackled on with Peter Haward's safety harnesses – they gave a great feeling of confidence. I was at the halliard, a heavy but straightforward job. She rode much more happily with the reefed main, but still careered along, half buried, half standing on her head. There was chaos below, with everything crashing everywhere. Reg managed to cook some stew. I had to change everything but vest and pull-overs (saved by my oily top). My shirt was soaked via my neck. I slept badly for a couple of hours and went on watch 0100–0300. It was exciting, certainly, like riding a mad racehorse of the highest class, but it was also cold, wet and miserable. I was thrown about the cockpit and was glad to feel that I was shackled on by my safety harness. I thought that the watch would never end, and was thankful when Peter Haward relieved me at 0300. Poor devil, having just got into all his heavy clothes he had a violent attack of diarrhoea. I offered to carry on at the helm to let him go back to lie down, but he would not, saying he was better on deck. In the twenty-four hours to 0800 that morning *Griffin* covered 134 miles, good going, but horribly uncomfortable. The weather moderated a bit as the day went on, and the afternoon turned fine and sunny. We managed to dry (or more or less to dry) most of our wet things. We had a visitor – the frigate HMS *Verulam*. Tim spoke to her on the Aldis lamp. *Verulam* asked whether we had on board '*Alaric's* third hand'. We replied, 'yes' (Tim). HM Submarine *Alaric* was Tim's last ship.

At 2245 I scribbled:

I take up this journal again just before going on watch from 2300–0100. We have just put in two reefs, largely as a precaution in case the wind, as forecast, pipes up. It was an easier job than last night – Peter Haward, Peter Comber and me. I was a bit more use, also it was not nearly so rough and we were not running. This time I did have the sense to put on full oilies. We have just seen North Ronaldshay light astern. After a day in which we managed to make only nine miles north after our splendid run the day before, we have just got going again. The engine seems to have packed up completely. All Peter Haward's work has failed to make it start. Anyway, we are supposed to be a sailing boat and we have our little auxiliary charging motor if the main engine won't do its job. Perhaps it will make up its mind to go again, or perhaps we can get something done about it in Iceland. I wish we didn't have to have an engine at all.

In the late afternoon of *May 6*, I wrote:

Not a good day. Am writing in extreme difficulties, sitting on the cabin floor, my knees propped up against what is left of our table. The table itself is not damaged, but Peter Comber and Allister McIntosh are suffering so much from seasickness that we are trying to abandon the fo'c'sle, which means that they have to sleep where the cabin table normally is – it takes down. This leaves nowhere to write. The heavy weather we have met was to be expected, but it has not been nice. The wind has been around Force 6–7 all day, with the sea steep and horrible. *Griffin* tosses about all the time, falling endlessly into great pot-holes – 'buck-jumping' I think Francis Chichester called it when *Gipsy Moth III* did it. It is the worst motion I have met so far – like going down in a lift without brakes. We are a shambles below decks – everything scattered everywhere, and nothing can be found. But people are pretty cheerful. All our bunks are wet. I have got the lifeboatman's suit that Pat Mulley gave me doing duty as a rubber cot mattress to try to keep off some of the water. Just before the end of my day watch (1100–1300) I saw a trawler damned close and called out. Peter Haward and Tim Lee came up, but neither could see anything. Goodness knows what it was I saw – gulls in the pattern of a ship? Pure hallucination? I certainly *did* see it. But the seas were so steep that there was no horizon and down in a hollow you can see nothing but the immediate crest. Nobody (except Peter Haward sometimes) reads anything: mostly when we are not on watch we lie down and doze. I write when I can, but lie down a lot. This awful motion is best survived lying down.

This is the point, I think, at which to record our experience of seasickness. Tim Lee and I were lucky: Tim was never sick at all, and I was sick only once, later in the voyage after our mainsail blew out for the first time; my sickness then, I think, was largely nervous reaction. Peter Haward suffered a little, very occasionally, but he is such an experienced seaman that sickness never worried him. Reg Garrod was afflicted in a curious way: for the first twenty-four hours or so after leaving port he was liable to be sick, but he just vomited, and that was that. He felt no ill effects – took out his pipe to be sick, and then went on smoking again. He never lost his appetite for food. Peter Comber and Allister McIntosh suffered so dreadfully in the early stages of our voyage, that I had to consider whether in fairness I ought to send them home from Iceland. They took the affliction in different ways. Allister gallantly struggled up to stand his watches, but for the rest of the time could do little but lie down. Peter Comber in some ways suffered even worse than Allister – Allister at least could generally keep down a cup of sweet tea, but Peter would vomit after even a glass of water. But he fought sickness, found jobs to do, never missed a watch, and even when it was bitterly cold, he tried to sit on deck. The effect of prolonged sea-sickness is double-edged. Not only is it a dreadful affliction in itself, but it steadily saps a man's strength, because he can keep down no food. I did ask both Peter Comber and Allister whether they would like to go home when we touched land, but both were reluctant even to consider the idea. In the end, they came to terms with seasickness. About half-way through the voyage Allister wholly recovered, and I think was not seriously bothered again even in rough weather. Peter Comber accepted that he would be sick for four days after leaving port, but by the end of the fourth day he began to look up, and on our longer passages he became perfectly fit after the initial period of sickness.

It was a calamity that the two members of the crew who turned out to be most prone to seasickness should have been given berths in the fo'c'sle. A ship's motion there is at its worst, as the bows climb and plunge through every sea. We moved them from the fo'c'sle as soon as it became evident that they were suffering. But we could not have known about this at the start of the voyage, and I fear also that both would have suffered wherever they slept.

The others used to say of Tim and me that we appeared to be immune from seasickness, but I don't think that anyone is ever wholly immune. We said of ourselves that we were lucky. Obviously, some people are more prone to seasickness than others, though why this should be so seems to be a mystery. I have felt seasick at odd times in my life, but rarely. For the most part I can be thrown about, either at sea or in the air, without any particular feeling of nausea. Tim Lee seems to be the same – there were one or two rather horrible occasions when he and I were the only members of the crew who felt like eating anything, and it seemed callous to cook a meal for just the two of us. But neither of us had any feeling of pride in not being sick – one may go without seasickness for years, and suddenly find oneself overcome. Experience of the sea itself is no guarantee against seasickness – Nelson was always sick on the first few days of a voyage, and other fine seamen have suffered in the same way. Normally, however, seasickness does wear off and after forty-eight hours or so, most people who suffer from it begin to get over it and to feel better. Peter Comber's and Allister's seasickness worried me because it went on for so long – I think that this was rather abnormal, brought about, perhaps, by the extreme discomfort of our crowded conditions in rough weather. Allister in fact had little experience of the sea, so that his sickness was less to be wondered at than Peter Comber's. Peter Comber had a good deal of experience of small-boat sailing, and at other times he has not suffered greatly. As a schoolmaster, he has sometimes taken crews of boys on sailing ventures, and on such voyages he has never felt sick. This is interesting psychologically, for it suggests that if your mind is occupied by other things, particularly by a sense of responsibility for other people, you can in some way forget to feel sick. This would be in keeping with other queer forms of travel sickness. My wife Helen, for instance, is liable to suffer from car sickness. But the moment she starts driving, she ceases to feel sick. In sailing our own small boat together she is liable to feel seasick when below, but as soon as she takes the helm she feels better. It is sometimes said that both car sickness and seasickness are largely matters of vision – that it is *looking at* the rising and falling horizon at sea, or the rapidly changing landscape from a car that brings about feelings of nausea. I doubt if there is more than half truth in this, because shutting one's eyes does not seem to bring much relief from either form of sickness, but vision may have something to do with it, and it may be that what really helps is to be able to concentrate one's vision, as one has to when driving a car or taking the helm of a vessel.

Before we sailed, the Burroughs Wellcome Company presented me with a supply of their Marzine anti-sickness tablets. Peter Comber got some relief from these and I think he and Allister might have been helped more if they had taken Marzine regularly, but both – understandably – were reluctant to rely on drugs. So the tablets were not much used. After Allister had been prostrated for some days I suggested that he should take a regular course of Vitamin C tablets. I put in a lot of propaganda about this. Whether it was the effect of

the propaganda or of the Vitamin C, I do not know, but he decided
that an occasional Vitamin C tablet did make him feel better. Perhaps a medicine glass of plain water would have been just as effective
if I had called it a magic remedy for seasickness – such things are
not unknown.

6

To the Faeroes

On May 7 we decided to put into the Faeroes. We had not met anything exceptionally bad in the way of rough weather, but it had been generally pretty rough and the rudder became more and more alarming. It also seemed imperative that we should do something to fix up better berths for Peter Comber and Allister. Allister was sleeping in the saloon where the cabin table ought to have been, and Peter Comber was on the cabin floor, alongside the mast, between Reg's and my bunks. This was a great nuisance, because it meant that at all times there seemed to be bodies everywhere, and since Reg's and my cabin was also a passageway from the saloon to the lavatory and fo'c'sle, anyone who wanted to move about at all below was always stumbling over somebody else. I offered to move into the fo'c'sle myself – I thought that I should probably be able to manage there, and Reg Garrod also offered to give up his bunk. But Peter Haward was against this, arguing that the two fo'c'sle berths were really of no use except in port, and that nobody should be expected to sleep there in rough weather.

Had the rudder been all right we should probably have stuck things as they were until we got to Iceland, but there was a disquieting amount of slackness in the steering, and with every day of fairly rough weather the rudder seemed to bang about more dangerously. There were other jobs that needed doing, and which could be done only in port. On *May* 7 I wrote:

We are going to the Faeroes. That rudder is alarming, and the bloody engine must be fixed. Also, Peter Haward thinks that we should have knees to strengthen our coach roof, in case we meet really massively bad weather off south Greenland. We may. And

I agree that the coach roof is vulnerable – if it should carry away in a heavy sea it would be very serious. True, *Griffin* is an ocean racer, and has been through pretty rough stuff in her time, but she is old, and in all her previous experience of heavy weather she never had to endure it for really long: her races were mostly a matter of days, and in an emergency she was never far from some place of refuge. This voyage is quite different – we may be exposed to dangerously rough weather for an indefinite time, so it seems sensible to get things strengthened, if we can, in the Faeroes.

We consulted the *North Sea Pilot* and it told us that there was a slip for fishing boats at a place called Tveraa, on Suduroy island, the most southerly of the Faeroes, and the nearest island to us. I thought that it would be a good idea to give notice of our arrival, and to see if we could make arrangements to get on to a slip before we got there. I was bothered in case delay might seriously interfere with my

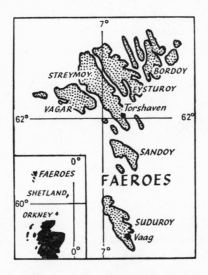

planning for the voyage. So Tim called up Thorshavn Radio (Thorshavn is the capital of the Faeroes) on our Kestrel, and asked to be put through to the harbourmaster at Tveraa. Thorshavn Radio dealt with our call efficiently and in excellent English, but the harbourmaster at Tveraa did not agree with the pilot book. He said firmly that there was no slip available for us there, but he was also helpful, and told us that there was a slip at another place called Vaag. So we called up the harbourmaster at Vaag, who said yes, there was a slip and he thought that we could probably use it. So we decided to make for Vaag, which is a small town of about 1,100 people, nestling at the end of Vaag Fjord on Suduroy Island. The harbourmaster was anxious to have an estimated time of arrival, and seemed a bit puzzled that we were unable to give one, until we explained that we were wholly under sail, with no engine. Then he understood. I wrote in my journal:

> I do hope that we are not going to be held up for ages at Vaag, and that it is all not going to cost much. It is a damned nuisance, but there it is.

In the way of things, when we could have done with some wind to help our passage to Vaag, we found ourselves all but becalmed. Apart from lack of wind, that evening (May 7) was lovely, with a gentle swell and a clean, open sky. The sun set in a mass of clear gold, without a touch of red, the exquisitely pale gold of a well-worn wedding ring. The whole seascape seemed suddenly very Northern, cold and surgically clean. We drifted more or less in the right direction and amused ourselves by trying to identify the gulls that came around us. None of us knew much about seabirds, but I had brought two bird books with which we hoped to be able to identify them. Our books, however, though no doubt theoretically accurate, were not of much practical help. Apparently you can identify gulls by studying their feet – but how can you look at the feet of a seagull when it is either swimming or flying? We decided that ours were the Common Gull, but we had a bit of doubt about their beaks. The book told us that the beak of the Common Gull is 'greenish-yellow'. The beaks of our gulls seemed to be more the colour of an egg yolk. But they looked lovely sitting on the water, gently rising and falling with the swell. A different kind of bird came along, more streamlined than the others, and we decided that this was a Kittiwake, or perhaps the Little Gull. On my watch Tim sighted land, about thirty miles away. He has far better eyes than mine and it took me about half a minute to find it. But there it was – a high island. It was no doubt the island for which we were bound. The pilot book told us that it had cliffs a thousand feet high, so it was reasonable that we should see it from a long way off on a clear evening.

There is nothing quite so dramatic as making a landfall on a small island – a dot in the ocean, which somehow you have to come to. Navigation always seems to me to be magic. I said to Tim: 'Is this our very own island? The one that we are going to?' He said, 'Yes, it is our very own island.' This was much better than our last landfall, in that foul murk off Buchan Ness.

I did not feel able to sleep when I came off watch on that calm evening, and took the opportunity to put down in my journal a good many general thoughts. They seem haphazard now, but this is how they came to me then:

> I do not really enjoy being on watch much; it is a responsibility which I feel heavily, and my glasses are a frightful nuisance. On watch, I think mostly about Helen. I don't think that it has been very fair to her to make this voyage, and yet in some way I *had* to make it. I cannot go on writing about other men's ocean sailing without doing something myself. Helen understands this, and has been wonderful throughout. But I have hated leaving her to cope with everything, and I'm just longing to be back with her.

On top of seasickness, Peter Comber had another trouble which bothered him, but about which, gamely, he said next to nothing. A plate holding a tooth had come adrift, and his mouth was in considerable discomfort. He had tried to repair the plate in various ways, but it was not successful. His tooth needed professional attention.

During the night of Saturday/Sunday (May 7/8), our calm changed to a strong headwind around Force 5, dead on the nose for where we wanted to go. This meant a hard beat to get into Vaag Fjord. *Griffin* put her lee rail under, and we had a rough, but marvellous sail into the fjord. Peter Comber was at the helm, and he told me afterwards that handling *Griffin* on this hard beat was something he would remember all his life. That morning was made memorable in another, minor way – scrambled eggs for breakfast. We had not had scrambled eggs before, and I decided suddenly that I would do

some. With *Griffin* half buried in the sea, and the galley at an angle
as steep as the roof of a house, the others regarded my performance
as a mixture of madness and heroism. I observed that *Griffin* herself
would do most of the scrambling. I collected twelve eggs from under
the floorboards in Reg's and my cabin, where they lived, got them
somehow to the galley, and into a saucepan. At that steep angle,
the saucepan was not really big enough to hold them, and the gas
flame burnt badly at such an angle of heel. But I mixed in milk
powder and by brute force in holding the saucepan to the cooker,
I managed to get them done – and they turned out to be jolly good
scrambled eggs. Not only was this breakfast of some value as a
morale raiser, both Peter Comber and Allister McIntosh felt able to
eat scrambled eggs, and what is more they kept them down.

Our call at the Faeroes I regard now as the direct intervention of
Providence in our affairs. First, it gave us precisely the break we
needed after what was in fact our shakedown cruise. And it gave us
that break in the happiest way imaginable; from the moment we
landed, the kindly Faeroese took us to their hearts, opened their
homes to us, and gave us everything they could. The shipyard at
Vaag, owned by the Dahl family – notable in Faeroese history –
must be, I think, among the most efficient in the world. The Faeroese
have been seamen for a thousand years or more, and they are used
to doing everything for themselves. They tackled work on *Griffin*
with exactly the same care that they would have given to one of their
own fishing boats. We could not have found more skilful workman-
ship anywhere. Looking back on what was done, that we were at
sea again four days after we landed now seems to me a miracle.

But I have more important reasons still for blessing our enforced
call at the Faeroes. Historically, the Faeroe Islands were the right
starting point for my voyage. I had scarcely thought of them when
planning the expedition (save as a possible place of refuge), but I
had not been in Vaag for more than a few hours before I understood
that in a curious way I was re-living tenth-century Norse history.
The Faeroes were settled by Vikings from Norway a generation or
two before their expansion from Iceland to Greenland, and on to the
Vinland colonies. The Faeroese today are the direct descendants of

those Norsemen whose history I was trying to unravel, and their way of life is nearer to the old Norse way than anything to be found anywhere. Icelanders are also direct descendants of the old Norsemen, but the economy of Iceland has been brought more into the modern world. Iceland has a wealth of natural power in its hot springs, and this is being put to a number of modern industrial uses. The Faeroese have nothing but their sheep and the sea. Mr Alec Forrest, an Englishman married to a Faeroese, who has made his home in the Faeroes, and who showed us much kindness while we were there, in conversation quoted a Faeroese proverb – 'Wood is gold in the Faeroes.' This gave me a sudden flash of enlightenment about the economic compulsion which drove Leif Eiriksson and his companions to look for new land to the west. The Faeroes have no wood of their own, and even today, when there are many new materials in the world, wood is vital to their economy: they still need it for their houses and for their boats. A thousand years ago, there was no conceivable alternative to wood, and the Norsemen could not survive without it. The discovery of a new source of timber would have meant more to them than discovering the Klondike. In other ways, too, the problems in the Faeroes today are precisely those that faced the Norsemen in Iceland and Greenland. The high moorland of the Faeroese cliffs and hills provides good grazing for sheep, but nothing else; apart from a few potato patches, there is next to no arable land, and there is next to no dairy farming. The sea and the sheep offer sustenance in return for continuous hard work, but practically everything else has to be imported. It was the same with the Norse colonies in Greenland – they had a compelling need to find new land to support them. A glimpse of life in the Faeroes brings home the meaning of the old Icelandic sagas. Leif Eiriksson called his settlement in America 'Vinland' because he found wild grapes growing there. He also found wild wheat, lush pastureland, and rivers rich in fish. You cannot read the sagas, even in translation, without feeling the force and freshness of the wonderment with which those rough Norsemen, accustomed to the harsh life of Greenland, found their American landfall. Later, their American land came to be known as 'Vinland the Good' – in the inscription on the Yale map it is described as 'this extensive and most

F

wealthy country'. After visiting the Faeroes, you understand why all this was so. Scholars have sometimes tried to argue that the root 'vin' in Vinland does not necessarily refer to grapes or wine, but may be from another old Norse root meaning simply 'pasture'. Other scholars have denounced this, holding that the word 'vin' in this context could not possibly mean anything but wine. You cannot read the sagas with any sense of their historical setting without concluding that these latter scholars are right – the Norsemen *did* find grapes and make wine, and their delight and wonderment at this lives on freshly in the ancient records. In a number of important ways the Faeroes offer a key to the rediscovery of Vinland.

But I must return to my narrative. As we beat in from the rough sea to the calmer waters of Vaag Fjord, our spirits rose. The little painted houses on the hillsides looked like pictures in a book of Hans Andersen's stories, and the whole fjord had a sort of fairytale air about it. Our engine was useless and Peter Haward handled *Griffin* beautifully as he brought her up to the little quay at Vaag under sail alone, going about at just the right split second to bring her gently to the quayside. I jumped ashore with a warp from the bows, and a knot of kindly people on the quay took our stern lines. Mr Einar Dahl of the shipyard had come down to welcome us, though I did not know this at the time – I took him for one of the harbour officials. He suggested that we should move round the quay to a more sheltered berth on the other side, so we warped her round. Then it was a question of waiting for the Customs. The Faeroe Islands belong to Denmark and we had run up our Danish courtesy flag. That was impeccably correct, but I wish very much that we had had a Faeroese ensign. I did not know it then, but the Faeroese have a flag of their own. Although it was a Sunday morning, a Customs officer and Mr Kjartan Midjord, the Assistant Sheriff, then acting as Chief of Police in Vaag, soon came down to the quay. While Peter Haward and the rest of the crew tidied up on deck, I went below with the officials to deal with our clearance and ship's papers. This can be an ordeal, but in Vaag our clearance was more a social occasion than a struggle with bureaucracy. Our papers were in order and soon dealt with, and at once we began a long conversation about Vinland, and the objects of our expedition. We also discussed dinner – I thought that a meal ashore would be good for everybody and I asked Mr Midjord whether there was an hotel or restaurant to which we might go. I did not realise it then, but this request put the Faeroese to a vast amount of trouble. We were, of course, talking in English – to my shame none of us knew more than a few words of Danish and not a single word of Faeroese. There was an odd delay while the Customs officer went off. I did not know what was happening, and thought that my request to be directed to a restaurant had perhaps been misunderstood. In fact, the Customs officer had gone off to see if anyone in Vaag had enough spare food to provide lunch for six stray Britishers – there is no hotel in Vaag, and only one small restaurant, which is really a boarding house and requires notice before extra meals can be provided. The Faeroese are not a rich community, and they cannot afford to risk wasting any food. It turned out that at such short notice on a Sunday, Vaag could not provide six extra meals, so the Customs man telephoned an hotel in a slightly larger place called Trangisvaag, about ten or twelve miles away, to order lunch for us. The Chief of Police got in touch with a man who owned a Volkswagen Microbus to come to drive us over, and himself came with us – all this on a Sunday morning with no notice at all. Although Trangisvaag is not really very far from Vaag itself, the road has to wind round fjords and inlets, and the drive there took the best part of an hour. The restaurant was spotlessly clean in the Scandinavian manner, and gave us a simple but splendid meal of soup and a kind of mutton stew. When I asked for the bill, I was told that the Chief of Police had already paid it. This incredible generosity to absolute strangers marked the whole of our stay.

Mr Midjord took us back to Vaag and arranged for the school-house to be opened on Sunday afternoon so that we could use the shower baths in its gymnasium. They were welcome baths, although, since it was Sunday and the heating was shut down, the water was no more than lukewarm. Feeling clean and fed, we went back to *Griffin*. What looked like being an exceptionally pleasant little holiday in the Faeroes was all very well, but until *Griffin* could be slipped I had no idea of what work might be necessary on her rudder, I had no idea what it might cost and no idea how long it might take.

I had given myself two months for the expedition, and if anything went seriously wrong I feared that the expedition would be a fiasco – that we should not have time even to look for Vinland. My timetable had to be strict. Peter Haward had commitments which made it imperative for him to be back in England by the first week in July, and Tim Lee also had to get back at the beginning of July because he had only so much leave from the Navy. Reg Garrod has his own business in London and although, being his own master, he was in a sense better placed than the rest of us to wander about the Greenland seas instead of earning a living, in fact he had pressing responsibilities in his business: it was a remarkable act of friendship that he had made time to come with me at all. Allister and Peter Comber were not quite such slaves to time – Allister because he was proposing to spend some months in Canada and the United States on his own, and Peter because, as a schoolmaster, he had at least the summer holidays: but without Peter Haward, Reg and Tim Lee the expedition would disintegrate. I, too, had planned to return as early as I could in July. But there was nothing to be gained by sitting down and worrying. There was work to be done, and we had to get down to it. I went to have a look at the slip in the Vaag shipyard, to see if it would take Griffin with her rather deep keel, while Peter, Reg, Tim and Allister made plans and rough drawings of the wooden knees to strengthen Griffin's coach roof, and of the various ways of devising new berths for Allister and Peter Comber. Peter Comber went over our stores to see what we might need in the way of supplies, and also tried to find a dentist.

On seeing the shipyard my hopes rose slightly. The slip seemed quite capable of taking Griffin, and the foreman, who had come down on Sunday afternoon to discuss things with me, seemed to be out-standingly capable. But Griffin could not be put on the slip on Sunday evening, and would have to wait until next day. I came away from the shipyard feeling that for the moment I had done all I could. Next, there was food to be arranged. If work was to be done on Griffin, it would not be possible for us to cook and feed ourselves on board, so I had to try to arrange meals ashore. Here Mr Forrest, who was a tower of strength throughout our stay in Vaag, came to the rescue. He took me to visit the woman who ran the little boarding

house in Vaag, and she agreed to give us meals, starting with breakfast next morning. By this time, practically the whole community
in Vaag had been down to the quay to have a look at *Griffin*, and to
offer any help they could, and I wanted to try to do something to
repay this hospitality. The only thing I could think of was to offer
to give a lecture about Vinland at the school. This offer was accepted,
and it was arranged that I should give my lecture the next night. I
was a bit dubious about the fact that I could speak only in English,
but I need not have been concerned. Unlike the English, who are
shameful about learning other people's languages, the Faeroese take
learning seriously, and all the upper forms of their schools study
English. What is more, they learn to speak English well. As things
turned out, I had a wonderful audience, deeply interested in Vinland
as part of their own Norse history, and fully capable of understanding
my talk in English.

I can best sum up our stay in Vaag by quoting from my journal
written at the time:

I am writing this sitting on my sleeping bag on the floor of a
woman chiropodist's studio (surgery?) in Vagur – Danish Vaag –
on Suduroy – Danish Syderø – Island in the Faeroes. I am going
to sleep here with a good Anglepoise light and all Dr Scholl's
foot powders (in Danish) around me. Why I am here requires
some explanation ...

We got here on Sunday, May 8, and intended to slip *Griffin* on
Monday. As it happened, she could not be slipped then because of
a strong wind howling up the fjord, but she was on Tuesday. Her
rudder fastenings are awful – all loose, and the bottom one nearly
broken through. How it survived even the bit of rough weather
we had is beyond me. We certainly could not have gone on without
disaster. All the rudder fastenings have to be redone. While the
metalwork is being done in the blacksmith's shop, they are getting
on with making knees to reinforce the cabin top, and with
interior carpentry to fix up berths for Allister and Peter Comber.
Allister completely recovered from his seasickness the moment he
set foot on shore, and he can do a lot of the joinery himself – this
proves how useful it is to have a ship's carpenter on board. Also,

it will help to keep down the cost – the shipyard people are very nice in letting our own man work with them. We are having meals at the little restaurant in Vaag. I went there with Alec Forrest to arrange for meals, and the woman who runs the place, who has no English at all, met us with a torrent of Faeroese. I took this to be a general denunciation of us for the demands we were making upon her, but I wronged her shamefully; she was apologising for not having been able to give us lunch when the Customs man had asked her on Sunday, 'because there was no food in the house'.

We slept on *Griffin* on Monday night, but when she went on the slip on Tuesday sleeping was a problem: it would have been uncomfortable enough anyway, with people working all over the place, and also although *Griffin* seemed securely propped on the slip I was not happy about having people sleeping on board. The problem was – where to sleep? Here Alec Forrest and his Faroese wife came to the rescue: they offered us the floor of a big room they had in their house, downstairs. Not only did they offer this, but Alec Forrest arranged for the shipyard's lorry to come and collect our bedding from the boat. Putting up stray foreigners seems to be accepted by the people of Vaag as part of the natural order of things. Last summer eighteen girls of the British Girls' Exploring Society who were stranded for the night in Vaag, apparently because the steamer for Thorshavn had left before they had expected it to, were all accommodated in the house of Mr Holm, the history master at Vaag school. He and his wife had two French girls staying with them at the time, and Mr Holm explained casually, 'We had twenty visitors sleeping all over the house that night.'

The Forrests' downstairs room turned out to be a sort of suite of rooms – one big room opening on to their own bedroom, with a bathroom and lavatory and the chiropodist's parlour next door: the chiropodist is a relation of Mrs Forrest's. They needed their own bedroom, but made us free of all the rest of the place, including the floor of the chiropodist's parlour. We must have been a fearful nuisance to them, but they showed not a sign of irritation and kept offering us food and coffee. I laid out four sleeping bags on the floor of the big room, put myself in the privacy of the chiropodist's room, with Peter Haward next to me in a sort of ante room. I don't know that the chiropodist's floor was really the best berth, but I wanted it chiefly because of the Anglepoise light, because I wanted to write in the small hours of the morning. Anyway, we are all pretty comfortable, and having a bathroom at hand is a godsend. There are no public lavatories in Vaag – at least we never have managed to find one. This makes things difficult! There is a lavatory in the little restaurant where we eat, and there are lavatories at the school – but they are about a mile apart.

I wrote on the floor here until around midnight and then dozed off. I woke with a start about 0230 and began frantically to get out of my sleeping bag, thinking: 'There is no one on watch – what on earth is happening to the boat?' Then I realised that I was in a house, and turned in again with some relief.

I am taking up this journal again on my second night on the chiropodist's floor. I had hoped to sail today, but the work was not finished and there are still jobs to be done. But I am fairly confident that we shall sail some time tomorrow. These Faeroese shipyard workers are incredible. Although I chafe at the delay, worry myself sick about it, they have done in three days what would have taken three weeks at most English yacht yards. I have damaged my left wrist, and have to wear my watch on my right wrist, which is rather irritating. I don't know exactly what I have done to the wrist, but I must have cut or scraped it in some way, and the wound has turned septic. I have put on some of the pencillin gauze that Dr Squires in Wantage recommended for our medical kit. I hope it will be all right. (In a couple of days it was.) On the injury front generally, things are looking up. Peter Comber found a school dentist who has dealt with his tooth. And dealt with it extremely skilfully, by Peter's account – he is full of praise for Faeroese (or perhaps it should be Danish) dentistry.

Tonight we had a sumptuous meal at the Forrests' – stew, ham and scrambled eggs, Danish pastries, cakes, all sorts of things. But tea, because we are English. I loathe tea, and couldn't take any. Mrs Forrest offered to make coffee for me, but I couldn't bear to ask her to make for me alone so I went without. Then, talk in the Forrests' sitting room, a nice long room, with that beautifully clean-lined Danish furniture. It was good talk, but I was desperately tired so I excused myself before midnight and came down to write this.

We have had some interesting gastronomic experiences, notably raisin soup at the little restaurant, and a sort of Mark II version of it with a thin jelly-like substance added. We don't know what this was – I called it 'whale blubber', though I am sure it wasn't. Allister rather liked it but Tim and I couldn't manage it.

We were given a send-off party by Mr Johan Dahl, who in addition to playing a leading part in the Dahl shipyard, was Mayor of Vaag, and one of the chief citizens of the Faeroes. He took us to his house, where we had more Danish pastries and much interesting conversation about the islands. The Dahls are a great family in the Faeroes and we were lucky to meet them. Like everybody else in the islands, they did everything they could for us, putting their whole shipyard at our disposal and giving *Griffin* the benefit of all their skill and experience and inherited knowledge of the sea.

7

A Rough Passage to Iceland

We sailed from Vaag and the Faeroes on the afternoon of Thursday, May 12, and pretty well the whole community of Vaag seemed to be on the quay to see us off. Unhappily, it was a filthy day, with stinging rain and the wind against us as we made our way out of the fjord. We had to beat out of the fjord in a series of short tacks, our No. 1 Yankee doing a fine job and pulling like a Shire horse. We thought that at least we could give our well-wishers on the quay a demonstration of nice handling of a yacht in beating out of their fjord, but within a couple of cables we were lost in the murk.

We left the Faeroes in infinitely better shape than when we arrived – in better shape both as a crew and as a ship. In human terms, we had shaken down together, rubbed off some rough corners, and become a community instead of a bunch of individuals. *Griffin* was both stronger and safer. The Faeroese had done a marvellous job on the rudder, reforging the fastenings and making it immensely strong. The knees that Peter Haward had designed for strengthening the coach roof were all through-bolted, and we felt confident that they could withstand even a massive sea. Below, we had refashioned our sleeping accommodation, to provide new bunks for Allister and Peter Comber. One was contrived at the expense of our cabin table: this had been sawn in two, leaving a sort of vestigial table, but giving a good boxed-in berth, opposite Peter Haward's berth in the saloon. The other berth was on the floor in Reg's and my cabin, but properly contrived so that it was raised a little from the floor, and fitted with a leeboard to prevent the occupant from being thrown out in heavy weather. This carpentry was skilfully contrived by Peter Haward and Allister, so that it did no structural harm to *Griffin*'s interior. The table top was plywood and could be replaced easily enough, and the other bits and pieces were made from additional wood: they could be taken down and *Griffin* restored to her original shape in an hour or so.

This rearrangement enabled everyone to have his own berth in either the cabin or saloon, but it added sadly to the discomfort of our already-crowded conditions. It meant that there were three people sleeping regularly in our small saloon, which robbed it of any pretence of comfort for anything else. The half-table that we had left ourselves was a little better than nothing, but it was a maddening affair, too small to write on, and capable of allowing only two people to eat at table at any one time. Still, it was the best we could do. The new third berth in Reg's and my cabin made the cabin overcrowded. It meant that anyone going forward to the fo'c'sle or the lavatory had to stumble over even more kit, and perhaps a sleeping body. Again, it was the best that we could do. The new saloon berth was regarded as a slightly better home than the floor berth in the cabin, so it was agreed that Allister and Peter Comber should take the two berths in turn – Allister to have the first fortnight in the saloon. We had not been able to add much to our stores in the way of fresh food in the Faeroes, for there was little that we could buy. It would have been nice to have had fresh milk and vegetables for the first few days of this stage of our passage, but we could obtain neither, except at the cost of depriving the Faeroese themselves. Peter Comber, however, did manage to buy some rye bread. But *Griffin* was well stocked and we had no anxieties about stores.

The mechanic at the Vaag shipyard had more or less rebuilt our ancient engine, and it consented to go again. But none of us had much confidence in it, and it packed up a few days later. This meant that we were wholly committed to sail, which did not bother us except for the slight nuisance of not having an engine for manoeuvring in confined places. But it also meant that we could not use our alternator for charging the radio batteries, and had to depend on the little portable charging motor that we carried with us as a reserve. This was a sturdy little engine, though it too was old and gave trouble later. Its main disadvantage was that it could be used only on deck, which required reasonably calm weather. However, I was not greatly worried about it because I felt every confidence in the heavy-duty Exides, and believed that as long as we could put some charge in them occasionally they would see us through. They did. We economised as much as we could in other demands on the batteries, using *Griffin's* electric lighting only for such imperative needs as lighting the compasses, Tim's navigating cubbyhole, and our navigation lamps. We were going north and the year was moving towards midsummer, so the long hours of daylight helped: our demands on the navigation lights were slender, for we used them only when there was other shipping about, or when we were closing land. The electrical work that had been done on *Griffin* at Dover was first-rate, and we had a pair of powerful floodlights on the spreaders to provide light for emergencies on deck. These floodlights were invaluable, but they made heavy demands on the batteries, so we rationed their use severely. We did use them, however, whenever we really needed them, and the batteries never let us down.

To economise with lighting in the saloon, we used a Tilley lamp instead of the electric light. This had the additional value of providing a certain amount of warmth, which was a godsend as we got farther north. One of the consequential difficulties that came with our rearrangement of sleeping accommodation was that the saloon became too crowded to use our oil stove with comfort. We did light it for short periods when it was bitterly cold, but with three people sleeping in such a tiny space, and others perhaps sitting there, it was not long before the oil stove began giving us headaches. If I were planning the voyage again I should give more thought to ventilation, to enable the stove to be kept going continuously. Our one pipehole over the oil stove was not enough – and ventilation was made particularly difficult in rough weather, because every instinct is to close holes in cabin or saloon to keep out the water.

Even the Tilley lamp was inclined to make the atmosphere heavy, and at night we put it out as often as we could. We had to compromise between the comfort of warmth and the discomfort of airlessness. We were all aware of the dangers of lamp or stove in confined quarters and we never, I think, ran any real risk. But we did have to endure more cold than we liked. We had, on the whole, fair winds for our passage from the Faeroes to Iceland, but it was

certainly rough. My journal for May 13, the day after we left
Vaag, records:

> Griffin is going like a train, under the double-reefed mainsail only.
> She has averaged seven knots for hour after hour. She needs some
> holding.

We began to find watchkeeping an ordeal, though we suffered
in different ways. It is hard to keep hands and feet warm in the open
cockpit of a small boat. I was lucky with my feet – I seldom had any
particular pain from them, but I think I suffered more than anybody
from cold hands. My hands have always been a bother to me in
cold weather, ever since I was sent to England from the West Indies
to go to school, and plunged from the tropics into my first winter at
a boarding school. You can't do much in the way of deck work on
a sailing boat in gloves, and in cold weather on Griffin I suffered
agonies from my hands. After even a few minutes of working with
bare hands I had to drive myself to go on using them. And sometimes
one or other hand would become so frozen that it was all but incapable of use. Fortunately, the others had better hands than mine,
although there was an equation of discomfort in that they tended to
have more pain in their feet.

The helmsman can – indeed must – wear gloves in cold weather,
but at that time none of us except Tim Lee, who had a pair of
Arctic naval gloves, had gloves that were any use. We had equipped
ourselves with rubber gloves in England, but the only sort we could
buy were more or less like gardening gloves, unlined and with next
to no warmth in them. These proved useless, and after being worn
for half an hour or so produced so much condensation inside that
they added to our discomfort. We tried wearing woollen gloves
under them, but although this gave warmth for a bit, the condensation inside the rubber gloves soon made the wool soaking wet. In
the Faeroes, Reg Garrod and I had bought thick woollen mittens.
These are what the Faeroese fishermen use. They were better than
nothing, but soon got soaked with rain or spray. Both the Faeroese
and later the Icelanders told us that the thing to do is to wear
woollen mittens (loose mittens are better than fingered gloves),
to let them get soaked with seawater and to be patient. They said

that after a little time of feeling cold with seawater, wet woollen gloves would become warm again. Peter Comber found that this worked to some extent, but the rest of us did not. Perhaps we were not patient enough, or perhaps we were not as tough as Faeroese fishermen. Peter Haward contrived for himself a weird loose sleeve made out of thin plastic sheeting, which he sewed to the sleeve of his oilskins. This enabled him to wear some sort of glove under the protection of the sleeve. This was ingenious but, like so many good inventions, suffered from the inadequacy of the materials available: the plastic sheeting was not strong enough for the job. Later, in Iceland, we were able to buy lined plastic mittens, loose enough for woollen or cotton gloves to be worn under them. This combination worked fairly well, and although my hands got cold whatever I did about them, the plastic-mitten/woollen-glove combination was a major help.

The weather continued rough and on our second day out I wrote in my journal:

It blew up during the night, but I slept through. Peter Haward and Tim Lee reefed the main and I woke to find us running in about Force 7 (soon Force 8) under the reefed main (two reefs down) alone. My watch (0900–1100) was horribly cold, with drenching seas over me. In spite of oilies some went down my neck and I had to change down to my vest when I came off watch. When I got below, I had to spend about twenty minutes thawing out my right hand by wrapping it in a towel. After this I decided to make an omelette à la Griffin for lunch. That sounds good, but it was really a sort of poor man's omelette, contrived with Marvel milk powder, and with a tin of baked beans in it. All went well in spite of difficulties in the galley, with Griffin more or less standing on her head.

Tim Lee has just put over a weather report to Wick Radio. Conditions were pretty bad. He tried to give them the 'seawater temperature' and they were puzzled by what they took to be our 'tea water temperature'. At 44°F the tea would have been pretty cold.

After a rough night we cheered ourselves up by getting down to good housekeeping.

We have just had a grand clearing up – Tim scrubbing out the saloon, me doing the galley while Peter Haward and Reg Garrod set the staysail. Feel much better for our tidy up. We had boiled eggs for breakfast and I saved the egg water (sea, of course) for shaving. Did quite well – I suppose a bit of salt had boiled out of it, perhaps. We are having a rough passage – Force 5 at the moment, and it seems quite gentle! The forecasts promised us everything up to Force 10 or so, but *Griffin* takes what comes and the weather mostly has not yet been as bad as the forecasts. We have had a fair bit of Force 8 and perhaps an occasional Force 9, but nothing worse. Got through to Brent well at 0800 GMT. Anne sounds so nice and secure when we are standing on our heads.

I am impressed by the persistence and survival value of *little* things. You lash down some big thing with 2 in. rope, and the wind and sea make short work of it. But my pocket watch, hanging on a bit of whipping twine, is still there. A bit of Helen's darning wool, tied to a backstay as a wind indicator, is still there. These things are like those pathetic lavatories and baths left ridiculously intact after an air raid.

We are listening to an absurd broadcast on the Light Programme of the BBC. I think that I have never heard such nonsense, and it seems about as far removed from *Griffin* as the moon, but it is making Allister laugh, which is a good thing.

The sea itself is marvellously clean and lovely. The sea is surely neutral towards human beings. It throws us about and hurls itself at us, but it does not *mind* about us. If we look after *Griffin*, the sea will let her be – she rises to each wave wonderfully well.

The weather continued rough, and the next evening (May 15) we lost our mainsail. This happened during my dog watch (1700–1800). We were going hard under the double-reefed mainsail in a wind that was pretty strong – somewhere around Force 8. It was all that I could do to hold her, but I was rather enjoying the rough ride, and *Griffin*'s supreme confidence in meeting the heavy seas that came at her. Suddenly I saw a line of light along the foot of the reefed mainsail, near the boom. I suppose I realised what was happening in some fraction of a second, but time scales in the crises of life are odd, and it seemed to me that I watched disaster unfold itself in a curiously leisurely fashion, like a slow-motion film. I yelled out, and Peter Haward, who had been asleep below, was up in an instant, rushing on deck in pyjama trousers and bare feet, ignoring the crashing spray and the bitter cold. He went straight to the mast, clawing at the sail to get it down, to save as much as he could from tearing further. The others followed at once, and soon everybody was on deck. I stayed at the helm, trying to keep *Griffin* under some sort of control while the others struggled with the sail. The strength of flapping canvas in a strong wind is all but indescribable: it seems to have an enmity that is wholly vicious towards everybody who tries to subdue it. And it is a mad viciousness, purposeless and horrible, like a demented man thrashing out and hurting himself as much as anybody else. The sail could be subdued only by brute force, but somehow it was got in and lashed to the boom. Then came a momentary breathing space, for the staysail kept *Griffin*'s head to the wind, and the helm could be lashed down. I persuaded Peter Haward to put on rather more in the way of clothes, and we set to work with needles and thread to do what we could in the way of temporary repairs.

I say we sewed – but that is getting a little ahead of events. The first problem was to find sailmaker's materials. I thought that we had some among our bosun's stores, but if we had nobody was able to find them, then, or at any other time on the voyage. Peter Haward – seaman that he is – had a palm and a few sailmaker's needles among his personal possessions, and by the grace of God I had hurriedly snatched up from my own *Mary Lane*, before joining *Griffin* at Dover, a little sailmaker's kit that I had carried for years. This kit, although small, has everything you need – sailmaker's palm, a selection of needles, reels of twine in various sizes, and a sailmaker's razor-sharp blade. I had this kit, living neatly in its own wallet, with my one set of respectable clothes, in a drawer under my bunk, and I could lay hands on it quickly. Then, and at other times, it was invaluable – it was the only sailmaker's kit that we had and, small as it was, it did its job.

Having assembled Peter Haward's needles and my kit, we returned to the sail, spacing ourselves along the boom, and each taking a couple of feet of tear to tackle. At once we ran into trouble. The will to work was there, but materials were sadly lacking. We had needles enough, but between the five of us we had only two palms – hard leather pads which fit over the palm of the hand to act as thimbles in forcing needles through thick canvas. We produced a few ordinary thimbles from the domestic sewing kits that most of us had with us, but an ordinary thimble is not much use for sewing sails. At first Peter Haward used his palm and I used mine; we could stitch away, but the others, without palms, could make little progress. Reg was working beside me, doing what he could with a thimble, and it soon struck me that he was a very much better sailmaker than I; Reg's business is concerned with carpets, and he is a professional at sewing and fitting carpets. So I gave my palm to Reg, and he did the sewing, while I acted as his mate, and kept needles threaded for him. Peter Comber did the same for Peter Haward, while Tim Lee struggled on with the best of our thimbles. I had a strange sense of being two people. One was clinging to the boom of a crippled and madly-tossing small sailing boat in the North Atlantic wondering for how long he could manage to go on threading needles with frozen hands. The other was a completely detached observer, looking down on *Griffin*, as it were, and finding the whole performance fascinating to watch. It was a mad sewing party in mid-Atlantic – a bunch of men stitching away and occasionally chatting to one another, for all the world like a village sewing bee before the annual fête. But it was a sewing bee with a difference – every few minutes the whole sewing party would be drenched with spray from a breaking wave, and instead of sitting down comfortably, they would be lying full-length across the boom at one moment, the next more or less standing on their heads. While all this was going on a gull, riding on the sea, rising and falling with the waves, looked on with complete unconcern. He was so near that I could see the brightness of his eyes. I felt half angry with him because he seemed so utterly at home in the storm.

We slaved at the sail for about an hour and a half, and then it became apparent that we were not winning. Although we were succeeding in cobbling up along the tear, it was more than doubtful whether this rough stitching would hold in even the lightest wind. We did succeed in making the sail safe and preventing the tear from spreading, but having done this, we decided to give up and wait for the weather to moderate. We had our trysail, a little triangular red sail, immensely strong, which could still be set aft of the mast. This trysail, very small in area, is primarily intended for use as a riding sail in storms, but although small it offered a chance of giving *Griffin* some sort of balance for a headsail, and of getting her sailing again. In the fitting out at Dover, Bernard Iverson had suggested that the trysail should be given a separate track on the mast, so that it could be set without having to unbend the mainsail to use the mainsail track. This was a most practical suggestion and, fortunately, we had acted upon it. So the trysail could be set quickly and without difficulty. This we now did, and it was a great relief to get under way again. *Griffin* could make headway under staysail and trysail, although we had to let her fall off from our former course. But the wind increased, and soon even these two pocket handkerchiefs of sails became too much for her. So we took in the staysail, and continued on our way under the trysail alone.

Nobody had thought about eating for hours. Peter Haward had made a stew for lunch, and some of this was left over. We managed to warm up the remains on the galley stove, at an angle of 30 degrees or so, and ate it gratefully. For me, this turned out to be a mistake. I felt glad of the meal when I had it, but soon after I had eaten I was sick, for the first and only time on the voyage. I felt no ill effects from this sickness: I was sick one moment, and the next I was feeling perfectly all right. I turned in for a couple of hours. My journal the next day says:

It was a rough night, with one terrific crash from a wave hitting my side of the ship, an inch or so from my bunk, just the planking between us. I woke with a start, for it sounded as though we had hit something, but we hadn't, so I dozed off again. My watch was 0300–0500, and I never sleep very well when I have an early watch. In fact, I did not try to do more than doze – did not get into my sleeping bag, but lay down fully dressed and ready to get up. By the time my watch came, however, it was quite a nice morning – the wind had moderated to about Force 6, enough in most circumstances, but seeming gentle in comparison with the Force 9

G

or so we had come through. It was an easy watch, with nothing to do but to keep *Griffin* gently sailing as close to the wind as possible. Without her mainsail she wouldn't do much better than south – nearly in the opposite direction to the way we want to go. We ended up the night some thirty-five miles farther away from Iceland than we were when the sail split. But this is partly deliberate: the forecast is offering us a *storm* – Force 9 or 10 – from the southwest, and we don't want to risk getting too near to the Icelandic coast and finding ourselves on a lee shore in a storm, with a dud mainsail. So we have been glad to make this offing by going backwards.

My morning call to Brent was OK, though we had difficulties in transmitting because the aerial lead blew off three times. Brent kept saying, 'We've lost you, *Griffin*.' They hadn't: we had lost our aerial lead.

During the morning we got the Yankee up and with the try-sail drawing well in a strong wind – Force 6–7 – we managed to make about northwest at 4–5 knots. Peter Haward and Reg Garrod during the afternoon got the rest of the mainsail stitched.

This really was heroic work. Peter Haward and Reg – far and away our two best sailmakers – got down to work on the mainsail as soon as the wind moderated enough. 'Enough' is a relative term. I doubt if the wind was ever less than Force 6 or so while they worked, and it remained bitterly cold. But they achieved a good strong repair. We could not risk setting the full sail again, but in any case there was too much wind for the full mainsail. But after their repair, in the late afternoon, we managed to reset the mainsail double-reefed. This made an enormous difference – *Griffin* was soon making 7 knots again, and she was handleable on something like her proper course. There was another gloomy forecast of a southerly storm going up to Force 10. The wind stayed strong, but mercifully the forecast, as far as we were concerned, was over-gloomy, and it never hit us at quite that strength. But we could not know this at the time of the forecast. We decided to make for a place called Vestmannaeyjar, in Southern Iceland. This was about one hundred miles nearer than Reykjavik, and the *Arctic Pilot* told us that there were facilities there which we thought might include a sailmaker who could make a proper repair to our sail. I did not want to put in at Vestmannaeyjar, because on leaving the Faeroes I had given Reykjavik as our next port of call, and had asked for all our mail to be sent there. I had also asked for various spare parts for our engine to be sent to Reykjavik in the hope of being able to make it go again. But with a southerly storm threatened, we had not much choice. Vestmannaeyjar was nearer, and we thought that we might be able to get there before the storm arrived.

But this particular storm didn't arrive – at least, it never reached our particular bit of the Atlantic. I wrote in my journal for May 16:

We had a good breakfast this morning – (tinned) sausages, bacon and tomatoes, and the last of the rye bread that we were able to get in the Faeroes. It was a jolly good meal. What was *particularly* good about it was that it was cooked by Peter Comber, who is coming out of his miserable seasickness. Even Allister ate some cold tomatoes.

My watch last night was 0100–0300, and I got up and got dressed to go on watch an *hour too early*. My wrist-watch is still on British Summer Time, so that I know what time it is in London and the office. Normally, of course, I make allowance for this, but last night I glanced at my watch and got up in a hurry by British Summer Time, whereas our ship's time has been Greenwich Mean Time since we left the Faeroes. What a pest British Summer Time is – I can't think why we still put up with it. It is always tiresome for children, for farmers and for hosts of people. If people in England want an hour more for themselves in the long summer evenings, why on earth can't we just get up and start work an hour earlier, without fiddling around with the clocks?

It was dark when I went on watch – but that means dark only by Icelandic standards, it was not really dark. It stays light until nearly midnight, and was light enough to read by at 0300. But when I went on watch it was too dark to read, and the wretched binnacle light in the steering compass had gone out. I had great trouble with my eyes: I fixed up my torch (*Mary Lane's* torch) over the compass, with a rubber glove to shade it a bit, and just managed to steer by that. But it was difficult, because every

time the compass swung on its gimbals a glare from the glass
dazzled me. It was difficult enough steering anyway, and once,
to my shame, I gybed her – fortunately not serious. It was quite a
nice night, apart from the difficulties of steering. Surprisingly,
I rather enjoyed the watch – it was unexpectedly warm. I had to
give such constant attention to the wheel that I could not look at
my wrist-watch – the sleeve of my oily is a two-hand job to get
up. So I did not call Peter Haward when he was due to relieve
me, and did twenty minutes unpremeditated overtime.

I have just shaved luxuriously with *hot* seawater. Not waste-
ful of our fuel, though, for I took a bit of the washing-up water
and did not heat it up specially. Shaving is magically better with
hot seawater, and I had quite a decent shave. I haven't tried the
electric razor that Helen gave me, yet. [I never did.] You would
have thought that the one thing the Atlantic could provide
readily would be a bucket of seawater. Just the contrary. First, it
is often impossible to go on deck unless one is in oilies, and it is
not worth dressing up for a bucket of water. Then, there is
always someone in the companionway. Next, you must find your
bucket: there must be about a dozen plastic buckets on this boat,
but what she does with them I don't know. Having found your
bucket, and got it on deck, you have to get it into the sea. If
Griffin is sailing upright, her freeboard is too high for a bucket to
reach the sea without a line – go and find a piece of string. If
she is hard over the sea is almost too much for the bucket and
nearly tears the handle off, or drags you into the water. Usually
it is impossible to fish up more than about half a bucketful.
Having achieved your half-bucket, the next problem is to get it
to the washbasin – not easy, with *Griffin* usually throwing you
about all over the place. It can be done, but it is a formidable
undertaking. But then every job on a small boat at sea is formidable – I reckon that every simple movement, like getting a
handkerchief out of a pocket, takes roughly four times as long as
the same job on land. You have to plan every movement in advance. Which hand to use? For one hand *must* hang on to the ship.
Then, just as you are getting hand to pocket she rolls the other
way, so *that* hand is needed to make a frantic grab to stay in one

piece. Then *things* – everything gets lost. *Nothing* stays where you put it unless it is in a drawer, and unless the drawer is latched, it will roll out, and everything in it will be scattered. I long for Helen to tell me where things are, but I fear that *Griffin* would defeat even Helen.

We are some forty to fifty miles from Vestmannaeyjar, but haven't decided yet whether to put in there or to get on to Reykjavik. The threatened Force 10 from the south hasn't showed up yet (not to say that it won't!). It is a temptation to go on to Reykjavik, for it would be much more convenient from every point of view. We are waiting for the next shipping forecast. Peter Haward's and Reg's work on the mainsail has stood up well. It has lasted through the night and we are now running under the reefed main and boomed-out jib, making nearly 9 knots. *Griffin*, for all her age (and some infirmities, it must be admitted), is a grand sailer.

The shipping forecast again offered gales from the south or south-east of Iceland. Just before the forecast I said to Peter Haward, 'You know that I want to go to Reykjavik, but the decision after this forecast must be yours. I won't say anything more because I don't want to influence your judgment.' The forecast, when it came, was pretty horrible, but Peter Haward reckoned that we had probably *had* a good deal of it already – the Force 7–8 that we had early that morning. The forecast promised bad visibility, but we might very well have had that during Tim's watch from 0700–0900. There was a crumb of comfort in the forecast, about improving visibility later – it seemed to be improving then. After the forecast and my discussion with Peter Haward, I wrote in my journal:

Although the glass is dropping quite sharply, we have decided to make for Reykjavik. It is a bit of a gamble, but I approve the decision. We shall just have to see. Ironically, it is the most beautiful afternoon (calm before storm?). The sea is almost blue, and the sun is shining. How quickly things can change!

At 1430 that afternoon, I thought I saw land, but although Peter Haward also *thought* that he did, we did not officially admit it. At

1700, we sighted land officially – fine on the starboard bow, and identified later by Tim as Surtsey Island. Soon a collection of rocky bits came into view, plus an extraordinary cloud, rising apparently from the sea, which appeared to be a volcano. Tim was on watch at the helm, and I was up – everybody else was asleep or dozing. Tim and I chatted. We were fascinated by the volcano – it seemed to be *our* volcano, for we had it to ourselves. It certainly *looked* like a volcano, but whether it was rising from the sea or from some bit of land behind the sea it was hard to tell. It looked just like a picture-book volcano, with whitish cloud rising up and spreading, a bit like a photograph of an atom-bomb explosion. I enjoyed the idea that perhaps it was a new volcano, and that we had discovered it. Rather to Tim's disapproval (he is more cautious than I) I decided to call it 'Lee's Volcano'.

Tim's caution was right. We could find nothing about the volcano in our pilot books, and when I sent my next message to the *Guardian* I wrote that perhaps we had discovered a new volcano and that I had called it 'Lee's Volcano', after Tim. Unhappily, our pilot books were a bit out of date, for although the volcano is a pretty new one, it had been going for some months, forming a new volcanic islet of Surtsey. So, regrettably, I cannot now claim to have discovered a new volcano!

My journal for that day ends cheerfully:

We have turned the corner to get to Reykjavik, and with luck should be there some time tomorrow afternoon. Tim radioed the weather report to Reykjavik Radio, and gave them our TR (traffic route), saying that we were bound for Reykjavik. The Icelandic radio people wanted our ETA*, and seemed rather surprised that we couldn't give a very exact one. This is just what happened in the Faeroes – people nowadays do not realise the peculiarities of navigating under sail, particularly under a torn mainsail!

At 0800 next morning (May 17) we were some twenty-six miles off Reykjavik, and going well. I thought that we should be in nicely by about 1100. But the wind turned against us, and it became a hard

* Estimated time of arrival.

beat all the way. Rain squalls came at us from the snow-covered hills around Reykjavik, and it was murderously cold. I went on watch from 1100–1300, and for the last half-hour of my watch I had to grip the wheel with my arms, because my hands were useless through cold. I blessed my mates when at last I was relieved by Peter Haward and able to go below, because they were so good and sympathetic. Reg Garrod gave me a glass of whisky, which I could scarcely hold. But I got it down, and it put a bit of warmth into me. Then I just sat for about twenty minutes with my hands wrapped in a towel. As feeling came back into them I felt rather ashamed of myself, and decided to prepare some lunch. Nobody felt inclined for an elaborate meal, so I made corned beef sandwiches with Ryvita (we had no bread left). They went down well. We were beating back and forth across the long fjord leading to Reykjavik, gaining a little on each tack, but it was a long process. After lunch I decided that I couldn't bear just to watch Reykjavik *not* coming nearer, so I turned in for a couple of hours.

8

An Ambassador Comes to Tea

After beating up and down the fjord all day, we made port at 1800 hours that evening (May 20). A launch, with pilot and Customs on board, came out to meet us, and brought our mail from the harbourmaster. The launch was skilfully brought alongside *Griffin*, and the pilot and Customs officer boarded us. I went below with the Customs officer to deal with our papers, while Peter Haward and the others brought *Griffin* into harbour. The Customs officer soon dealt with my papers, and did not seal our few bottles of whisky and gin. I had a bit of a job getting up the floorboards to show him our stores in the bilges, to which we had transferred the bottles as soon as we left Scarborough and could break open the clothes locker that the Customs at Dover had selected for sealing. Perhaps the Reykjavik Customs officer thought it was such a job to get at our liquor anyway that a seal was scarcely necessary. He put me on my honour not to bring anything dutiable ashore. I came up to find *Griffin* at rest, secured to a small Icelandic gunboat called *Maria Julia*, which in turn was made fast to an elderly trawler, next to which was the big Icelandic gunboat, *Thor*. So we were fourth vessel from the quay, and had to climb over the other three ships to get ashore. But it was a good berth, and our harbourmates were always friendly. Waiting on *Maria Julia* as we came alongside was a group of Icelandic press and radio representatives, and photographers. One of the reporters was a woman, Miss Palmasdotter – I was delighted to find the old Norse form of personal name, explaining that one is son or daughter of one's father, still in use. Miss Palmasdotter told me later that one Icelandic family can have a whole batch of names: the father taking his name as the son of *his* father, the mother taking her name as the daughter of *her* father, sons and daughters similarly taking their names from their own father. The system goes right back to the sagas. It may seem rather complicated, but it works. And in a tightly-knit community, where genealogies are important, it tells you at once on meeting somebody not only who he is, but something of his family background.

Reykjavik is a metropolis in the true sense. Iceland may be a small and rather remote island, but it has played a notable part in both European and American history, and the Icelanders are rightly proud of their place in history. During the war Iceland, which had previously come under Denmark, became an independent nation – as it was in the time of the sagas. It is a fiercely-guarded independence, maintaining the traditions of the oldest democracy in Europe.

Iceland was naturally interested in our Vinland project: crowds of people came to look at *Griffin*, and although the newspapers were full of an election campaign then taking place in Reykjavik, they gave much space to us. I was invited to broadcast – in English – over the Iceland Radio, and we had a stream of visitors offering their views on where the Vinland colonies may have been – interesting and useful views. I made one mistake which was corrected quickly: in one early conversation I referred to Leif Eiriksson and his father Eirik the Red as 'Norwegians' – at once I was told firmly, 'They were Icelanders.'

Although our stay in Reykjavik was a pleasant social interlude in our voyage, there was a great deal of work to be done. First, we had to find a sailmaker to mend our mainsail. A friend of Tim Lee's family, Mr Breen, was on the quay to meet us, and he offered to find a sailmaker. He was as good as his word – went off and telephoned, and came back to say that he had found a sailmaker who was prepared to tackle our sail, who understood the urgency of it, and who would get down to it first thing next morning. Next, we had to eat. It was not easy to cook on *Griffin* in port – there was always so much to be done that there was never time to prepare meals, and since the blessed stability of being at anchor or tied to a quay offered the only real chance of tidying up, we always tried to eat ashore when we could. I felt that this was also important from the point of view of keeping up everybody's spirits – a meal ashore is a good change from eating out of tins. Here again Mr Breen helped. He took us to the

Hafna Budir, the Seamen's Mission in Reykjavik, and explained who we were. The Mission invited us to use both its restaurant and its shower baths. These showers were a joy – Iceland has constant hot water laid on by Nature from its hot springs, and I have seldom enjoyed baths so much.

We couldn't eat at the Hafna Budir that first night, because we took so much time over our baths that the restaurant was closing when we came out. So Mr Breen took us to another restaurant in Reykjavik. We were a bit concerned about our clothes – we had come off *Griffin* dressed as we were, in our working clothes, sail-cloth trousers and heavy sweaters, and we scarcely looked the part for a civilised meal in a capital city. I felt that we were rather letting down our hosts. But a word of explanation in Icelandic from Mr Breen ensured us a welcome, without raised eyebrows, in the restaurant to which he took us.

We got back to *Griffin* to find Mr Brian Holt, the British Consul in Iceland, waiting for us. Late as it was, he had come down to the harbour to see whether we needed any help that he could give. It was pleasant to meet one of our own countrymen like this, and after chatting for a time Mr Holt went away saying that he would tell the British Ambassador about us, and that he hoped that we should be invited to visit the Embassy.

It was long after midnight when I turned in. My hurriedly scrawled journal recalls:

Slept rather uncomfortably in *vest* and pullover, no shirt – wanted to keep a clean shirt for next day! Up at 0710 GMT and did tea for Peter Comber, Allister and Reg, and coffee for Peter Haward, Tim and me.

After breakfast at the Seamen's Mission, I allotted tasks. Peter Haward and I went off to the sailmaker, Reg undertook to find a bank to get some Icelandic money. Tim Lee went off to establish relations with the Icelandic meteorological people, and I asked Peter Comber and Allister to try to find a laundry, and to make arrangements for getting our clothes washed quickly. Peter Haward and I found the sailmaker, who took us back to the harbour in his van. He collected our sail and took it off to his workshop, promising to do his best to let us have it back, mended, that evening. Our social life took a surprising and slightly embarassing turn: the Consul was again waiting on the quay, this time with the news that instead of inviting us to the Embassy, His Excellency the British Ambassador had asked if he might come to see us! Our little *Griffin* seemed scarcely suitable for entertaining ambassadors, but at once I invited His Excellency for tea. We set to work to scrub and tidy our tiny and overcrowded saloon as best we could. His Excellency, Mr Holford Macleod, came promptly at 1500, bringing with him his Head of Chancery. It must have been one of the oddest ambassadorial tea parties on record. We had no crockery but our plastic mugs, and nothing much to offer in the way of eatables, but biscuits. At least, it may have been a change from normal diplomatic functions. The Ambassador stayed for over an hour, drinking tea from a plastic mug and discussing learnedly the objects of our Vinland expedition. He was deeply interested in Icelandic history.

I had hoped to be able to sail next day, but I had to postpone our departure for twenty-four hours because it turned out to be a public holiday in Iceland, and there were still things that we needed to do, but could not do over the holiday. I grudged this delay at the time, but it turned out happily, for our next visitor was Professor Thorhallur Vilmundarson, who has the Chair of Icelandic History at the University of Reykjavik. He came both to discuss our expedition, and to offer to take me in a private aeroplane to fly over that part of Iceland – Breidaford – from which Eirik the Red had sailed to Greenland. I asked whether Tim Lee could come too – there was just room for the two of us in the aeroplane, so this was all right. Professor Vilmundarson took us in his car to Reykjavik Airport, collecting on the way Mr Bardur Danielsson, by profession a civil engineer and architect, but also President of the Iceland Private Pilots' Association. Mr Danielsson had put his own aeroplane at our disposal, and came with us to pilot it himself. We had a memorable flight, flying low over the Icelandic hills, and getting an invaluable first-hand impression of the geographical background to the Icelandic sagas that it would have taken months to acquire on foot. It was a moving experience to fly over the archipelago of rocky islets. 'These islands were the nursery of the Vikings,' observed Professor Vilmundarson. It was a precise observation, for one could see how utterly dependent on boats anyone who tried to carve a living for himself out of those bare rocks must have been. Moreover, the intricate channels between them must have nurtured seamanship of the highest order. I imagined Leif Eiriksson as a boy, clambering in and out of boats, absorbing knowledge from his father, and acquiring that instinct for the sea which enabled him to achieve his Vinland voyage later.

Our sailmaker had kept his promise, and delivered our sail – strongly mended – on the evening before the public holiday. We sailed in the late afternoon of the day after the holiday, after a hectic morning. Peter Comber had found a laundry, and our clothes came back clean, but in a dreadful muddle. We had made up individual parcels of our personal washing, but the laundry had washed the lot together, leaving us to do all the sorting out. We could identify most of our own things, but some bits and pieces either went astray, or were lost in some odd corner of *Griffin* – we never saw them again. Another big work was the restowing of *Griffin*. Looking at her across the water from the far side of the harbour, I thought that she seemed rather down by the stern, and asked Peter Haward what he felt about this. Peter had been thinking about the same thing, and we decided to get more weight forward and less aft. The main stores to be moved were jerry cans of petrol and water. Peter Haward got as many of these shifted forward as the fo'c'sle would take, and *Griffin* certainly seemed to lie more happily after the transfer. It had a result that might have been disastrous later.

An unexpected but welcome visitor that last morning was the Icelandic representative of the Shell Company, who had had a cablegram from the Shell people in London, asking him to provide us, free of charge, with any fuel that we might need. This was a generous act. We needed only a few gallons of fuel because, with our engine out of action for most of the time, we had used little. But the thought behind the Shell Company's cablegram was heart-warming: it seemed to me an outstanding example of the humanity of industry that a great oil company should find time to consider our small affairs in such a way. I fear that we gave the Shell man in Iceland a good deal of trouble, for he was more accustomed to supplying fuel in bulk to big ships than in jerry cans to a little sailing boat. But he made light of it, and all we asked in the way of petrol and paraffin was promptly delivered. He also helped us in another way – he asked an expert mechanic to have a look at our engine. Peter Haward, Reg Garrod and the mechanic – Peter and Reg both seem to have a natural ability for tinkering with engines – managed to get the thing going again. The spare parts which Anne Bradbury in London had ordered from the makers to be sent to Iceland, had not arrived, and since there was no knowing when they might arrive I decided not to wait for them. Without them, the ancient engine was still in poor shape. It kept going just about long enough to get us out of the harbour, and then packed up again.

Other visitors that morning included Mr Henry Halfdansson, the secretary of the National Life Saving Association of Iceland, the equivalent of our Royal National Lifeboat Institution. Mr Halfdansson brought an invitation for lunch which, regretfully, I had to decline, because there was no time for lunch that day. I wish I could have spent longer with Mr Halfdansson, because he is a mariner of long experience, and has made a deep study of early Icelandic navigation. He came on board, we talked in the intervals between doing a host of other things, and I found his views of the American landfalls of the Vinland voyages of considerable value to me later. The secretary of the Odinn Yacht Club at Reykjavik also called, and presented us with the club's burgee. I undertook that *Griffin* should wear this on leaving Iceland. She did, and it was a rather proud piece of ship's millinery, for the yacht club had only recently been formed, and *Griffin* was only the second ship to wear its burgee.

The day before we sailed from Iceland, I had a navigational-and-timetable conference with Peter Haward, Tim Lee and Reg Garrod. Greenland had always figured in my plans, but I was not absolutely committed to landing there. Leif Eiriksson had sailed from what is now called Julianehaab, and all that was really necessary for me was that I should make my departure for the Vinland stage of the voyage from somewhere off this part of the Greenland coast. A fair bit is known about the Norse settlements around Julianehaab, and there has been devoted archaeological work there. I am in no sense an archaeologist, and had neither time nor means to add anything to what had already been found at Julianehaab: I was concerned with the sea. But Greenland was so important to the Norsemen of Leif Eiriksson's day, and it is such an interesting place in itself, that it seemed a pity not to land there if we could. One thing, however, was certain: we could not get into Julianehaab, because of ice. Coastal ice off southwest Greenland seems more severe today than it was a thousand years ago, and the fjord leading to Julianehaab was barred at this time of year. Godthaab, farther north, and the site of the Vikings' western settlement in Greenland, was ice free, and it might be possible for us to put into Frederikshaab, between Julianehaab and Godthaab.

The movement of ice around Greenland needs a little understanding. The ice that concerned us – that is, the ice along the west coast of Greenland – comes from *eastern* Greenland. The glaciers of the east coast bring great masses of ice to the sea, where they break off and form icebergs. They are caught in the current that flows clockwise around the southern tip of Greenland, and are carried round Cape Farewell and northwards up the west Greenland coast. The north-going West Greenland Current is a flow of relatively warm water, and as the ice is carried north, it gradually melts – normally it melts shortly before reaching Godthaab, so that Godthaab is usually ice-free. This West Greenland Current curls anti-clockwise across the Davis Strait until it meets the south-going Labrador Current that flows along the eastern seaboard of the northern part of the American continent. The relatively warm ex-West Greenland Current and the cold Labrador Current flow southwards side by side, meeting but not mixing, until finally they merge with the Gulf Stream south of the Grand Banks of Newfoundland. Their relative temperatures are an extraordinarily interesting study; sometimes there is almost a 'temperature wall' between them, a line on one side of which the temperature of the sea may be several degrees higher than on the other.

The rate of movement of ice around the Greenland coast, and the quantity of ice, varies from year to year, and we could not be quite sure precisely where we could put into in Greenland until we got there. We also had to be careful not to be trapped: we might be able to put into an ice-free fjord one day, and find on the next that it was closed by pack ice. So planning was a tricky business.

It was then May 19, and my original planning had envisaged getting to Greenland, or to a point in the sea off southwest Greenland from which we could take our departure for Vinland, by the end of May, leaving a month to cross the Davis Strait, and to investigate the other side. Thanks to the good work of the Faeroese shipyard, and of the sailmaker at Reykjavik, we had more or less caught up with our programme. There seemed time to go to Greenland, so we decided to go there. Peter Haward had a private ambition to see Cape Farewell, one of the great capes of the world – and one of the most forbidding. Its ominous name is justified. It would have been satisfying to have seen this formidable cape, but it was out of the question: the ice there was liable to be so dangerous that we could not approach it in our small wooden sailing boat. Tim Lee got the latest ice reports from the Met office in England, and from the Icelandic Met people in Reykjavik, and the general picture was of a great tongue of ice curving into the sea southwestwards from Cape Farewell. We had to allow for sailing outside this tongue of ice, which meant keeping from 90–100 miles south of Cape Farewell, and going a considerable distance more to the southwest before we turned north again for Greenland. There seemed to be just about enough time to permit this, and to give us at least a couple of days somewhere in Greenland.

What came next? I had now to go again over all that the sagas tell us about the Vinland voyages, to try to work out where we were most likely to end up. I could not, of course, know this yet, because the whole object of the voyage was to try to find out, but I had to make my own guesses in order to plan for our own twentieth-century needs. There is a Newfoundland school in modern Vinland history, which holds that the main Norse settlements in Vinland were on Newfoundland. This theory has attractions, but there are grave objections to it. The more I considered my own studies, and what I learned in Iceland, the more improbable it seemed to me that Vinland was to be found in Newfoundland. I could not know this, and it might be that our voyage would end by taking us logically to Newfoundland, but I thought this less and less likely. I had to give somewhere for our North American destination, to arrange for mail to be sent, and for such facilities as we might need after crossing the Atlantic. So I decided to put in at Halifax, Nova Scotia, in any event. We might or might not call in at Newfoundland on the way.

9

Beards and Other Matters

We left Reykjavik at 1710 on the afternoon of May 20, our engine consenting to go for just long enough to get us out of harbour. It packed up again soon afterwards, and we were without it for the rest of our passage to Greenland. That evening I headed my journal 'At Sea' and wrote:

> It is good to lose the corruption of the land. But it is hard to write. One can write on land, as long as boats are in the far past or future. One can write after weeks at sea. But boat-land, land-near-boat, you can't write – or, at least, I can't.

We had a long discussion in *Griffin's* little saloon that evening about the ships in which the Norsemen sailed for Vinland. The picture that comes into one's mind whenever one thinks of Viking ships is of the long, lean, open boats from which the Vikings raided the coasts of Europe. These are seaworthy vessels, and the form exists still in the traditional open fishing boats of the Shetlands and the Faeroes. But the Viking longships were essentially *warships* – ships in which all considerations of comfort took second place to the need for carrying armed men. There is no doubt but that the Norsemen made long voyages in their warships, but it seemed to us quite impossible that they should have made regular ocean passages in them. We recalled our own storm on the way to Iceland – rough weather, admittedly, but weather as rough, and often rougher, is to be expected in these seas. The Viking longships must often have survived such weather but often, too, they must have foundered. Crowded, as the sagas tell us, with cattle, they would have faced serious trouble whenever the weather in the open sea turned nasty. A good deal is known of the longships, but less is known of the

H

trading vessels in which the Norsemen of the tenth and eleventh centuries made long voyages. They were ships of a type quite different from the warships. We concluded that seamen as experienced as the Vikings would certainly have found some means of decking their vessels for long trading voyages, and that the ships in which the Vinland voyages were made must surely have been fully, or mainly, decked. They carried cargo and cattle, and they must have carried fodder for the animals. Moreover, on the Vinland voyages they also carried women – perhaps children – and no seaman would expose women and children to conditions worse than they need be. We know that the Norsemen cooked at sea, because the sagas tell us of their need for firewood: they must have cooked in some form of wood-burning brazier or stove, probably standing on a box of sand. Even in the conditions that we had experienced, rough, but not exceptionally so, cooking of any sort would have been impossible in an undecked boat – it would have been impossible to keep any form of galley fire alight. Moreover, occasional hot food or an occasional hot drink is not a luxury in bitter weather or a long voyage – it is all but a necessity.

It seems probable, therefore, that the Vinland ships were sturdy, broad-beamed vessels, of the type of the medieval Swedish *knorr*; if not fully decked in the modern sense, at least planked over, with substantial space below the planking for cargo, or for places where people could huddle and be protected from the weather. They may have had, too, some form of doghouse, or enclosed shelter for a galley – indeed, they *must* have had shelter of this sort. Another misconception conjured up by the traditional pictures of Viking longships is that they were primarily rowing boats. For inshore raiding, the Vikings certainly used oars for propulsion, to give them mobility in estuaries and rivers, and to be independent of the wind for coastal work. But they could not have depended on oars for regular ocean passages. Boats have been rowed across the Atlantic, but not boats of the size that the Viking trading vessels must have been. We debated whether a crew of three or four times our numbers could possibly have rowed *Griffin* through the weather we had met, and we decided that it would have been impossible. The ocean swell alone would have made oars hard to use, and in rough waves oars would have been unusable: they would have snapped off. So it seemed to us quite certain that the Vinland ships must have been essentially sailing ships, probably capable of far better sailing performance than is commonly imagined about medieval ships. Probably the Vinland voyagers used oars or sweeps for manoeuvring inshore in confined waters – they would have used them just as a modern sailing yacht uses her auxiliary engine (if she has one!). There were times when we, with a useless engine, would have been glad of stout sweeps and men to use them. But such oars or sweeps could seldom have been of any use to propel a heavy vessel on an ocean passage. The Vinland ships must have been sailing ships.

Next morning, there was a crisis. Tim Lee, wise navigator that he is, took a bearing of the sunrise and found that our two compasses were both mad. They were showing a wild deviation that bore no relationship to the deviation cards worked out for them when the compasses were adjusted at Dover. What had happened was evident: in re-stowing *Griffin* at Reykjavik to improve her trim, we had moved forward most of our steel jerry cans of fuel. These had been stowed aft when the compasses were adjusted, and their removal had altered the magnetic field round the compasses. Had we relied upon them without realising what we had done, we should have met disaster. Tim Lee's training and self-discipline as a navigator undoubtedly saved the ship. He got to work at once on a series of true bearings on the sun – it was merciful that the sun appeared that morning – and worked out new deviation cards for the compasses. The Greenland sea is a bad place for compasses, anyway. In those waters you are getting fairly near to the earth's magnetic pole, and this is liable to produce large variations in magnetic compass readings. These geographical variations are bad enough – I still turn cold with thinking what might have happened to us had Tim Lee not spotted quickly what had happened to our compasses.

We had other compass troubles on our voyage, which I mention now to put other small-boat sailors on their guard. After Tim Lee had corrected our compasses, we were puzzled by an occasional recurrence of odd compass behaviour. Peter Haward noticed, during one of his watches, that although we were on course according to the steering compass, the main compass showed us to be several degrees off course. I was in the cockpit with him, and we were discussing this, rather gloomily blaming our compasses, when I noticed that somebody had put down the exposure meter for his camera on the cabin hatch near the main compass. On moving this, the compass corrected itself. Exposure meters, being electro-sensitive, can have disastrous effects on compasses. So can small portable radio sets. So can even small objects made of iron or steel. I have mentioned that one night, when our binnacle light failed, I rigged up a torch over the steering compass so that I could see it. I did this again when the bulb in the binnacle broke another time, and fortunately Peter Haward noticed it: the metal body of the torch deviated the compass by two or three degrees. After this, I was always particularly careful, whenever a torch was anywhere near the steering compass, to check it against the main compass and to allow for any deviation. Tinned foods can also affect compasses if the tins are stowed anywhere near them. It is therefore of the first importance not merely to adjust compasses when a small boat sets out on a passage, but to keep an eye on them as tinned stores are consumed, and empty tins go overboard. It is better, of course, not to stow tinned stuff, or anything else containing iron or steel, anywhere near the compasses, but this is not always possible on a small boat. The important thing is to be constantly on one's guard about possible compass deviation.

Soon after leaving Reykjavik, we met rough weather again. The Denmark Strait between Iceland and Greenland is notorious for bad weather, and although we were crossing it well to the south of where the worst conditions are usually met, we had our share of bad weather. At midnight on May 21 I wrote:

Have just got into my bunk – did the 2000–2200 watch, made coffee for Peter Haward and me when he relieved me, and made a small independent supper for myself (Ryvita and cheese), pottered, and am now in bed. Writing is difficult, with *Griffin* doing about 8 knots under reefed main and staysail. I had a wild ride during my watch.

My journal here changes from ink to pencil. It continues:

Pen out of ink, but I am not getting out of my bunk again to fill it. In any case, the Tilley lamp is going out with a damaged mantel, and the saloon is dark. About crew – Allister is much better but Peter Comber, again, is sadly seasick. I hope that our voyage may be giving him something worth having in his life, but he is paying heavily for it. He is a marvellous worker, though.

We had our last glimpse of Iceland during my morning watch – a lonely white mountain, far astern, half cloud, but looking very beautiful and cold. I thought it looked a bit like pictures of Mount Fujiyama in Japan – a perfect mountain shape. We were a long way off – 50–60 miles, at least. Tim thought that our mountain might be Hekla, but then decided that this was dubious. So I don't know what mountain it was – in a way, I don't really want to. It was just beautiful, all quite white, a magical last glimpse of Iceland. I suppose that we saw only its snow-covered peak. I expect that it looked just the same when Eirik the Red sailed, with his boy Leif with him.

The weather continued rough and made things uncomfortable. Heavy seas threw us about, but they didn't bother us all that much. *Griffin* is a magnificent seaboat and, although naturally I worried a bit about our mended mainsail, I never had a moment's anxiety about her ability to stand up to the sea. Our next trouble was with our radio – not with the performance of the radio itself, for I think that the Kestrel would probably go on working from the seabed, but with a bit of its subsidiary mechanism called the 'starter relay'. This began sticking, upsetting the making of a radio call. To my private horror, Tim Lee took the thing to pieces. But he knew what he was doing, and he put everything together again, and made the starter relay work.

Odd jottings from my journal for May 21, written in pencil in the small hours:

Peter Haward and other people did a noble job in cleaning out the forepeak bilges this afternoon. I turned in after washing up, because I didn't get much sleep last night. With the forehatch open it was bitterly cold, and I couldn't get warm in my bunk, in spite of being fully dressed. After the work in the forepeak was finished and the hatch shut, it was better.

Peter Haward did further good work with polythene sheeting to try to stop drips coming down the mast, where it goes through the deck, from soaking Peter Comber's bed.

Reg Garrod did sailmaker's work on the canvas forehatch cover – patient, self-disciplined work, sewing away with cold hands on the open foredeck. That forehatch cover is a disgracefully ancient thing. It ought to have been renewed at Dover.

Allister borrowed my darning needle to darn his socks. He had wool, apparently, but no needle. Peter Comber refastened the thimble on the jib sheet – another cold job in the open. The air temperature this evening was 40 degrees, the water temperature a good bit warmer at 46 degrees, but we are moving towards colder water and I fear that we shall have real cold to put up with before long.

Meals this day:

Breakfast (me) – scrambled eggs. Lunch (Tim Lee) – soup, brisket and bread and butter. Dinner (Peter Haward) – steak in gravy with mashed potatoes and spinach (tinned). I didn't eat any dinner because I was on watch when Peter Haward cooked it, and eating on watch in the rough weather was just too difficult. That is why I had a private dinner when I came off watch.

Sunday, May 22, brought a spell of gentler weather, the first really fine day we had had at sea since leaving the Faeroes. The sun shone, the wind was light, and the sea a lovely deep-sea blue. The maximum air temperature was only 43 degrees, but the sunshine was warm and cheerful. We hung *Griffin* with wet clothes, so that she must have looked rather like a sailing clothes line. Things didn't get all that dry, but at least they were well aired, and mostly wearable again. Allister covered himself with glory by sighting our first whales – a small school of them playing around. My journal for May 22 begins again in ink:

With all our troubles, it is a miracle that my small ink bottle has survived (so far) intact. This is because I have been *ruthless* in keeping it wedged-in in our one cupboard in the saloon, and **in putting back the top the** moment I have used it.

Peter Comber is *much* better today and is reading *A Midsummer Night's Dream*. I am sitting on the saloon floor – cabin sole in the vernacular – to write this. Really, I think that the floor is the most comfortable place on *Griffin*. In spite of our radio troubles we had a good call to Brent this morning, and George Gardiner (Marconi) diagnosed possible faults in our starter relay. Tim Lee has again taken the poor old radio to bits and is fiddling with its innards. Oh dear. I *think* he knows what he is doing – I hope so, at any rate. [I wronged Tim Lee here. His naval training has made him an extremely efficient radio officer.] I am quite cosy on the floor except, of course, that I am sitting in our only passageway and everybody has to walk over me. But now we take it as a matter of course that if you want to get anywhere you have to step over someone else. Peter Haward is making coffee – thank goodness he likes coffee, it is good to have somebody who is not a tea drinker. I think Tim Lee is really a coffee man, though he has a weakness for tea occasionally. I have my private ash-tray beside me – a St Bruno tobacco tin, ex-Reg – Lord, the real values of things! My ash-tray tin is real wealth and so, above all, is the Edgworth tobacco tin that I bought in the Faeroes solely for the tin. I gave the tobacco to Reg (Edgworth is pipe tobacco). This tin is the only cigarette case I have, and it is the only thing I possess to prevent cigarettes from disintegrating in my pockets. It is of almost infinite value.

We must put our clocks back today, which means that we shall be an hour in advance of GMT, and two hours in advance of BST. We shall work our usual watches, but cut out the dog watch, because the clock change will have the same effect. We are completely cut off from the world. I suppose that if we tried hard enough we could listen to some BBC news, but the BBC's programmes are all BST, and we always seem to be doing something else with the radio at BST times. Well, it doesn't matter much. If we survive this passage, news will catch up with us again, alas.

Griffin had only a sixty-gallon water tank, and we could carry about another forty gallons in plastic jerry cans. The traditional sailing-ship ration of fresh water at sea is half a gallon a day per man. With six of us on board, this meant three gallons a day. All my planning was based on the possibility that we might have to spend up to thirty days at sea without putting in anywhere. In fact, our longest passage – from Greenland to Nova Scotia – was only twenty days, but prudence required that I should estimate for at least a month. With a ration of three gallons a day, the fresh water we could carry just allowed for thirty days, with ten gallons over – a pretty small reserve. The half-gallon ration itself is not generous: I have lived on it myself at various times, and found it adequate for drinking and for the fresh water needed in cooking, but it allows nothing for washing or anything else. I sought advice on fresh water needs from various medical people before we sailed, and their view was that half a gallon a day is not really enough: we were sailing into cold waters, and although in extremely cold weather one may feel that one does not need much to drink, in fact this is not so: in extremely cold conditions the human frame requires a good deal in the way of fresh water for health, for hot drinks and hot food, as well as for drinking water directly. So although I allowed for a basic minimum of half a gallon a day for survival, I felt that we should almost certainly use more – and we did, because on our various passages there always came a time when we knew that the chances against our having to spend a month without replenishing supplies were negligible, and at this point we were able to use water rather more freely. But at the start of each passage, it was imperative that fresh water should be rationed strictly, and as a matter of self discipline, we continued to be extremely careful with fresh water even when we knew that the strictest rationing need not be maintained. Tim Lee and I could have made fresh water go further by using seawater for some of our cooking – we both like salt – perhaps rather need it in our personal metabolisms, and we can cheerfully eat potatoes and other hard vegetables cooked wholly or partly in seawater. Apart from one or two small experiments, however, we could not use seawater for cooking on *Griffin* because other members of the crew disliked things cooked in salt. So we cooked almost wholly with fresh water and, until the last day or so of any passage, allowed no fresh water at all for washing, either ourselves or any of our clothes. Reg Garrod, Tim Lee and Peter Comber formally decided to grow beards, and gave up shaving with intent, as it were. Peter Haward more or less abandoned shaving on passage, but not with the intention of growing a beard – he always shaved on nearing port. Allister McIntosh half decided to grow a beard, and produced an impressive one, although I think his heart was never wholly in his beard – it was more a matter of the convenience of not shaving. Reg, Tim and Peter Comber tackled beard-growing seriously, and all grew handsome beards. In the earlier stages of the voyage, Reg Garrod's beard, tinged with a distinguished grey, was, I think, our best. I called him 'our Viking' and he looked much like a picture-book version of a Viking, huge and broad and with a beard that would soon have been flowing, had he left it. Unhappily, he turned against his beard when our voyage ended, and it came off in America. Peter Comber's growth was closer and less flowing – more dapper than Viking, but still quite a good beard. He also turned against it when we landed in America, and it came off. Tim Lee's ended up by being the best beard of all. As a naval officer he had a fine tradition of beards to live up to, and he took his beard more seriously than did the others. When he was able to get ashore to a barber and have it trimmed, it became a most distinguished adornment. It returned to England with him, but alas, when I last saw him in London it had joined our other beards in history.

I am not hostile to beards for other people, but I am hostile to them for myself. I have never tried to grow a beard at sea – or any-where else – and have always contrived to shave somehow. I regard shaving as slightly necessary in keeping up my own personal morale, and the worse the physical conditions in which I may find myself, the more I feel the need of a daily shave. I think that there were only four days in our two months on *Griffin* when I did not shave, and I never went longer than two days without shaving – if I missed one day because I was simply too tired to tackle shaving, I always shaved the next. I shaved normally in cold seawater – sea-water to save fresh water, and cold to conserve our gas supplies, which were also limited. Personally, I felt rather proud of my cold-sea-water shaving, but I think that the others regarded the performance as slightly mad. I cannot pretend that it is either efficient or pleasant to shave in cold seawater, but it can be done. By using an extra ration of brushless shaving cream, and by using a new safety razor blade at least every other day, you can get the bristles off your face and keep up to date with shaving; but it is not a process to be recommended in any normal circumstances. There are checks and balances in life, and later in the voyage, when we met ice, and cold-seawater shaving may have seemed additionally unpleasant, it became in one sense a little easier. The sea is less saline in the presence of ice, because of fresh water melting from the ice, and I noticed this with pleasure in my shaving. The icy seawater was horribly cold, but at least it lathered better, and the razor hacked off my bristles slightly more efficiently.

I washed at least face and neck daily in cold seawater – again a discipline rather than a pleasant process. We had some seawater soap on board; this lathers in seawater better than ordinary soap, but I was seldom able to find our seawater soap, and I didn't like it as much as the Wright's Coal Tar soap I normally use. So I did what I could with my ordinary soap: it wouldn't lather at all well, but at least it smelt nice and fresh, and gave me a feeling of having washed. Occasionally, if time and circumstances went together (which they seldom did), I used a bit of hot seawater, saved from washing up, for my personal washing and shaving. These occasions are always recorded in my journal with a sense of pleasure – hot seawater is undoubtedly more kindly than cold. There would not have been much additional strain on our supplies of bottled gas if I had regularly heated seawater for washing and shaving, but having started off by using cold seawater, I went on with it – more, I suppose, as a matter of personal pride than of strict necessity. There is no dust and not much dirt at sea, so the need for washing is less imperative than it is on land. After a day or two of sleeping in one's clothes, one begins to long for a bath, but baths were out of the question on *Griffin*. When we made port, almost the first thing we did was to try to find somewhere to have baths.

Washing clothes on passage was also all but out of the question. You can do a little with seawater soap, and I have found that under-clothes – or anything that does not need ironing – can be washed tolerably well by tying them to a line and towing them through the sea for a few hours. I did this occasionally on *Griffin*, and so did Reg

Garrod from time to time. The main problem, however, is to get things dry. This is extraordinarily difficult. Even on a fine day, clothes hung in the rigging may get spray thrown over them, and even if there is no spray there is nearly always so much moisture in the air at sea that clothes hardly ever dry properly. It can be done in the tropics or on rare days of blazing sunshine elsewhere, but for the most part it is scarcely ever possible to get washed clothes really dry at sea. Tim Lee and Peter Haward used to wash smalls and other bits and pieces whenever half a bucket or so of fresh water was going, but mostly we relied on having enough spare clothing to get by until the next port. After baths, the next thing we tried to find whenever we made land was a laundry.

At sea, we needed both watch-keeping and ordinary clothes, and again our attitudes were individual and varied. Peter Haward always changed into pyjamas when he turned in – a practice that I thought heroic (at least as heroic as my seawater shaving). Peter Comber normally undressed down to his long pants to turn in. Tim Lee and I slept more or less fully clothed. Reg Garrod and Allister McIntosh came somewhere in between. My normal wear off watch, during the colder stages of the voyage (most of it was pretty cold) consisted of string vest, shirt, two pullovers, short underpants, long underpants, pyjama trousers, drill or sailcloth trousers, and long socks of Norwegian wool. To go on deck I added a second pair of socks and another pair of trousers, sometimes one, sometimes two more pullovers, and on top of all this Henri-Lloyd's waterproof nylon trousers, jacket and hood. Gloves I have already discussed. Always on deck we wore rubber boots. Some of us wore rubber boots most of the time, but mostly we changed into canvas yachting shoes below deck – I always did, finding them more comfortable for prolonged wear than rubber boots. The Henri-Lloyd waterproof garments, made of ICI nylon, were superb. Before this voyage, I did not really believe that nylon could be anything like as efficient in keeping out the sea as the normal PVC oilskins, and supplied the crew with PVC smocks as well as our nylon clothing. Now I would never wear at sea anything but nylon. It is vastly more comfortable to wear than the stiff and heavy PVC, and it stood up to everything that our voyage brought – and we experienced conditions, particularly off Iceland and south Greenland, that were a severe test of any clothing. Twice, I was thrown into the scuppers while working on deck, and the sea drenched over me – on both occasions my nylon clothes kept me completely dry underneath. Once I was lying full-length on deck, working near the forehatch, when a sea swept over me, going up my trouser legs. This did mean changing my undertrousers but, even so, the nylon kept out most of the sea. Short of wearing something like a frogman's suit, I do not see any way of preventing the sea from going up the bottom of one's trousers if one is so placed that it is able to. At no time did my nylons ever let a drop of water pass through their cloth – even after a long watch in rain and drenching spray, they were not even damp inside. Moreover, they were so well designed that they were also well ventilated, and I never suffered from condensation under them.

Our PVC smocks were interesting garments in that they were specially made to incorporate safety harnesses of Peter Haward's own design. These harnesses were fixed outside the smock on Velcro self-sealing pads, which held the harnesses in place so that they could be put on automatically with the smock. We started off by wearing the smocks in bad weather because of the safety harnesses, but when we found that our nylons stood up to everything, we detached the safety harnesses and wore them over our nylons. These harnesses were a godsend – at least twice mine saved me from going overboard. They are quickly fastened, and can be put on in a moment: and Peter Haward has designed them with two lengths of strong synthetic line which can be snap-tackled to a shroud, safety rail or lifeline wherever you may be on dcek, to give you a long or a short 'tether'. The two lengths of line on the safety harness are contrived by snap-shackling a loop of line to a buckle on the harness itself – you can use the line either long or short by undoing the belt shackle.

In fog, we wore lifejackets whenever we were on deck, and it was a ship's rule that everybody below should have his lifejacket beside him, whatever he might be doing. The main danger to a small boat in fog is of being run down, and if we had been hit by another vessel there would have been perhaps only a matter of seconds before we sank. So everyone put in some private practice with his life-jacket, adjusting the fastenings so that it could be put on quickly, and in fog either wore it, carried it around, or used it as a pillow for sleeping. I obtained our lifejackets through my friend Pat Mulley, of a firm called Vacuum Reflex. Pat Mulley and his company have done valuable research work in lifejackets, and those that we had seemed to offer the highest possible chance of survival at sea. They were of a pattern made primarily for lifeboat crews, and others liable to be exposed to extremely severe weather at sea. They provide some permanent buoyancy to help to keep one afloat whatever happens, and are also inflatable by carbon dioxide gas – the inflation is automatic on pulling a small toggle. In addition, they carry a lamp which lights automatically on hitting the water, and are equipped with a whistle and a strong lanyard for use either to lash oneself to something or, to assist someone else to haul one's body from the sea. These lifejackets look rather bulky, but they have been designed so skilfully that they are surprisingly comfortable to wear – I wore mine for long periods without discomfort. Had we been cut down in fog, our lifejackets would have been our only hope of survival; they were a great comfort in the days of fog that we met off Newfoundland and Nova Scotia later.

10

'Ice now dominates our thoughts'

On that Sunday, May 22, we found ourselves about a hundred miles northeast of the British weather ship *Weather Adviser*, stationed in position Alpha between Iceland and Greenland. These weather ships have a lonely but important job, lying to or steaming slowly to keep their position in a given area of sea in all weathers, to collect and record the meteorological information on which weather forecasts are based. They act also as rescue stations in case an aircraft should be forced down at sea anywhere in their vicinity. The weather ship service is international, and several nations share in maintaining the ships, taking it in turns to man the various positions.

We had learned from the Meteorological Office before we left England that a British ship would be on duty in position Alpha at the time that we were likely to sail by, and the Met people at Bracknell invited us to call on the weather ship for supplies or for any other assistance that we might need, if conditions made this possible. We were not in need of any assistance, but we all liked the idea of paying a social call on *Weather Adviser* in mid-ocean. Also, although we had no lack of food, there were various luxuries that it would be nice to have if the weather ship's stores could provide them, and it would be useful to be able to take on a little more fresh water. I had arranged with the Met office, when planning the voyage, to pay for any supplies that we might get from the weather ship in cash, and the master of the weather ship Captain Sobey had been asked to meet our requests if he could. With the possibility of calling on the weather ship in mind, I had been careful throughout the voyage to keep a small supply of British currency in hand – her stores were Government property, and it would be necessary to pay for anything we had in British money. So when we were about a day's sailing distance from *Weather Adviser*, we sent the following signal to her master.

To: Captain Sobey
From: Mr Anderson
1. Expect to be in your vicinity tomorrow pm. Looking forward to calling on you. Would be most grateful if you could supply any of the following stores:

    5 lb ground coffee or ten tins of Nescafé if not available
    56 lb potatoes
    20 lb carrots
    20 lb any other root vegetable
    6 lb green vegetable if available
    4 bottles of whisky
    1 tin light oil
    600 tipped cigarettes
    10 gallons fresh water
    8 large white loaves bread
    8 pints fresh milk
    24 bars fruit and nut chocolate
    24 bars plain chocolate
    6 lb demerara sugar
2. Would you like one seasoned haggis in part exchange?
3. Assuming unable to come alongside what method of transfer would you like to use?

That haggis was a bit of an embarrassment to us, and I considered it a stroke of genius on my part to have devised this satisfactory way of disposing of it. It had been brought aboard by Allister McIntosh when he joined us at Scarborough, but he had never got around to eating it. None of the rest of us ever felt any passionate desire to consume the haggis, so it hung in the galley looking like a rather pale ghost, and occasionally hitting people on the head when *Griffin* kicked around. I wondered from time to time if I really ought to send it overboard, but Allister was somewhat attached to it and I did not like to hurt his feelings. Since Captain Sobey of the *Weather Adviser* is a Scotsman it seemed fitting that we should offer him the haggis on our visit, and Allister approved of this. *Weather Adviser* replied to our signal by calling us up, and I spoke to Captain Sobey. He said that he would do what he could in the way of supplying our shopping list. He was a bit guarded about the haggis, observing that he thought he would like it 'if it had been freshly shot'. I assured him that it had been shot on the best moors in Scotland, and for the moment we left it at that.

We estimated that if the wind held, we should come up with the weather ship early on Monday afternoon, and we told Captain Sobey that we would hoist our radar reflector in the hope that he would be able to pick us up on his radar screen long before he could see us. We gave him our course, and he promised to steam slowly in our direction for as long as he could without getting off station, to cut down the sailing distance between us.

Just before noon next day, we sighted *Weather Adviser* as a smudge on the horizon. She was about six miles away, and when the distance between us had closed to about three miles we saw through the glasses that she was lowering a boat. I thought it a wonderful piece of navigation by Tim – a ship is tiny compared with even the smallest of islands, and out of the vastness of a whole ocean Tim had brought us to precisely the right spot, a point so minute that it would not show even as a dot on a large-scale map. The weather stayed benign, although there was a considerable swell – the launch coming towards us disappeared and rose again as we watched her. It is a tricky business for one boat to come alongside another, even in calm weather, in mid-ocean and we put out all the fenders we had to receive the launch. She was beautifully handled by *Weather Adviser*'s men, who brought her alongside us without a scratch to our paintwork. It would be a break for all of us to visit a larger ship, but clearly we could not leave *Griffin* unmanned. While waiting for the launch I had arranged that we should go across to *Weather Adviser* in two parties – first Peter Haward, Allister and I, leaving Reg Garrod, Tim Lee and Peter Comber to look after *Griffin*; then we would come back, and the others would have their turn. Although the sea was fairly calm, I asked people to wear lifejackets for the trip across: it is in getting on and off boats that accidents happen, and I have always tried to make it a rule for myself, and anyone who may be sailing with me, to wear lifejackets for all dinghy work. On this occasion, too, it would be useful practice with our lifejackets.

We felt a pleasant sense of excitement as the first three of us transferred to *Weather Adviser*'s launch. It was the first time that any of us had had a chance of actually seeing *Griffin* at sea – when you are on board a boat you cannot see what she looks like in mid-ocean. *Griffin* was beautiful as she lay there, hove to, rising and falling with the swell. To be able to see her like this for the first time gladdened all of us.

The powerful launch took us quickly to her parent ship. *Weather Adviser*'s side looked like a cliff as we came up to it, and I was a little nervous of the vertical rope ladder up which we had to climb. But all went well, and in a moment we were shaking hands with Captain Sobey and his crew on deck. Captain Sobey had spent his life at sea, and he knew what we wanted without asking – he took us straight to his own quarters, and invited us to use his shower bath! After our cramped living conditions on *Griffin*, *Weather Adviser*, although she is not really a very big ship, seemed palatial. The water in the shower was gloriously hot, and the bath a great luxury. It distressed Captain Sobey that I had been able to bring only half *Griffin*'s crew with me, and while I was having a bath he discussed, through the doorway, how the rest of us could be brought over. The first mate of *Weather Adviser*, Mr L. Sutherland, was a sailing man, and Captain Sobey suggested that Mr Sutherland should take a crew from *Weather Adviser* to look after *Griffin* while the whole of our party enjoyed his hospitality. This was a suggestion both generous and practical, so the launch went back to *Griffin*, taking Mr Sutherland and a crew of volunteers to man her, and a message from me asking the others to return with the launch to join us. Soon all *Griffin*'s people were on board and, after everyone had had a bath, Captain Sobey's steward produced hot buttered toast in man-sized quantity – another great luxury which Captain Sobey's seaman's imagination provided for us. That toast, however, was only the *hors-d'oeuvre*, for, after we had consumed toast and chatted for a bit, we were taken into the officers' saloon for a sumptous meal, beginning with soup, going on to steaks, and ending with ice cream. Our shopping list was met bountifully

I

from *Weather Adviser*'s stores. Everything for which we had asked
was there, and in addition *Weather Adviser* presented us with a bag
of fresh pears, beautifully fresh from her refrigerator, and with
some crisp white cabbages. I was able to buy four bottles of whisky
(duty free), and *Weather Adviser*'s officers added two more as a
present. When we got back to *Griffin*, we found that Mr Sutherland's
crew had brought on board a crate of Guinness as a present. Captain
Sobey had had eight loaves of bread baked specially for us. *Weather
Adviser*'s baker knew his job, for not only was his bread delicious,
but it kept almost miraculously, far better than any other bread we
were able to buy anywhere on the voyage. Allister went off to the
canteen with Captain Sobey's steward, and came back laden with
chocolate and other sweets.

Captain Sobey gave us one piece of interesting news – the day
before, *Griffin* had been sighted by an aircraft, and reported to the
weather ship as an iceberg! There was some excuse for this – a small
sailing boat is such an improbable sight nowadays in the Denmark
Strait that, seen from a great height, we might easily have been mis-
taken for an iceberg. The Met people on board the weather ship knew,
however, that there were no icebergs then in the vicinity, and since
they also knew of our presence in the area, we did not confuse the
ice charts!

The weather held, but we could not risk staying too long away
from *Griffin* in case it might deteriorate suddenly and we should
find ourselves marooned. After three most happy hours on Captain
Sobey's ship, the launch took us back to *Griffin*, and re-embarked
Mr Sutherland and his crew, who had enjoyed sailing her around
Weather Adviser, and had handled her well. Just before leaving
Weather Adviser, I formally presented Captain Sobey with our
haggis. He accepted it politely and with apparent gratitude,
but its ultimate fate I have not inquired about since. I do
know that Captain Sobey and his crew returned to the Clyde
after their tour of duty, apparently in good health! Our ship's log
reads:

1640 Crew return on board, washed, fed and provisioned.
1645 Took departure from *Weather Adviser*. Streamed log.

My own journal, scribbled at midnight while lying in my bunk, records a near disaster to me personally:

The whole thing nearly came to an end today with a broken leg for me. It was the narrowest escape I have ever had. Climbing down the ladder from *Weather Adviser*, carrying our film camera, I was so intent on getting the camera safely into the launch that I got a rung too low on the ladder, and the heavy launch, rising on the swell, trapped my leg against the ship's side. A wicker fender, plus good pushing work by the crew of the launch, just saved my leg, though it hurt a lot.

It was a wretched accident, and although I was able to keep going all right, my leg troubled me for the rest of the voyage and, indeed, troubles me still. My journal continues:

Our call on *Weather Adviser* was an extraordinary mid-ocean meeting, and I hope that they were as glad to see us as we were to see them. When we were in the launch, waiting to cast off from the ship, I called on the Griffins for three cheers for Captain Sobey and *Weather Adviser*. My crew responded well, though there were only six of us and our cheers sounded pretty thin in the waste of ocean. It was rather ridiculous, I suppose, but I think that *Weather Adviser*'s people understood.

Quickly, we slipped back into our routine on *Griffin*, and continued on our course towards Cape Farewell, although making well to the south of it. My journal for May 24, dated 'midnight, ship's time; 0100 GMT', says:

Ice now dominates our thoughts – mine anyway, and I think Peter Haward's and Tim Lee's. At about 2000, ship's time, we entered an area where theoretically we could meet an iceberg, though I think it is not very probable. The question of lookout is bothersome – I feel sometimes that we are not good enough. There is a tendency for the watchkeeper to concentrate on steering. Steering a compass course on any small boat is difficult enough, anyway, and I don't reckon that *Griffin* is all that easy to steer. For the past couple of days, we have been mostly running, fast, making 7–8 knots, and our courses have often been on the edge of gybing. It is hard to concentrate on such a course *and* to keep a good lookout. Also, *Griffin*'s steering position is not good. However, these things cannot be helped, and we must just do our best.

Allister is vastly better. He cooked a slap-up meal tonight with very professional chipped potatoes – he has turned out to be a brilliant potato chip chef. I didn't have any, because I had to go on watch. Peter Haward made a cabbage and grated carrot salad while I was on watch and he was waiting to relieve me, and I was looking forward to having it when I came off watch at 2100. But *Griffin* dealt with it. When I went to get it, it was already in the bilges, plus broken plate. When running, *Griffin* does roll dreadfully. She is rolling now, and it is hard to write.

I have just closed the door from the forehatch into the lavatory as a precaution, and I want to try to keep it closed whenever we can. It is by no means a watertight bulkhead, but if we did hit ice and the bow got holed, I reckon that the door would hold for quite a few minutes. I mustn't get too worried about ice.

Odd, the relativities of things! Helen and I have always reckoned Force 5 an ugly wind, and too much to go out in from choice. Now it seems quite a gentle breeze! I think that in mid-ocean things *are* a bit different: you are *in* the wind, part of it in a sense, and not just experiencing it. *Griffin* enjoys Force 5, anyway – it is a good wind for her. Even the Force 9 that we had the other day didn't really seem too awful.

Reykjavik is a most efficient radio station, and answers remarkably quickly. Reykjavik Radio has been very nice to us. We got through this evening, I expect for the last time, because we are getting a long way away, and the man was very friendly and wished us a good voyage.

I have added another pair of pyjama trousers to my underwear for watchkeeping. The wind this evening seemed to come straight off the ice.

By May 25 we were about a hundred miles off the Greenland coast, and were becoming more and more conscious of the possibility of meeting ice. Tim Lee had a copy of *The Mariners' Handbook*, published by the Hydrographic Department of the Admiralty, and all of us in turn read and re-read the chapters about ice. We discussed icebergs, 'bergy bits' and 'growlers' – a 'bergy bit' is defined in the *Handbook* as 'a massive piece of ice, generally less than $16\frac{1}{2}$ feet above sea level, and about the size of a small cottage'. A 'growler' is defined as a 'smaller piece of ice than a bergy bit, frequently appearing greenish in colour and barely showing above the water'. We decided that although icebergs might look perilous, they would mostly be so enormous that we should see them well in time to be able to keep out of their way, and that bergy bits and growlers would be the main hazard. At that time we had none of us experienced ice. We began getting daily ice reports from the Meteorological Office, passed on to us when we made our regular radio calls to Brent. Tim Lee charted the reported positions of ice as we got them. Considerable ice fields were reported up to seventy miles off the Greenland coast. We studied what the *Handbook* had to say about 'ice blink', described as 'a whitish glare on low clouds, above a distant accumulation of ice'. We kept our eyes open for ice blink, which we thought might give us the first warning that we were really in the neighbourhood of ice. At that stage of our voyage, we saw none, and my journal for May 25 records only domestic details:

I had to miss my watch this morning because of the Brent radio call. I didn't like doing this, but couldn't help it, and I tried to make up for my missed watch by doing a good stint of housekeeping. I washed and tidied up the saloon table, which had become a tip, and did floors with dustpan and brush. I thought all the time how much better Helen would have done the job.

That night I had a long and rather philosophical discussion with Peter Haward about risks, and the taking of risks. Everybody else was asleep and, when he relieved me from my watch, I stayed up and talked to him. We had many of these long conversations together, and Reg Garrod and I also had long discussions about everything under the sun from time to time when I relieved him on watch, and he stayed up and talked to me. There is a wonderful

sense of intimacy and of human companionship when two people
are alone together in the cockpit of a small boat far out at sea:

> Peter Haward argued, and I am sure that he is right, that the man
> who is hazard-unconscious does not amount to anything – it
> is no credit just to ignore risks. But calculated risk taking is all
> right: you know that there is a risk; you assess it; take what pre-
> cautions you can against it; and the rest is with God. That is fair
> enough. Also, we decided that a man mustn't *not* do things that
> involve risk simply because he may have a wife and children.
> Clearly there is a real problem here, and risk taking, to be justi-
> fied or not, is a matter of degree, but the point is that you must
> not pack up being a *man* because you have a wife and children.
> There may be things that you can do justifiably if you are a single
> man that it would be better not to tackle if you have a wife and
> children, but this is something that you must decide for yourself. I
> don't want to die in these Greenland seas, but I've got to die
> some time, and to wind up on an expedition like this would
> not leave a bad taste in the children's mouths – to say Daddy
> was lost at sea off Greenland would not be bad. But I hope that
> we are not lost – I have a lot of things still to do, or to try to do
> somehow.

My leg was bothersome, and hurt a good deal, but the broken
skin seemed to be beginning to heal. It was still badly bruised, but I
was so thankful not to have broken the leg that I ignored it as much
as I could.

The weather worsened, and we began setting ice watches as well
as our ordinary watches at the helm. This meant doubling up on
watch, and losing a certain amount of sleep, but this was where
Peter Haward's system of single watches which we had adopted paid
off, for we had all been getting as much sleep as we needed and were
fit for the extra work. My journal for May 26 is so badly written that
I can scarcely read it – the handwriting is all over the page as *Griffin*
threw me about:

> Writing is near impossible, with *Griffin* standing on her head in a

heavy confused sea with a Force 6 wind. We are rounding Cape Farewell, and a horrible time it is giving us. Christiansund Radio in Greenland gave us a warning of Force 7 – it came. I went on ice watch at midnight, with Tim steering. It was pretty rough. At the relief of watch, Peter Comber came to the helm and Peter Haward went on ice watch. At the change of watch, Peter Haward decided – rightly – that it was time our big jib came in, and he and I went forward to hand the sail, wearing safety belts. While we were up on the foredeck she gybed – I don't blame Peter Comber, for it was vilely difficult steering. The mainsail came across like thunder – fortunately a good bit of the strain was taken by the preventer. It carried away, but it did its job before carrying away – that is what it is for. The rope held, but the top of the cleat to which the preventer was made fast forward broke clean off. Tim rushed up to help, and made up the lee runner, which helped to take the strain. There was general chaos for a bit, and the main sheet got tangled in the steering wheel. Peter Haward and Tim Lee gradually restored order, and Peter Haward and I were then able to set the yankee. While trying to get hold of a sheet, I was flung practically over the life rail – fortunately my safety belt was shackled on to a shroud and everything held – otherwise I wouldn't be writing this. Next, a shackle on the yankee came adrift and I went right forward to fix it. My hands froze. I was thankful to get below, and gradually thawed out. I was on watch again at 0500, so did not get much sleep. In Reg Garrod's watch, before mine, the yankee was handed, and I took over *Griffin* running fast under the double-reefed main alone.

May 27 brought a change for the better. My journal – more readable – says:

Helen's birthday. Many happy returns to her. We are now off Cape Desolation. Life is full of surprises. Cape Farewell saw us off with plain hell – thirty hours of tumultuous swell and strong winds of Force 6–8. We could carry only the double-reefed mainsail, and in spite of this did a hundred miles in twelve hours.

Conditions were dreadful, with *Griffin* rolling her gunwales under and tossing in the steep seas, running all the time, with the ever-present fear of another gybe. Now the surprise – Cape Desolation is another fearful name, but it is giving us quite a nice day. Long may it last. We are steering to avoid a kind of island or tongue of ice extending from the coast, and it looks as if we may be able to get into Frederikshaab.

There was a crisis in the middle of our radio call to Brent this morning when something got tangled with a spreader and the aerial had to come down in a hurry. Poor Brent! I just gasped out, 'Stand by!' while Peter Haward dealt with the crisis. They kept saying, '*Griffin, Griffin,*' and Anne kept saying, 'We've lost you.' I could hear them but we could not transmit until we had saved our spreader and got the aerial back.

Julianehaab was hopelessly barred to us by ice, but the reports from Frederikshaab were encouraging. The ice, moving slowly northwards at this time of year up the west Greenland coast, had not yet got to Frederikshaab in any quantity, and it looked as if we might be able to get into the fjord that leads to the small settlement there. We had to be careful in case the ice should come up while we were in the fjord, and entrap us. But the reports suggested that we ought to have time at least to spend a few days there. Next day – May 28 – I wrote:

Cape Desolation did us proud. Prinz Christiansund Radio promised us everything hellish up to Force 10 or so, but instead we had a magical night of almost dead calm. I was on watch 0100–0300 and succeeded in making just under 1½ miles in the two hours. Peter Haward, who followed me, did 1·3 miles! During my watch *Griffin* at times barely had steerage way, and twice I had to put her right round in a circle to get back to our NE course – she just wouldn't move to port and had to be left to herself to go round, slowly, and with great dignity, to starboard. It was an exquisite night, with the sea calm enough for the moon to be reflected in it, while the sun was getting ready to rise in the east. There was virtually no darkness at all, a clean sky with a few pale stars. I slept too well after turning in from my 0300 watch, and woke in a panic at 0745 (GMT), just in time for my 0800 radio schedule with Brent.

Anne Bradbury gave me all the information she could collect about Frederikshaab as a place, and the ice conditions there, and passed on a message from the Danish Embassy in London, suggesting that we should try to get in touch with the Danish naval base at Grönne Dal in Greenland. Prinz Christiansund Radio is being a good friend. He speaks good English, and is clearly rather interested in us. When we tried to get through to Julianehaab Radio, Prinz Christiansund answered and explained that Julianehaab did not listen always on our frequency. He got through to Grönne Dal for us – he knew our position, and seems a very nice chap. Reykjavik Radio in Iceland was always good to us, too. We got through to Grönne Dal after a bit, but they didn't seem to understand us clearly and asked us to call back in half an hour. We did. The chap there seemed a bit puzzled about us, and asked us to report our position twice a day. We undertook to do this at 1100 and 2300 GMT. GMT is my one link with sanity in all this messing around with time.

I had a good shave in some hot seawater today. The air temperature was 37 degrees and the sea temperature 38 degrees, so it was not warm. Now fog has come up.

We were about a hundred miles south of Frederikshaab, and the coming of this fog brought a sort of change of gear to the voyage. Until then it had been more or less normal ocean sailing – we had met some severe weather, but nothing that *Griffin*, once her rudder had been repaired, could not take. With this fog, we began to experience conditions that were formidable indeed to a small wooden sailing boat, and I began to realise that we had undertaken not merely a long voyage but an ordeal that would be a harsh test, both of our ship and of ourselves. The fog did not come down thickly at once: for the next twelve hours or so it came and went, lifting for periods of fair visibility and then enclosing us again. In one of these periods of fair visibility, we saw a whitish glare under the distant sky – unmistakably ice blink, though it seemed a long

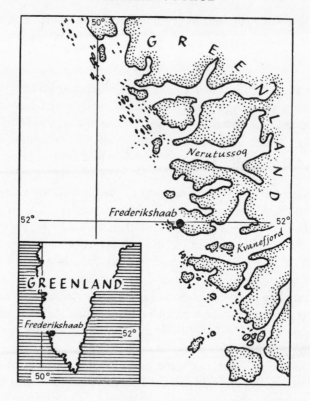

way off. On my watch that afternoon – May 28 – we met our first icebergs:

In the afternoon watch (1300–1500) I was bothered by a flicker of white on the horizon. I watched it closely, but it disappeared. I asked Reg if he could see anything, but he couldn't. A few minutes later I saw it again, and reported, 'Iceberg or ship almost dead ahead.' Peter Haward brought up the glasses and it *was* an iceberg – our first! We logged it at 1330. About half an hour later I saw another. This was about 2½ miles away, and seemed rather smaller than the first. Tim Lee suggested that there should be a prize of an ice lolly for me as the sighter of our first icebergs. As we haven't got any ice lollies, and no means of making any, my prize will have to remain an honorary one. I don't want an ice lolly in this temperature, anyway. I am not quite sure what the iceberg-sighting prize ought to be – to get away from them, I should think.

We were half fearful, half as excited as children about our icebergs, anxious both to keep away, and to get near them to see them at close quarters. There was not much wind, and as the icebergs were being carried by wind and current more or less on our course, it was nearly four hours before we got up to them. The air was noticeably colder, but – oddly – the sea temperature in the vicinity of the icebergs was a little warmer. This, however, was in accordance with the textbooks – seawater has a lower freezing point than fresh water, and as the ice from an iceberg melts into fresh water it raises the temperature of the surrounding sea a little. This phenomenon is a rather frightening reminder of the immense mass of ice in an iceberg.

We wanted photographs of *Griffin* among the icebergs, and as the only way to get such photographs was to take them from the dinghy, we prepared to launch the dinghy. It was unthinkable to lose the opportunity of photographing our first experience of ice but, privately, I was a good deal worried about letting anyone go off in the dinghy. The horizon was grey with fog ahead, and it might have closed down quickly, making it difficult for the dinghy to return to *Griffin*. I did not like the idea of anyone being adrift in a dinghy off that part of the Greenland coast. Two people were needed for the dinghy trip, one to row and one to take photographs with both our cine and still cameras. There were eager volunteers. Peter Haward was particularly anxious to take photographs, and the others were all keen to have a row round the ice. But I made up my mind to go with Peter Haward myself. If we did have trouble with fog, Peter Haward seemed to me to be about the most capable of all of us of getting out of it, and if anyone else was going to spend the night adrift in the dinghy I felt that it had better be me. So I ruled that the dinghy party should consist of Peter Haward and me – it says much for the loyalty of the expedition that this ruling was accepted without a murmur, in spite of the disappointment it must have caused. I took the precaution of putting some cartons of Horlicks emergency rations into the dinghy, and Peter and I went off. I rowed, and he looked after the cameras.

It was a queer feeling to be rowing a dinghy in that lonely sea within a couple of cables of an iceberg: the act of rowing and the bobbiness of the dinghy were precisely the same as on a river or lake at home, but the familar behaviour of the dinghy made the loneliness of that icebound sea seem more acute. We took our photographs quickly, for the fog was closing in and, although we were away for barely half an hour, we could only just make out *Griffin* when we got back to her. I was glad when we and the dinghy were safely on board again. Glancing at the log a little later, I noticed that Tim Lee, who automatically became *Griffin*'s sailing master while we were away, had duly logged both our departure in the dinghy and our return. This was another example of Tim's fine sea training. Such things ought always to be logged, but many yachtsmen are slack about log-keeping. Had anything happened to Peter Haward and me, the precise time of our departure in the log, with the known position of the ship at that moment, might have been a major help in locating us, when the fog lifted. I blessed Tim for his meticulous standards of log-keeping, and thought again how lucky I was to have him with us.

While Peter Haward and I were rowing around in the dinghy, and before the fog thickened, Tim measured the iceberg by taking sextant angles of it. This berg was 350 ft long and 75 ft high – a small thing in comparison with the gigantic icebergs we met later, but to us an enormous mass of ice, as big as a large factory.

The log for 2250 that night reads:

Pack-ice sighted to the east. Grinding noises quite clearly heard.

We were more closely involved with ice than we realised. The fog, which had lifted a little to show us the pack-ice, soon came down again more thickly than ever. By 0300 in the morning, it was dense, and we set double watches. That was one of the most miserable nights of the whole voyage. It was cold enough in the vicinity of the ice in any case, but the fog seemed to freeze as well, so that our whole world was wrapped in a kind of icy cloud. Everything on the ship froze – sheets, halliards, and rigging were covered with ice, and bitterly cold to handle. The man on ice watch had to stand right in the bows, away from the shelter of the cockpit, exposed to everything. People suffered severely from their feet, and when one had done one's turn and gone below, one could hear one's mate on duty stamping on the deck to try to keep some feeling in his feet.

By 1000 that morning, the fog cleared a little, and the ice on the ship began to melt. This brought a new hazard, for bits of ice about the size of large marbles broke off from *Griffin's* upper rigging, and pelted down on the deck with the force of thrown stones. I felt that I ought to have equipped the crew with steel helmets. Fortunately, this particular hazard did not last long, and no one was hurt, although there were some near misses. The clearing fog showed that we were coasting along a sort of shoreline of pack-ice. It looked grim and forbidding, and the sea was dotted with bergy bits and growlers. Our engine having packed up soon after we left Iceland, we were wholly dependent on our sails – a nice test of sailing seamanship, but, at such close quarters with ice, a reliable engine would have been a comfort. Although I blamed myself for not having discovered the engine's idiosyncrasies before we started, in a way I felt a curious satisfaction at being engine-less. I felt that this put us on a par with the old Norsemen, and with men like the Elizabethan seaman John Davis – who gave his name to the Davis Strait – and others who had explored these seas and investigated ice long before engines were invented. Thanks to them, we had charts – because of them, we knew where we were. They did not. They had sailed into the unknown with ships that were often unhandy, and with food that was nothing like as good as our well-balanced diet. If they could sail among the icefloes, so could we. And, in *Griffin*, we had an infinitely better sailing machine than their ships ever were.

My journal for that day (May 29) is a mixture of domestic jottings and descriptions of ice:

Radio call to Brent at 0800, not a good call, but just got through. Aerial all iced up. Then three-hour watch – we are working three-hour watches to fit in ice duty. Did two hours, all but five minutes, right forward, wearing everything I've got. Walked up endless flights of stairs, slowly, to keep feet alive. Spent the whole time staring into fog, thickening and thinning, but the sun was not far away. It glistened on gulls' wings about fifty feet up.

Next to no wind. The flywheel has come off the engine – no one knows just when or how. We bolted it on, and tried to start it, but at the first turn the nut came loose. No good. Discussed with Tim the possibility of asking by radio for a tow into Frederikshaab, but it is still quite a long way, a tow would probably cost a lot, and it would be rather a confession of failure. Discarded idea. Discussed the possibility of towing *Griffin* with the dinghy – decided that it just wouldn't work: that with one pair of oars in our small dinghy we could scarcely move this heavy boat. Oh for Leif Eiriksson's rowers with their sweeps!

Made coffee (tea for Peter Comber and Allister McIntosh). What do you *do* with these wretched tea bags? Curious that the most civilised conversation seems to go with coffee. (Does it?)

I *think* we pick up a pilot to get into Frederikshaab. According to Frederikshaab Radio, the meeting point for picking up pilots is an island called Satuarssugssuaq, at least I think it's that. When we tried to pronounce it, they said, 'You don't pronounce the Gs in Greenland.' So it sounds like 'Satuasuak'. We couldn't give Frederikshaab an ETA because there is no wind.

Took some photographs of the ice around us. Wonderful blues in the dazzling white. TV detergent whiteness isn't in it. We drift on. Am on watch in an hour. Owing to the three-hour double-watch procedure, we have got all messed up and are now on at even hours instead of our normal odd ones.

During my watch that evening, we got a little wind and gradually closed the coast through a sea dotted with bits of ice. The fog had lifted, and with steerageway on *Griffin*, it was not difficult to keep out of the way of ice, though one needed a sharp lookout to see the smaller bits. Even a small footstool of ice on the surface of the sea might be as big as a packing case below the surface, and might do serious damage to *Griffin* if she hit it. Gradually, we closed the coast and tried to identify landmarks. The coast was a mass of rocks and skerries. Which rock or islet was Satuarssugssuaq? According to the chart, there was a lighthouse on Satuarssugssuaq, visible for twenty-one miles. That would mean a pretty substantial lighthouse and we ought to have been able to see it. But we could see nothing that looked like a lighthouse. Peter Haward and I ranged the coast with glasses, but couldn't make out precisely where we were. Somewhere among that mass of skerries was the channel into the fjord that led to Frederikshaab, but where? I thought that we were still too far south, and should go north around the next headland. Peter Haward was not convinced of this (and he was right). Finally, we called Tim. He had turned in after coming off watch when we were still a long way offshore and more or less becalmed, but the little wind that had sprung up had taken us in more quickly than had seemed probable when he went off duty. When he came back to the cockpit he looked at the coast, and seemed to sniff the air like a pointer. I wanted to discuss my feeling that we were still too far to the south, and began talking to him. But he shut me up, saying, 'Leave me alone for a minute or two.' Tim was calling up his navigator's sixth sense, and it was badly insensitive of me to interrupt him. After sniffing the air and studying the chart, he decided that we were on course as we were, and that an islet ahead of us was the one that marked the entrance to the fjord. The puzzle about the lighthouse was explained. We were using a Danish chart, and the '21m' marked on it beside the lighthouse was not in English – it did not mean that the lighthouse had a range of twenty-one miles, but that it was twenty-one metres high. A few minutes later, we saw a fishing boat come round the islet and knew that all was well. The men in the boat waved to us in a friendly way, and held up a bit of rope as the international sign for offering us a tow. I felt tempted to accept the offer, but declined. We had come so far under our sails alone that it seemed a pity not to make Frederikshaab under sail. We were moving slowly, but we were still moving, and the hesitant little wind never quite failed us. At last we entered the fjord and could see the houses of Frederikshaab ahead. It was after midnight, but still quite light. In the early hours of the morning, we ghosted up to the quay of Frederikshaab, and made fast alongside a Danish liner called *Erika Dan*.

I I

Greenland

Late, or rather, early in the morning, as it was when we made fast
to *Erika Dan* in Frederikshaab, the harbourmaster, Mr Peter Jensen,
came on board to make us welcome. He had heard about us over the
Greenland Radio, exempted us from all formalities, and offered any
help he could give. I said that our chief need was to try to find a
workshop which could fix our engine: he was doubtful if we could
get spare parts in Frederikshaab (we couldn't) but said that there was
a Danish Government engineering shop which would certainly do
what it could for us. By then it was about 0300 Greenland time, but
almost broad daylight, and boatloads of interested teenage Greenlanders were milling around *Griffin*. They began climbing on board,
and I had to ask them not to, because we were all too tired for visitors.
I don't think that many of them had more than a word or two of
English, but I think they understood that we wanted to be friendly
but could not receive them then, for they went away at once,
without fuss. The harbourmaster left us, promising to come back
later in the morning, and at last we were able to turn in. By GMT it
was then well after 0500, and I had to be up at 0800 (GMT) for my
radio call to Brent, so I couldn't risk falling asleep too deeply, and
in the event did not sleep at all. Reg Garrod, our official radio officer,
loyally undertook to be up to help with the call to Brent, so he and I
got up as quietly as we could, leaving the others to get a bit more
sleep.

Our radio call was futile: we were tied up to a steel ship, and although we could just hear the people at Brent, they could not hear
us at all. I was not greatly bothered by this, for I knew that Brent
would realise that we were in harbour, and not be worried about our
safety. Strictly you are not supposed to use a ship's radio for long-

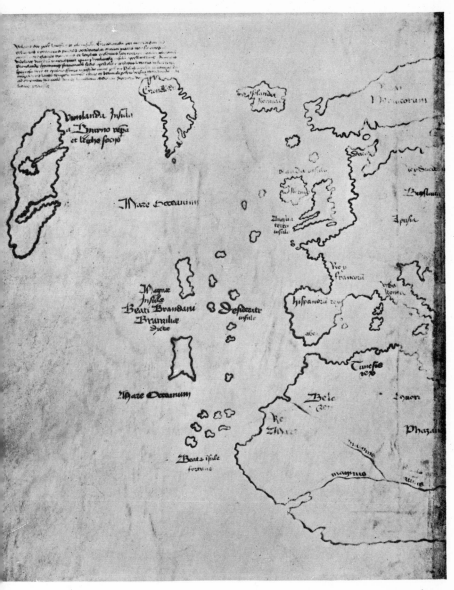

The Vinland Map – copied about the year 1440 from a still unknown original.
The Latin caption in the upper left-hand corner records a visit by Bishop Eirik
Gnupson to Vinland as Papal Legate 'in the last year of our most holy father
Pascal' (Pope Pascal II, who died in 1118)

The author

Peter Haward

Lieutenant (now Lt-Commander) T. R. Lee, RN

Peter Comber

R. A. Garrod

Allister McIntosh

Fitting out in Wellington Dock, Dover

Above: A pontoon has just been brought alongside *Griffin* for painting her topsides

Left: Checking stores

Five thousand miles to go. *Griffin* leaves Scarborough escorted by a fishing boat

Allister McIntosh. The 'beehive' by the ensign is the screened box of the thermometer for daily Met. observations

Our link with the rest of the world. Reg Garrod at the radio telephone

Top: The journal – writing in good conditions

Bottom: The journal – what it looks like half an hour later

Peter Comber investigates
his sea boots

Peter Haward does some
tricky work on the boom.
Note the safety line for
his feet

Heavy weather. The author at the helm off Newfoundland

Heavy weather. Tim Lee repairing a sail

The statue of Leif Eiriksson at Reykjavik

Moment of calm. (What sailing *can* be like!)

Weather Adviser, the weather ship at Station Alpha

Dangerous ice (a 'bergy bit') in Frederikshaab harbour

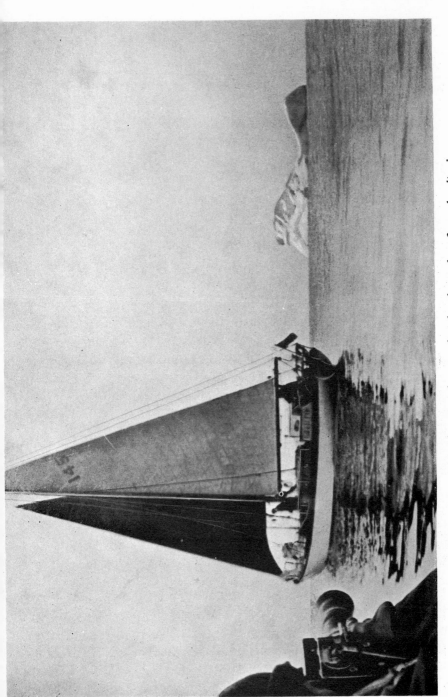

Iceberg and fog. This photograph was taken by the author from the dinghy – Foreground, Peter Haward photographing *Griffin*

The *Griffins.* (back) Allister McIntosh, Reg Garrod, Peter Haward, the author; (front) Tim Lee, Peter Comber

Under way – in a rare spell of warm weather

distance communications in territorial waters. In both the Faeroes and in Iceland I had invoked official after official to get permission to make one radio call in port, but in Greenland I was just too tired: I hope that the Danish Government will understand and forgive me: as I was unable to communicate, perhaps it did not matter.

After our failure with the radio, neither Reg nor I felt like turning in again, so we climbed up a ladder on to *Erika Dan* and went ashore. It was a sunny morning, and we both felt rather excited at setting foot on Greenland. We walked from the harbour towards the settlement, locating as, we went by, what seemed to be the Government engineering shop about which the harbourmaster had spoken.

Frederikshaab, with a population of around 1,100, nestles, well-protected, at the end of a fjord, or inlet, called Kangerdlunguak. It is one of the oldest of the modern settlements in Greenland – 'modern', that is, as distinct from the old Norse settlements before the fifteenth century. After the collapse of the Norse colonies there, little was known or heard of Greenland for some three hundred years, until the eighteenth century, when Moravian missionaries from Denmark set out to try to re-establish Christianity among the Greenlanders – then thought of as Eskimoes. 'Re-establish', because the old Norse colonies in Greenland were devoutly Christian. Bishop Eirik Gnupson, who went to Vinland as Papal Legate in 1117, was Bishop of Greenland, and it remained a bishop's See until the collapse of the early Norse civilisation. Modern Frederikshaab dates from 1742, when the Moravians established a settlement there, with a church and school, and a trading post to encourage the Greenlanders, who were then nomadic, to adopt a more settled way of life.

The collapse of the Norse colonies in Greenland, some time in the fourteenth or early fifteenth centuries, is commonly regarded as having been absolute and final. No one really knows why these well-established settlements, which had lasted for some four hundred years, should suddenly have disappeared. They may have been largely wiped out by the pestilence known as the Black Death, brought from Europe by some trading vessel, leaving a remnant of their former population that was too weak to survive either the rigours of the climate, or attacks by local Eskimoes. It is conjectured that, even without pestilence, a climatic change for the worse made

K

life too hard for the Norse colonists to sustain. It is suggested that the native Eskimo population, originally overcome by the Norsemen, gradually recovered strength, became more and more aggressive, and at last wiped out the settlements. All these things may have happened – or happened at least to some extent – but the real facts of history are seldom either absolute, or final. Civilisations that are supposed to have vanished from the earth live on in all sorts of ways, in folk-memories, or in the sub-conscious minds of the men and women who make up their successor civilisations.

Throughout the eleventh and twelfth centuries Norse-Greenland flourished as an independent country, maintaining the vigorous democratic traditions of the Icelanders who founded the settlements there, and trading regularly with Europe. I believe that these Greenland colonies, and their trade with Europe, were sustained by imports of food, timber, furs and other valuable products from their own colonies in Vinland. Certainly they flourished, and furs, which could have come only from North America, certainly reached Europe via Greenland. In the second half of the thirteenth century trade began to decline. People have looked for reasons for this in conjecturing about what may have happened *in Greenland* – I think it far more probable that the decline of European life in Greenland reflected happenings in the Vinland colonies in North America. In 1261 Norse-Greenland ceased to be independent and accepted the sovereignty of Norway, becoming subject to Denmark as the Danish Scandinavian kingdom embraced Norway. In exchange for giving up independence (and having to pay taxes to Norway), the Greenlanders were promised two royal ships a year, to bring them goods from Europe and to collect the goods that they themselves wanted to sell. For the next hundred years these 'treaty ships' called more or less regularly, but no ship came after 1367, and for the next three centuries Greenland practically disappears from European history.

It makes for tidy history to assume that Norse-Greenland simply *did* disappear: to suggest plausible reasons for its disappearance, and to leave it at that. I do not believe that human history is ever quite so neat and tidy, and I am sure that there are living traces of the old Norse-Greenland, and of its daughter-colonies in Vinland, still to be found by patient research. For one thing, Christianity in Greenland did *not* wholly disappear in the fourteenth century. The captain of one of the vessels in the little fleet with which John Davis explored the Davis Strait, sent a party ashore for wood and water at the mouth of one of the west Greenland fjords: they came upon a recent grave, marked with a cross. The West Greenlanders today are a mixed race of Eskimo and European (mostly Scandinavian) stock. It is assumed too lightly that their European blood goes back no farther than the eighteenth century, when Danish traders began to follow the Moravian missions, and the whaling fleets began to visit Greenland. No doubt there was a new admixture of races then, but why should all the old Norse blood die out? I came across a fascinating bit of evidence that it did *not* die out in conversation with a Danish police officer, Mr Hans Moller. He told me of a legend, told to him by an old Greenlander living in a remote part of the Frederikshaab district. According to this legend, Greenland was once three islands (Greenland, Markland and Vinland?), and it used to be possible to sail to a richly-favoured part of the Greenland islands by sailing *westwards* from a fjord near Frederikshaab. The old man apparently believed that if you chose the right fjord, and knew the old sailing directions, in some miraculous way this western route would bring you to an Elysium on the *east* coast, of Greenland. This is understandable: Greenland was his world, he knew that there was no Elysium to be found on the west coast, and therefore the richly-favoured land must be somewhere on the east coast. The real east coast of Greenland, harsher far than the habitable west, is separated from the west coast by the vast sub-continental ice-cap of central Greenland. Naturally, there would be legends about it. What I found so fascinating about this legend is the belief that you can get there by sailing *west*, and the belief that there were once *three* great islands of Greenland.

I did not know of the old Greenlander's legend as Reg and I explored Frederikshaab that first morning, but my mind was full of thoughts about Norse-Greenland history. I wished that we had been able to put into Julianehaab, the site of Leif Eiriksson's old home, but at least we were in Greenland. As things turned out, I was even grateful to the ice which barred us from Julianehaab, because the Frederikshaab district in some ways is more interesting, Not far to the south was the 'Middle Settlement' of the Greenland Norsemen, between the Eastern Settlement around Julianehaab and the Western Settlement at Godthaab, and later I had reason to think that this area of Greenland may have been of particular importance in the last chapters of the Vinland story. Apart from the geographical setting, however, there was not much to remind one of old Norse Greenland, as Reg and I explored that morning. The place looked to us like a film set for a story about the Yukon or the Klondike – buildings, mostly of wood, and mostly small and looking temporary, set down higgledy-piggledy apparently wherever anybody thought that he would put his house or store. No flowers, no trees – the only vegetation a thin, coarse grass clinging here and there where an inch or so of soil covered the bare rock. Between the houses were rough tracks – in the whole Frederikshaab area of Greenland there are only about four miles (seven kilometres) of road. But the little church, with its fairy-story steeple, was brightly painted and attractive, and magnificent, snow-capped mountains dominated everything.

We began to think about breakfast. We came to a building that had a wineglass painted on the door; through the windows we saw chairs and tables, and we took the place to be a restaurant. I knocked on the door, intending to ask if we could have meals there, and after a longish wait a man came to the door. He was in pyjamas and I had clearly got him out of bed. But he was wonderfully civil, spoke some English, and in reply to my questions explained that the place was not a restaurant, but sold drink. He added that there was no restaurant in Frederikshaab, but that there was a small hotel, and he told us how to get there. We thanked him, and made our way back to *Griffin*.

To reach *Griffin* we had to walk across the *Erika Dan* and, passing her galley, there was a most appetising smell of breakfast. I asked a mess-boy if he would convey my compliments to the chief steward and ask if we might buy breakfasts for ourselves and for the rest of *Griffin*'s crew. The messboy was Danish, and he had learned some English in the Danish schools. He came back a moment later and said, 'The chief steward says that you cannot *pay* for breakfast . . .' indicating that we were invited to have breakfast as guests of the *Erika Dan*. How long, the boy asked, would we be? I said, 'About half an hour,' and went down the ladder to *Griffin* to get the others up, with the promise of a breakfast that none of us would have to cook. This bright prospect overcame sleepiness from our late night, and soon all six of us were installed in the stewards' mess room on the *Erika Dan*, tucking into a splendid breakfast of two eggs, bacon, coffee, bread and butter and jam.

Pleasant as it was to sit at the *Erika Dan*'s breakfast table chatting to members of her crew, we had work to do. First, *Griffin* had to move, for the *Erika Dan* was sailing that morning, so we could not stay tied up to her. Then I wanted to get the engine looked at as soon as possible, and I wanted to try to arrange with the hotel for the crew to have meals and baths ashore. There were the usual domestic needs to be seen to – travellers' cheques to be changed into Greenland money, the post office, to find out about sending letters home, and also I had to find a cable office to send messages to the *Guardian* while I could not use *Griffin*'s radio. So after breakfast we divided forces as we had done in Iceland. I asked Peter Haward and Reg Garrod to open negotiations with the Government workshop about our engine, and I asked Peter Comber and Allister McIntosh to see what they could do in the way of arranging meals and baths for all of us at the hotel. Tim Lee and I stayed with *Griffin* to get her moved to her new berth.

The harbourmaster had promised to show us where he would like *Griffin* moored, and soon after the others had gone off on their various jobs the harbourmaster arrived with a launch to tow us across the harbour. He wanted us to moor, stern first, to a ringbolt set in the rock on the other side of the fjord. A boy in the launch took our warps ashore and we made fast, lying in the clean ice-cold water of the fjord about fifty yards offshore, with an anchor led from the bows as well as the warps holding us to the ringbolt in the rock. It was a snug anchorage, protected as long as the wind did not start blowing strongly down the fjord. The weather seemed reasonably settled, and the harbourmaster promised to warn us in good time if conditions looked like becoming dangerous. In fact, they did not, and we lay comfortably where we were for the rest of our stay at Frederikshaab, moving back to the quay just before we left, to take on fresh water, and to make it a bit easier for the Danish engineers to make last-minute adjustments to our engine.

Our new mooring had one disadvantage – being offshore, it meant that we had to use the dinghy to get ourselves and our supplies to and from *Griffin*. The dinghy was pretty well loaded with three of us, so for all of us to be on shore together meant normally three trips. This dinghy work was a slight nuisance (though useful exercise), but it was offset by the relief of not being immediately accessible to the general public. The people of Frederikshaab were much interested in us, and bands of children constantly thronged the little harbour to look at us. We answered all the questions we could, and did our best to be hospitable, but I did not want to have people coming on board without being invited.

Tim and I had just finished tidying up at our new anchorage when there was a hail from the shore, and we saw Peter Haward and Reg Garrod waving to us. Tim rowed across in the dinghy to fetch them. They had done well, and arranged for a mechanic from the Government workshop to visit *Griffin* that afternoon. A few minutes later the other Peter and Allister also reappeared. They, too, had done well. They had found the hotel, and fixed up for the whole crew to have breakfast, lunch and supper there while we were in Frederikshaab. They had also persuaded the proprietor to provide six hot baths, one after the other – and we were expected forthwith. So we collected towels and clean clothes and off we went. To get the whole crew ashore in two dinghy trips meant that one trip had to take four people (somebody had to row the dinghy back). In the still water of the harbour we just managed it, but the overloaded dinghy had precious little freeboard. I was happier with a limit of three.

To conserve hot water, we staggered our baths, and Tim volunteered to have his after lunch. This was as well, because we all wanted to wash clothes, too, and 'bathing' took rather a long time.

There are no regular posts from this part of Greenland, but there is a post office, and mails go by ship or aircraft when one calls. We learned that an aeroplane was expected to fly to Godthaab next day, so we got down to writing letters and postcards – all were eventually delivered. Peter Haward, Reg and the Government mechanic dismantled the engine, and discussed possible ways of making it go again – the main need was to devise some way of refastening the flywheel to the shaft, without benefit of any spare parts. Tim Lee and I went off to find the radio station, and Peter Comber and Allister went shopping, to see what (if anything) in the way of fresh food was to be had. There was not much, for practically everything but fish has to be imported – and even the fish which is Greenland's wealth seems mostly to be exported and to come back in tins. But we did manage to get some freshly-baked bread, oranges, and some useful replacements for our tinned supplies. The radio station, to which we had been talking as we approached Frederikshaab, was glad to see us – it is not often that voices from a ship at sea become real people to radio operators on land. The radio station also undertook to send press messages for me to the *Guardian*.

I was anxious to get away from Frederikshaab, because ice was gradually coming up the coast. The day after we arrived I was disturbed to see an iceberg just off the coast at the mouth of the fjord, but it was a solitary monster, and there was no close pack-ice near it. Still, it was a sign of things to come. Later that day a small bergy bit drifted into the fjord and came right into the harbour. The water was clear enough to see its underneath parts, massive spears and broken ridges of ice projecting many yards from it. To a small vessel under way, to graze it would have meant foundering, and even among moored boats it was not a pleasant neighbour. The crews of two small Danish naval survey vessels tackled it with boathooks, trying to push it off and send it away from shipping to the other side of the fjord. They had a hard job: it was as heavy as a huge block of concrete. They managed it in the end, and we breathed more freely.

The appearance of this piece of ice right inside our fjord made me more than ever anxious to get away, but we had to stay at Frederikshaab for another thirty-six hours to get our engine repairs completed. Restoring the flywheel to the main engine was a big job, made more difficult by the lack of spare parts. The heavy wheel had to be sweated onto the shaft after long heating with a blowlamp, in the hope that contraction of the metal as it cooled would help to hold the wheel to the shaft. It *seemed* strong enough when it was done, but none of us was happy about its possible behaviour under load, so Allister constructed heavy wooden knees, to Peter Haward's design, to strengthen the bulkhead behind the flywheel, so that if it came off at speed

at least it would meet some resistance before crashing into the saloon.
But the Danish mechanics did their work well, and Allister's wooden
buttresses were never needed, though it was always a relief to know
that they were there. That ancient engine did us good service a few
days later when we were in grave danger of being trapped in ice,
so I must not be too hard on it. But it remained a constant anxiety,
and although it ran again after the work at Frederikshaab it never
seemed to give much power. Perhaps that was as well: the flywheel
might not have stayed in place.

The main engine was not our only mechanical trouble. While
it was being repaired, we brought on deck the little charging motor
to put some charge into our batteries, and *that* engine suddenly
coughed and stopped working. Reg took it ashore in the dinghy to
the Government workshop, and the diagnosis was not good – in the
opinion of the mechanics there, the engine was just worn out, and
would never go again. Back on board *Griffin*, we discussed the
situation gloomily. The condition of our main engine was uncertain,
and if that failed again the little charging motor was our only means
of keeping the batteries going. If that failed too, it looked as if our
radio would have to go off the air, to say nothing of our navigation
lights and binnacle lights for the compasses: all depended on the
batteries.

Reg was not altogether satisfied with the official diagnosis on the
charging motor. 'It's old, of course,' he said, 'but I don't think it's
quite as bad as all that. If I could have a go at it with proper workshop
tools – well, I'd like to have a go. But I don't think they'd let me.'

Reg had a London boyhood, and saved his pocket money for a
third or fourth-hand motor bicycle as soon as he was old enough to
be allowed to ride one. That was boyhood in the years between the
wars, when teenagers seldom had much money, and if you wanted
to ride a motor bicycle you had to learn the hard way to be your own
mechanic. Reg had a passion for motor bicycles, and had gone in for
motorcycle sport. As some people have 'green fingers' in gardening,
so Reg has miraculous fingers for persuading small petrol engines to
keep going. I felt that if anybody could do anything with our
charging motor, Reg could. The question was, would the Government workshop allow him to use its workbench and its tools? We

could at least ask. Reg and I rowed ashore in the dinghy and went to the workshop.

We found the manager, who spoke good English, and I put our case as well as I could. It was a delicate business, because the workshop's own mechanics had said that there was nothing to be done with the engine, and to ask if Reg could use their tools to have a go looked as if I distrusted their skill. Furthermore, we were foreigners in a community dependent on the Danish Government. I had said that of course I would pay whatever charges were due for the men's time and for work done on *Griffin*; to ask if our man could use the Government workshop might also look as if I were trying to get out of paying money. I tried to explain that none of these thoughts was in my mind; that I had been deeply impressed by the skill of the workshop staff in tackling our flywheel, and was most grateful for all the help that we had been given; that I did not doubt their diagnosis about the charging motor, but that Reg understood that engine as nobody else did, and that it was just possible that he could make it go again for long enough to see us through. Good as the manager's English was, it was still a foreign language, and I was uncertain how much of my explanation was really understood.

I need not have worried. Whether or not the whole of my diplomatic effort was appreciated, I do not know, but the manager was kindness itself. Certainly Reg could use the workshop, he said, and he wished us luck. I left Reg there with the engine and went back to *Griffin*.

I found visitors on board, the police officer in charge of the Frederikshaab district, Hans Moller, and Constable Anders Nielsen, the resident policeman in Frederikshaab, on whom we had called earlier to get our passports stamped. They were interesting visitors, and spent more than an hour with us, discussing life in Greenland. Hans Moller has travelled much in Greenland, and it was he who told me of the old Greenlanders' legend about sailing westwards to reach a richly favoured part of Greenland's 'three islands'. Constable Nielsen invited us all to his home that evening for supper, and to have baths.

In spite of my worries about engines, and about having to spend another day in Frederikshaab, that was a good evening. Reg came back cautiously optimistic about the charging motor, and we enjoyed our visit to the policeman's home. When we said good-bye to him and his wife, we did not go straight back to *Griffin*, for we had been invited to go on to the house of a Dane living at Frederikshaab who had expressed great interest in our expedition. He was a student of Greenland history, and we talked long into the night about the old Norse colonies. He showed us a set of prints – the originals, I think, are in a museum at Copenhagen – from paintings by a self-taught Greenlander about a hundred years ago, depicting a series of in-cidents in the life of the Norse colonies. Most of them were of sadly bloodthirsty battles with the indigenous Eskimoes – the artist was a Greenlander-Eskimo, and it was clear where his sympathies lay. What interested me particularly was his painting of a Norse ship – not in the least like a Viking warship, but a beamy, decked vessel of a type that I am sure the Norsemen must have used for trading voyages. Perhaps this conception of an old Norse ship was at least partly de-rived from the nineteenth-century whalers which were familiar in Greenland waters. Perhaps, also, it reflected a folk-memory in the mind of the Greenland-Eskimo people of the sort of ship in which Eirik the Red and his descendants came to their shores. To me this was another fascinating glimpse of the historical *reality* of the old Norse-Greenland which I am sure lives on in Greenland still.

Coming on deck after a sadly short night, for a moment I found it hard to believe what I saw. About a couple of cables from us, made fast to the quay where the *Erika Dan* had been, was a new ship – and her name, in white letters on her handsome bows, was *Vinland Saga*. I *had* to pay a call on her, and during the morning an opportunity presented itself. On our rough passage to the Faeroes most of our supply of distilled water for the batteries had found its way into the bilges, and at Vaag we had replenished them with water that seemed to have been distilled perhaps a long time ago. It was all we could get. Tim was now worried about the batteries, because the hydrometer readings were not what they should have been. I was not greatly worried: not having Tim's training in naval engineering, and being more accustomed to the rough expedients of life than the precision of a submarine's engine room, I had more faith in the batteries than in the hydrometer. Still, it would do no harm to call in a second instrumental opinion, as it were, and to check the hydrometer's dubious view of the state of the batteries by measuring their output with a voltmeter. We had no voltmeter. I decided to go across to the *Vinland Saga* to ask if we might borrow one.

Peter Haward came with me, and we introduced ourselves to Captain Vinskol, the master of the *Vinland Saga*. His immediate reaction was that our battery troubles could safely be left to a first-class electrical engineer among his engineering officers, and that the matter of most moment was to celebrate the remarkable coincidence of finding our Vinland Expedition and his ship the *Vinland Saga* together in this same remote Greenland fjord. So we adjourned to his cabin for whisky (me) and excellent Danish lager (Peter). These comforting formalities over, Captain Vinskol, his electrical engineer, and a passenger travelling on his ship, came back with us to visit *Griffin*, where we were happy to return whisky for whisky, and Whitbread's for Danish beer. The electrical engineer's voltmeter confirmed my private opinion that there was nothing wrong with the batteries, and the engineer himself went straight to my heart by saying that in his view they were best left alone. That problem settled, Captain Vinskol invited the lot of us to a party on board the *Vinland Saga* that evening.

I had hoped to be able to sail this day, but it was already midday, and at the earliest we could not have left before late afternoon. The mouth of the fjord was still clear of pack-ice, but for thirty miles or so offshore there would be icebergs and bergy bits – the outriders of the pack. We needed as much daylight as possible to try to clear the ice, if we could, before our first night out. It seemed sensible, therefore, to postpone our departure until early the next morning. Full of good resolutions about leaving promptly at 0300, we accepted the *Vinland Saga's* invitation.

There was still much work to be done before we could think of party-going. I had to change travellers' cheques and pay our bills at the hotel and the Government workshop. Tim had to get the latest ice reports from the radio station, and there were bits and pieces of shopping to do. More, Peter Haward and Tim Lee, in some fit of masochism or saint-like martyrdom, had voluntarily undertaken the vile job of trying to make *Griffin*'s lavatory work. They had stripped and cleaned out the thing, but it had to be put together again.

All these things got done. After paying my bills I had about thirty shillings left in Greenland currency, and I asked Allister to go ashore and invest the lot in rolls of kitchen paper. His Scottish thrift revolted. 'All thirty shillings on paper?' he said. 'The lot', I said firmly. Loyalty overcame thrift, and he went off, to return with his arms full of kitchen rolls. It was the best investment I have ever made. We blessed them for the rest of the voyage.

Work done and ready to sail, we changed into reefer jackets and (more or less) respectable trousers for the *Vinland Saga*'s party. It was a marvellous party – as things turned out, perhaps a bit too marvellous. But I had been working everybody hard (more fairly, the crew had been working themselves hard) and I felt that a break was needed. We sang songs in English, Scots (Allister) and Danish until it was unclear in what language anybody was singing – our hosts never let a glass rest empty for a moment. I felt a brute as I got up to say that we simply must go back to our ship – but if we were to sail at 0300 we had about two hours' sleep left. Tim and I dutifully dragged ourselves up at 0245, and Peter Comber was getting up, when I felt that this was really driving men too hard. It seemed wiser to wait until 0700 – in this latitude near mid-summer there should still be plenty of light for negotiating the ice-belt. Tim and Peter Comber (I would have given both medals if I had had medals to give) were reprieved and went back to sleep, and I let the others sleep on. I had much to think about and did not feel like going back to bed myself, so I sat and wrote my journal. In spite of the party there was a brisk turnout at 0700 and at 0825 we slipped from Frederikshaab, and with a cautious eye on the flywheel, used our ancient engine to motor gently down the fjord. By 0845 we were clear of the entrance, streamed the log, and hoisted mainsail and genoa. There were a few icebergs and the sea was dotted with floating ice, but there was no sign of impacted ice. It was a clear sunny morning, with a wonderful display of pastel-coloured clouds over Greenland's icy mountains.

12

Navigational Detective Work

In any attempt at historical reconstruction you must start from
certain assumptions. You must be convinced at least that there is
something to reconstruct – in my search for Vinland I had no doubts
of that. Eirik the Red and Leif Eiriksson were real people, and
the Vinland voyages of Bjarni Herjolfsson, Leif Eiriksson and
Leif's brother-in-law Thorfinn Karlsefni were historical realities:
I think that few would now question their reality. But where
were their North American landfalls? Where, on the vast eastern
seaboard of the American continent, did Leif establish his *budir* or
settlement which became the first European colony in America?
How, after nearly a thousand years, did one set about looking
for it?

My first basic assumption after accepting the historical reality of
the Vinland colony or colonies was that the sea which took Leif and
his companions there could also take me. The sea is trackless, but on
any *long* voyage, ships setting out *from* the same place *to* the same
place will tend to cover much the same route. Even high-powered
steamships on ocean passages have recognised routes – routes that
are either the most direct or the most convenient from place to place.
A sailing ship cannot choose its route in a way that a powered vessel
can, but it is even more subject to the geophysical conditions that
affect its track across an ocean. Over any small area of sea ('small' in
this context may be an area of hundreds of square miles) a sailing
ship may be blown anywhere, but over the thousands of square
miles of ocean a sailing vessel, well rigged and under command, will
tend to go the way of other sailing vessels in getting from Point A
to Point B, provided that Points A and B are ocean-distances apart.
The clipper ships in the great days of sail had recognised routes for

sailing from Europe to the Far East and back. Francis Chichester, in *Along the Clipper Way,* discusses their sailing routes:

> This great clipper way was like a broad path curving down through the North Atlantic and the South Atlantic, passing between 300 and 800 miles south of Cape Town, and then running down the easting for 6,600 miles to Bass Strait, either keeping within the Roaring Forties, or south of them. . . . After leaving Sydney the clippers either passed between or south of the New Zealand islands, then again they ran their easting down in the Forties or the Fifties. The next landmark was Cape Horn, 5,000 miles on from New Zealand, and once they had doubled the Horn the sailors reckoned they were as good as home, though in fact they had another 8,000 miles to sail through both Atlantics.

You can draw a line round the globe – as Chichester has – and call it correctly 'the Clipper Way'. At any given moment of time on different voyages ships may be hundreds of miles north or south of this invisible route, but their passages *as a whole* will tend to follow the route. So, I felt, with the Vinland voyages. I could not hope to *reproduce* Leif Eiriksson's voyage exactly: he left no log (or none that has yet been found), and since in any case he could not reckon longitude there is no means of knowing where his ship moved from noon to noon. But I knew where he had started from, certain facts about his voyage can be deduced from the sagas, and if the descriptions of Vinland in the sagas are accepted as factual (as I think they must be) I knew within broad geographical limits where he must have ended up. Given all this, and given a sailing boat subject to all the forces of wind and sea that have affected sailing vessels in the Davis Strait and the Labrador Sea since the dawn of time, it seemed to me that I might reasonably attempt, not to *reproduce* but to *reconstruct* Leif's voyage to Vinland. Moreover, although I was primarily concerned with Leif's voyage, because where he got to determined where other Norsemen followed, I was also concerned with *all* Norse voyages relating to Vinland – Bjarni's and Karlsefni's as well as Leif's – and anything that could be deduced about one voyage would help to interpret another.

At what time of year did Leif Eiriksson sail? There is not much evidence in the sagas, but one of the key passages is this, from the *Graenlendinga Saga*, recording Leif's arrival at an island off Vinland:

They went ashore and looked about them. The weather was fine. There was dew on the grass, and the first thing they did was to get some of it on their hands and put it to their lips, and it seemed to them the sweetest thing they had ever tasted. Then they went back to their ship . . . and steered a westerly course round the headland . . . They carried their hammocks ashore and put up booths. Then they decided to winter there, and built some large houses.

This is a summer scene, and late summer rather than early summer. The decision 'to winter there' means that it was certainly not winter when they landed, but it also implies that the summer was sufficiently advanced for thoughts of the coming winter to be in their minds. I think, therefore, that Leif's arrival in Vinland can be dated as in July or August. How long did the voyage take? Here our own navigational needs seemed relevant. We needed daylight, as many hours of daylight as we could have, for meeting the perils of ice; and in any case, if one is sailing into the unknown, the more daylight the better. I chose the weeks around midsummer for our voyage from Greenland to Vinland because those weeks give more daylight than any other time of the year. I think that Leif would have done the same, and left Greenland at about the time as we did, in early June.

We left Frederikshaab in Greenland in the early morning of June 2, and reached what I believe to be Vinland on the evening of June 27, having spent forty-eight hours at Halifax, Nova Scotia, on the way. That is roughly a month. Leif made at least two stops, putting in to Helluland and Markland, and while the *Graenlendinga Saga* suggests that he was anxious not to waste time at either place – being as keen to get to Vinland as I was – one cannot say precisely how long these visits took. Helluland, in Northern Labrador, or perhaps Baffin Island, may well have been farther north then we went, so Leif may have sailed a rather greater distance than we did in his total voyage from Greenland to Vinland. Also, he made two stops to our one. So

I think that he probably took rather longer than our month. I was
sure that he would have set out on the right side of midsummer, at
least a week or two weeks, perhaps a bit more, before midsummer's
day. That would bring him to Vinland in July or early August. Any
date in July or August would fit with what the sagas tell us, and with
what I reckon to have been his navigational need for maximum daylight for the northerly part of his voyage. Thus I feel confident that
Leif sailed, and we sailed, at about the same time of year.

The next piece of this navigational detective story was to try to
work out what course Leif took on leaving his father's settlement at
Eiriksfjord (modern Julianehaab). One can be misled here by the
modern map – we know too much about the land masses, and precisely where they lie in relation to one another. At first glance Leif's
obvious course would seem to be more or less due west, or west with
a bit of south. But Leif certainly started off by going north. I do not
know what the ice was like off Julianehaab in early June a thousand
years ago. It may have been less formidable than it is nowadays, but
there was certainly some ice, and a prudent navigator would have to
reckon with it. Leif would have had to sail north to get round it, and
he would have been helped in going north by the north-setting West
Greenland current. Relating Karlsefni's voyage to Vinland, which
followed Leif's, to Leif's own voyage, there is some evidence that
a northerly course was the established route on setting out for
Vinland. *Eirik's Saga* tells us of Karlsefni's voyage: 'They sailed first
up to the Western Settlement.' Now the Western Settlement (the
names 'Western' and 'Eastern' are a bit confusing here, though one
can see how they came about in the minds of the early settlers) was
around Godthaab, well to the north of Julianehaab, and, as I explained earlier in discussing the movement of ice around Greenland, more likely to be ice-free than the coast of southwest Greenland. Moreover, the Davis Strait narrows as one goes north. The
Norsemen of the Greenland settlements certainly hunted north of
Godthaab; they were in touch with the native Eskimoes, whom
they fought and sometimes captured – and when they were not
fighting, doubtless they tried to trade. The nomadic Eskimoes migrated from the Canadian Arctic to Greenland, and from Greenland
to the Canadian Arctic, and the Greenland Norsemen may have

learned from the Eskimoes, or found out for themselves, that from the north of Greenland there is land not far to the west. From modern Holsteinborg, north of Godthaab, to Cape Dyer on Baffin Island is not much more than two hundred miles. The Norsemen were accustomed to coastal sailing, and at the outset of an exploring voyage it may have been a comfort to feel that there was a coast of some sort not far away. Although it is unrecorded, there is little doubt but that the Norsemen in Greenland discovered Baffin Island before they had any thoughts of Vinland.

Karlsefni may have had reasons for visiting the Western Settlement before setting out for Vinland – he may have had friends there who wanted to join him – or he may have sailed north to get round the ice, or to be nearer to a known western land before leaving Greenland. Whatever his reasons, he is recorded as having sailed north on leaving Julianehaab. I am sure that Leif set off in the same way, though whether he went as far as the Western Settlement at Godthaab, or turned west before he reached it, as soon as he could conveniently get round the ice, there is no means of knowing. My own guess is that he did not go as far as Godthaab, but turned west some way north of Frederikshaab, as we did. Since the saga-writer says definitely that Karlsefni went first to the Western Settlement, I feel that he would have recorded Leif's visit also, had he gone there.

I believe that the European colonies in Vinland were both more extensive, and were maintained for longer, than is commonly supposed. Vinland was first colonised from Leif Eiriksson's Eastern Settlement in Greenland, but as time went on there must have been regular voyages from the Western Settlement, too. And as the climate of southwest Greenland became harsher (from the twelfth to the fourteenth centuries), and ice around the Eastern Settlement became more severe, it seems probable that Vinland's main links with Greenland would have been with Godthaab rather than with Julianehaab. But the Godthaab Settlement collapsed before the Julianehaab colony.

Neither historical record nor archaeology has yet been able to explain precisely what happened, or why things happened as they did. What is known is that at some time towards 1340 the Godthaab Settlement was wiped out by Eskimoes (called by the Norsemen 'Skraelings', the generic name given by the Greenland Norse both to

Eskimoes and to the American Indians in Vinland; it means roughly 'savages'). Why were the Norse Greenlanders of 1340 incapable of resisting Greenland Eskimoes whom they had successfully withstood for the past three centuries?

Climatic change and the slow deterioration of Norse stock as the climate worsened may be in part the answer. The culture and the economies of the Greenland Norse and of the Greenland Eskimoes differed radically. The Norse were *settlers*, establishing settled farms and homesteads, from which they went out to trade, to explore, to hunt and fish, but to which they returned. The Eskimoes were a nomadic folk who had come to terms with the Arctic, living by specialised forms of hunting and fishing from their kayaks, developed for survival in their ice-bound world. In a climate slightly kinder than that of Greenland as we know it today, the Eskimoes would have been content to roam in the far north, and would not have had much need to contest the fjords of Godthaab and the south with the Norse invaders. Undoubtedly they once lived there, for one of the earliest of Iceland's historians, Ari Thorgilsson, writing about 1127, records the finding of human dwellings and skin boats by the first Norse colonists in both the Eastern (Julianehaab) and the Western (Godthaab) Settlements. But they may have largely abandoned these southerly fjords and migrated northwards before the Norsemen came. Such fighting as there was would have been sporadic, with isolated fragments of the Eskimo peoples, whom the Norse could have subdued or driven away without much difficulty.

With the worsening of the Greenland climate the situation changed. The Eskimo economy is wonderfully adapted to survival in the Arctic, but in persistent extreme severity of cold no human life can survive. If life became insupportable in the far north, hunger would have driven the Eskimo folk south again. And if climatic deterioration affected the Canadian Arctic too there may have been an influx of Eskimo peoples into Greenland, adding to population pressure on food resources and intensifying the movement southwards in search of food. 'Population pressure' here is not to be understood in modern terms of hundreds of thousands of extra mouths to feed. In an Arctic economy the arrival of two or three more families in search of food could bring about a crisis.

So, for climatic or other ecological reasons that upset the delicate balance of Arctic economy, the Eskimoes moved south again, and in their southward migration attacked the Godthaab Norse. Maybe the Norse beat off the first Eskimo attacks, but always there were new bands of these hard, hungry people coming from the north. And, in a worsening climate, the Eskimoes were better fitted than the Norsemen to survive. In the end the Godthaab homesteads fell, and the Western Settlement disappeared from history. This must have had profound influence on the fate of the Vinland colonies, the collapse of Godthaab leading ultimately to the collapse of European Vinland. But I do not think this happened quickly. People do not give up their homes easily, and the Norse were formidable fighting men (and women). It is more probable that the Godthaab Norse were worn down gradually: and that the Vinland colonies, getting less and less support from Greenland, gradually succumbed to attacks by American Indians. Here the Middle Settlement may have become important. As Julianehaab as a base for Vinland was closed for more and more of the year by ice, and as Godthaab was made untenable by Eskimo attacks, the Middle Settlement, based on the fjords around Ivigtut to the south of Frederikshaab, would have become the last effective base for Vinland trade. But the Middle Settlement appears to have been more thinly populated than either the Eastern or the Western Settlement, and however the Greenland Norsemen may have tried to develop it in those last years, they had not the resources to succeed. There has been less archaeological work here than in other parts of Greenland, and much remains to be discovered about the Middle Settlement and its links with Vinland. Archaeology here, and particularly the new techniques of underwater archaeology in places where ships may have been wrecked, can, perhaps, add much to our knowledge of Vinland's history.

Norse Greenland and Norse Vinland were interdependent for nearly four centuries, from Leif's voyage in 1001 until late in the fourteenth century. The *Icelandic Annals*, regarded as a good historical source, record the arrival in Iceland in 1347 of a ship loaded with timber from Markland, which had been making for Greenland but had been driven off course by a storm. Trade in timber is not a snatch-and-run affair. Sea raiders can seize gold or jewels or other personal valuables and make off quickly, but timber cannot be cut and loaded in a day. A timber trade requires haulage ways from forest to shore; even if the forest lines the shore there must be haulage ways to the beach, and some form of jetty or causeway from which to load heavy tree trunks on to ships capable of carrying them. A natural rock-causeway with deepwater alongside might serve for a jetty, but it would have to be defended, and there would have to be some sort of settlement where woodcutters and longshoremen for handling the timber could live during the cutting and loading period. Logging settlements need not be permanent, but they must be capable of providing food and shelter for the logging force, for weeks or months at a time. If a timber trade between North America and Greenland was going on in 1347, there must have been settlements capable of maintaining logging camps. The loggers *could* have been migrant workers brought each year from Greenland, but wood was so vital to the economy of Greenland that it seems to me more probable that the timber trade was organised by permanent settlers in America, so that ships could arrive from Greenland and be sure of finding cut timber stacked and ready to load. The timber-ship in 1347 is recorded as having sailed from 'Markland'. I think that this was probably not Leif's 'Markland' of two hundred and fifty years earlier – the name simply means 'wooded country' – but either a wooded part of the Vinland settlements, or a wooded area nearer to Vinland than southern Labrador, capable of being controlled by the Norse settlers.

There is no evidence that this ship in 1347 was the last of the timber-ships from America to sail for Greenland – there is nothing to suggest that the trade did not go on for years after 1347. But there is evidence that as the fourteenth century drew to its close the Greenland settlements, and with them, I think, the Vinland colonies, were finding it harder and harder to survive. The last of the regular royal ships from Norway – the 'treaty ships' – reached Greenland in 1367, and after that trade with Europe seems to have died. Some trade with Iceland lingered on, but there is no reference to Greenland in the *Icelandic Annals* after 1410.

As life in Greenland became harder to sustain, and attacks by Eskimoes more frequent, why did not the Greenland Norsemen emigrate to the richer and infinitely more favoured lands that their kinsmen held in Vinland? I think that almost certainly they did; that the Vinland colonies lasted until well into the fifteenth century, and that one of the reasons for the apparently sudden disappearance of Norse Greenland from history was that most of the Norse Greenlanders emigrated to America. Why did these European colonies in America fail, when the New England settlers of the period after Columbus survived and flourished? There must be many reasons, but I think that the most important can be summed up in one word – 'gunpowder'. These early Norse colonies were colonies without gunpowder. European settlers in America, after Columbus, had guns, which gave them an immeasurable superiority in weapons over anything that the native inhabitants could bring against them. Given a musket, one courageous woman could hold a stockaded dwelling against twenty or thirty attackers without gunpowder. Ten determined men with muskets and perhaps one cannon were a force that a tribe of Indians could not subdue. The early Norse had no muskets – they were no better armed than the Indians whose land they tried to settle. The Norse had iron and therefore better swords and spears, but a superior sword or spear is significant only in hand-to-hand fighting: it may enable one strong man to subdue two or three opponents, but he will tire in the end, and be brought down. The Indian bow may have been a better weapon than anything the Norse archers had. In struggles with the Indians, therefore, the Norse had no superiority of armament, and must always have been outnumbered. The Indians attacked on interior lines, and every Indian who fell could be replaced quickly from his tribal homeland. A Norseman who fell could be replaced only when the next ship from Greenland called. Ships might be lost, and there might be months, perhaps even a year or more, between the coming of ships from Greenland.

Where the Norse did have an absolute superiority was at sea. The American Indians had nothing in the way of sea-going vessels remotely comparable with a Viking ship: nor had they anything approaching the knowledge and experience of the sea that the Norsemen had. This absolute superiority at sea made it possible for the Norse to conquer and to hold local maritime areas. They would be stockaded and strongly defended settlements, open to the sea, which the Norse controlled, and capable of sending help to one another by sea. But they could not extend inland beyond a certain point – a point strictly limited by whatever natural features capable of strong local defence might exist. I doubt if any of the Norse Vinland settlements extended more than a mile or two inland, but I am also confident that small, strongly defended coastal colonies existed for centuries. Norsemen and Indians were not always fighting. No doubt the Indians would attack the invaders whenever they felt strong enough to drive them out, but the Vikings were formidable fighting men, and in a defended position, with their backs to the sea, they would not have been easy to drive out. There must have been periods, perhaps long periods, of truce or more or less peace, when the Norsemen and Indians co-existed and traded with each other, the Europeans secure in their sea-defended settlements, but unable to go far beyond them, the Indians secure in their countryside, but unable to penetrate the settlements.

In the end, manpower told. We know from the sagas that the Norse settlers brought women with them, and that children were born to them in Vinland. But the population of the Norse colonies could never have been enough, or been left alone for long enough, for natural increase to produce a community capable of over-running Indian territory and extending permanently inland. However secure a Norse settlement may have seemed, and some of them must have endured for generations, the Norse remained dependent on sea-power. There were never enough Norsemen in Vinland to create a sea-power based on Vinland itself – to create a Vinland nation (as post-Columbus European settlers created a nation). Their sea-power was based on Greenland, which in turn was sustained by ships from Europe. As the Greenland settlements declined, and ships stopped coming from Europe, so the power of the Greenlanders to sustain their Vinland colonies declined. As a last effort at survival it seems to me probable that the remnants of the Norse Greenland population emigrated to America. But there were not enough of them to survive in America – not enough to fight and to find manpower to build the ships with which they could have made a Vinland nation. One may deplore the savagery, recorded in the sagas, which marked the Norsemen's battles with American Indians, but in the setting of its time such warfare was regarded as part of the lot of man. The Vikings had a bloody history, redeemed at least to some extent by courage and tenacity, and by their insistence on a rough form of democracy in their own institutions. They would kill enemies, and enslave captured enemies, but such slavery was not the brutal institution it was in the Mediterranean world. A captured slave would have to work for his master, but if he worked well he was treated as a member of the family, and was generally given his freedom. The sagas record a number of touching instances of this. Our modern world owes much to those old Norsemen for inventing and preserving the idea of parliamentary democracy – the idea that power in a community should derive from an assembly of equals, and not from the autocratic word of any individual. The British parliament is commonly called 'The Mother of Parliaments', but the Icelandic parliamentary assembly is older, and has a better claim to the title. Since the British have written their own history books – and English is more widely read than Icelandic – the name 'Mother of Parliaments' has stuck, and the Icelanders now call their assembly 'The Grandmother of Parliaments'. Historical justice here is with the Icelanders. Monarchies arose in Scandinavia, as they did elsewhere, but the ancient Norse institutions never wholly foundered. Scandinavian monarchy today is a pattern of what monarchy in a democratic community should be, offering respected leadership without separating Crown from people by ranks of privileged hangers on. In their attitude to women the Norsemen of a thousand years ago could give lessons to many later societies. Their women had equal property rights with men, they could divorce their husbands if they wished and retain their own property, and a woman who had qualities of leadership was as much respected as any leading man. Throughout the genealogies in the sagas, as much attention is paid to the mothers and grandmothers of people as to fathers and grandfathers. It was an age of violence and hard living, but the Vikings clung to ideals of human behaviour which are not always acted upon, even today. Their attempted conquest of Vinland was bloody, but no worse than the more efficient wars against the Indians by the European settlers in America who succeeded them. The Norse conquest of Vinland nearly succeeded. It was at least a gallant failure.

But where *was* Vinland? In studying Leif Eiriksson's voyage, and the other recorded Vinland voyages, I have said that I knew 'within broad geographical limits' where they must have ended up. But those limits were *very* broad – from Hamilton Inlet in Labrador perhaps to Cape Hatteras off North Carolina. They would have to be defined much more closely. I thought it could be done.

The key to Leif's voyage, and to the location of the Vinland settlements, must be in Bjarni Herjolfsson's earlier voyage, which Leif was attempting to re-sail. The saga records have become rather mixed and confused. *Eirik's Saga* ignores Bjarni, and credits Leif with the discovery of Vinland when he was blown off course on a voyage from Norway to Greenland. This was a discovery as accidental as Bjarni's, except that Leif did go ashore to find 'fields of wild wheat and vines'. There are no navigational details of any sort. The caption to the Vinland map credits Leif and Bjarni as having sailed together to discover Vinland – not impossible, but there is no other evidence for it. The *Graenlendinga Saga*, however, has an account of Bjarni's voyage so coherent and consistent that I feel it must be true. Why invent a story about Bjarni's having found new lands to the west and *not* gone ashore, if the accidental discovery had been Leif's and he *had* gone ashore? Ninety-nine sea captains out of a hundred, on discovering an apparently attractive new coast line, would have wanted eagerly to go ashore to have a look at it. Bjarni's behaviour was so unusual, improbable even, that I cannot believe it was invented. Moreover, the facts of the story provide at least an explanation for his eccentric behaviour, in his compelling desire not to waste time, but to get his laden ship to his father in Greenland as quickly as he could. All this hangs together. The caption to the Vinland map, recording Leif and Bjarni as having sailed together, is understandable as an ellision or summary of rather vague historical memories: the compiler of the map was concerned with the existence, place and shape of Vinland, not necessarily with its discovery.

So I think that one may turn fairly to the *Graenlendinga Saga* for the version of this part of the Vinland story that seems likely to be the most accurate. This is what the saga says:

Bjarni arrived in Iceland at Eyrar in the summer of the year that his father had left for Greenland. The news came as a shock to Bjarni, and he refused to have his ship unloaded. His crew asked him what he had in mind; he replied that he intended to keep his custom of enjoying his father's hospitality over the winter. 'So I want to sail my ship to Greenland, if you are willing to come with me.' They all replied that they would do what he thought best. Then Bjarni said, 'This voyage of ours will be considered fool-hardy, for not one of us has ever sailed the Greenland sea.' How-ever, they put to sea as soon as they were ready, and sailed for three days until land was lost to sight below the horizon. Then the fair wind failed, and northerly winds and fog set in, and for many days they had no idea what their course was. After that they saw the sun again, and were able to get their bearings. They hoisted sail, and after a day's sail they sighted land. They discussed among themselves what country this might be. Bjarni said he thought it would not be Greenland. The crew asked him if he wanted to land there or not. Bjarni replied, 'I think we should sail in close.' They did so, and soon they could see that the country was not mountainous, but was well wooded and with low hills. So they put to sea again, leaving the land on the port quarter, and after sailing for two days they sighted land once more. Bjarni's men asked him if he thought this was Greenland yet; he said he did not think this was Greenland any more than the previous one – 'for there are said to be huge glaciers in Greenland'. They closed the land quickly, and saw that it was flat and wooded. Then the wind failed, and the crew all said they thought it advisable to land there, but Bjarni refused. They claimed they needed both firewood and water, but Bjarni said, 'You have no shortage of either.' He was criticised for this by his men. He ordered them to hoist sail, and they did so. They turned the prow out to sea, and sailed before a southwest wind for three days before they sighted another land. This one was high and mountainous and topped by a glacier. Again they asked Bjarni if he wished to land there, but he replied 'No, for this country seems to me to be worthless.' They did not lower sail this time, but followed the coastline and saw that it was an island. Once again they put the land astern and sailed out to sea before the same fair wind. But now it began to blow a gale, and

Bjarni ordered his men to shorten sail and not to go harder than ship and rigging could stand. They sailed now for four days until they sighted a fourth land. The men asked Bjarni if he thought this would be Greenland or not. 'This tallies most closely with what I have been told about Greenland,' replied Bjarni, 'and here we shall go in to land.' They did so, and made land as dusk was falling at a promontory which had a boat hauled up on it. This was where Bjarni's father, Herjolf, lived, and it has been called Herjolfsness for that reason ever since.

This is not much to go on, but what there is is coherent and consistent. Three days out of Iceland, apparently with a fair wind, which would be taking them west or a little south of west, they met northerly winds. 'Northerly' does not necessarily mean 'from due north'. In fact, the phrase implies to me that, while the wind was predominantly from the north, it was not due north – seamen still today, and, as far as I know, in all languages, will talk of winds as 'northerly', 'easterly', 'southerly' or 'westerly' meaning that that is the *general* direction from which the wind is coming, but it may veer or back a point or two from time to time. There could not have been any west in Bjarni's norther, because that would have sent him off towards Ireland: on one abortive voyage to Vinland from Greenland, described in *Eirik's Saga*, a ship was blown to Ireland and then came home. Norse seafarers knew Ireland, and the British Isles, well enough. Bjarni's new land was certainly not there.

From due north, Bjarni's norther would have sent him towards the Azores or perhaps the coast of Africa. That would have taken so long that it may be doubted if any of his ship's company would have survived to get back to Greenland, and there is nothing to suggest either the Azores – obviously small islands – or an African coast in the story. They may be ruled out.

A touch of east in his northerly wind would have sent him towards an area between Newfoundland and Nova Scotia, a part of the Atlantic notorious for fog. After 'many days' in fog, we are told, he saw the sun, and was able to get his bearings. We do not know precisely what this means. Norse navigators of that period had neither chronometer nor compass, and no means whatever of reckoning longitude. They could take accurate observations of the sun, which gave them a good idea of latitude – their north-south position on the earth's surface. They could not assess their east-west position with any accuracy, though inherited skill in known waters perhaps enabled them to interpret Nature's small signposts, seaweed, the flight of birds, the trend of swell, the colour, even the smell of the sea, in ways that we have long forgotten. In unknown waters this skill could not have helped much. Bjarni would have known that he was far to the south of Greenland. He could not have known how far he had been driven east or west. Moreover, in fog, such wind as there is is commonly light and variable – a decent wind tends to disperse fog. In his fogbound days, therefore, he would have drifted considerably. He may have tried to keep his dead reckoning up to date, recording every small shift of wind, but with no compass he could not have done much more then guess at the direction of light shifts of wind.

When the fog cleared, he was lost as far as his position east or west of Greenland was concerned, though he could work out pretty accurately how far he had been driven to the south. He would know that he had to make north, and he would get as much north in his course as the wind permitted. We are not told what wind he had when the fog lifted, but evidently there *was* wind, for they were able to sail, and when they sighted land they were able to 'sail in close'. Where was the land? Newfoundland? Nova Scotia? Long meditation on the problem has convinced me that it was probably Nova Scotia. The description of the coast, 'not mountainous, but well-wooded and with low hills', fits the Nova Scotia coastline around the modern Halifax to perfection – just how dramatically it fits I was to discover later. The existence of this coast to the west told Bjarni that he had to make north and east – he could not go north and west, because the land stood in the way. By this time, too, I think, Bjarni must have had a shrewd idea that he had sailed west of Greenland, and needed to get east as well as north.

Leaving the land to port, they sailed north and east for 'two days' when they sighted land again. Newfoundland? Or did they round Cape Race without knowing it, and next sight land in Southern Labrador? This one cannot know. If the wind was westerly on leaving

Nova Scotia Bjarni may have decided reasonably to make as much easting as he could before turning north again. Cape Race is such a decisive landmark that I feel that some record of it would have got into the saga if Bjarni and his crew had had to weather it. So I think it more probable that they did not see Cape Race, but passed it unawares, well out to sea.

Bjarni's second land may have been either the east coast of Newfoundland or the southeast coast of Labrador, perhaps both, for there is no indication anywhere in the sagas that these early Norsemen realised that Newfoundland was an island, and they could have taken Belle Isle Strait to be a fjord, merely a deep indentation in a continuous coast. The Norwegian Captain J. Kr. Tornöe, who has made an outstanding contribution to studies of early Norse navigation and whose hypothetical reconstruction of Bjarni's voyage greatly influenced my own thinking, attaches importance to Bjarni's choice of words in replying to his men when they asked if this second land might be Greenland. The saga quotes him as saying that he did not think it could be Greenland 'for there are said to be *huge* glaciers in Greenland'. Captain Tornöe makes the shrewd suggestion that Bjarni's emphasis on the *hugeness* of the glaciers in Greenland implies that they had seen *some* snow or glaciers on approaching their second land; and they could not have seen snow-capped hills or glaciers in summer before reaching northern Newfoundland. Captain Tornöe suggests that after seeing or glimpsing northern Newfoundland the land they closed next was around Château Bay in southern Labrador: knowing nothing of the Belle Isle Strait or the St Lawrence river they would have assumed a continuous, indented coast. It seems to me a reasonable suggestion.

What about time and distances? Could this have been done in two days from Nova Scotia? Here one comes up against the maddening old Norse word *doegr*, which has confused practically everyone who has tried to study the Vinland voyages, because it is translated as 'day' – and whatever it means, it does *not* mean day. Magnusson and Palsson, whose admirable modern translation of the *Graenlendinga Saga* and *Eirik's Saga* I have drawn upon for all quotations in this book, put a cautionary footnote about *doegr* when it occurs in Bjarni's voyage:

doegr: this term is ambiguous. Strictly speaking, it means 'day' in the sense of twelve hours, but it is also used in the sense of the 'astronomical day' of twenty-four hours, and there is often doubt about the particular meaning in many early texts.

The conception of *doegr* as 'day', or even as a 'sailing day' in terms of time has cast doubt on attempts to interpret the Vinland voyage because if they are to be interpreted in terms of real distances they demand sailing speeds for the old Norse ships that are all but impossible. Even Captain Tornöe, whose approach to the problem of Vinland navigation is unquestionably right, has to accept fantastic speeds for the Vinland ships. Analysing Bjarni's voyage, he is forced into this time-and-distance-run table (on p. 38 of his *Norsemen before Columbus*).

from Nova Scotia to south-eastern Labrador:

approx 600 miles in 2 *doegr*

from Labrador to Loksland (Baffin Land):

approx 700 miles in 3 *doegr*

from Loksland to Greenland:

approx 600 miles in 4 *doegr*

approx 1,900 miles in 9 *doegr*

The average speed for the distance will thus be 8·8 knots.

This seems to me to be impossible. Sailing ships *can* travel at 8·8 knots; depending on their waterline length, they *can* sail much faster. But I do not believe that any medieval sailing ship could *average* 8·8 knots over the mixed weather of nine days. That would be a fantastic performance for the best of modern racing yachts – just possible, perhaps, in exceptional conditions, but almost unbelievable. *Griffin*, designed as an ocean-racer, and a fast boat, averaged 4·15 knots on the passage from Greenland to Nova Scotia – and that was remarkably good going in the conditions we met. I do not believe that Bjarni's ship *could* have averaged 8·8 knots over much the same route.

I write here with knowledge of *Griffin*'s actual average speed for the passage, whereas in planning the voyage I could not know this.

I did know, however, something of the speed of sailing ships. The Viking ships were good vessels, ably handled, but I could reckon their *average* speed for a passage at not more than about 4 knots – more probably, I thought, it would be between 3 and 4 knots. So here was something inexplicable, and irreconcilable with everything else that it seemed that one might learn from the sagas. Navigational probabilities were consistent and seemed to me to make sense, but the times and distances simply did not fit. The more I considered Bjarni's voyage, and my own attempts to reconstruct it, the more strongly I found myself agreeing with Captain Tornöe's interpretation – but I could not accept his table of times and distance run. I mulled over this dilemma, feeling that if everything else seemed right, then the interpretation of the *doegr* must be wrong. I wondered if the *doegr* in a navigational sense perhaps did not mean a fixed time at all, whether it might be the period required to work through a set of watches at the helm, which would vary with the number of helmsmen in the crew. Suddenly I hit on a solution which was not really a solution at all, but which at least enabled me to avoid trying to define the *doegr*. I decided to consider the *doegr* purely in algebraical terms, as an unknown quantity of time, or x. Thus two *doegrs* in one voyage would relate to the same time or distance as two *doegrs* in another voyage, but the elapsed time would be considered merely as $2x$ – days or hours, or anything; it did not matter. Captain Tornöe's table thus became acceptable: if Bjarni took two units of time to cover six hundred miles it was reasonable that he should require three units for seven hundred miles, and four units for the next six hundred miles was consistent with the vagaries of sailing boats. As I have admitted, this did not solve the problem of the *doegr*, but it did cut through the arithmetical barrier between existing interpretations of the *doegr* and navigational reality.

After my return to England from our voyage, Mr A. N. Ryan, of Liverpool University, sent me extracts from an article in the *Bergens Sjøfartsmuseums Årshefte* for 1964, in which Mr R. Morekin puts forward what I am sure is the correct interpretation of the *doegr* as a navigational term. Doubtless the word was also used in old Norse in a non-navigational sense to mean 'day', and this must be why confusion has arisen. *Navigationally*, according to Mr Morekin, the *doegr* had nothing to do with actual time, but was a distance based on Norse conceptions of latitude, which were remarkably accurate. The Norse unit of nautical measurement, based on Eratosthenes' measurement of the circumference of the earth, not Ptolemy's, used elsewhere in Europe, was the *vika*, which equalled six nautical miles. The word *vika* originally meant 'a watch of rowing', and a band of fresh rowers were supposed to be able to cover six nautical miles in one watch of two hours. The *doegr* began by meaning 'a day's rowing', but it did not mean a day's *actual* rowing, but the distance of twelve *vikur* or seventy-two nautical miles that *theoretically* could be covered in a day's rowing. When applied to sailing vessels, twenty-four hours' rowing was equated with twelve hours under sail, so that the *sailing doegr* became twice the *rowing doegr*, or 144 nautical miles. Sometimes, particularly in coastal work, and traditionally in Greenland in the thirteenth century, the *half-doegr* was used as the unit of sailing distance, meaning seventy-two miles.

Contemplating Bjarni's voyage in terms of nautical *distances* instead of sailing *days* gives interesting results. Taking the *doegr* as 144 nautical miles, the distance from anywhere on Baffin Island to Herjolfsness in southern Greenland is rather far for four *doegr*. From northern Labrador it is about right. I had always been a little uneasy about a reconstruction of Bjarni's voyage sending him as far north as Baffin Island, where ice is liable to be formidable; even assuming some worsening of ice conditions since his day. I like northern Labrador for the Helluland landfall much better, and as the distances fit in terms of the *doegr*, I am inclined to place Helluland in northern Labrador. And perhaps not all that far north. Bjarni estimated the distance from Markland (southern Labrador) to Helluland as three *doegr*, which is approximately 450 miles. This would put him somewhere around Ford Harbour or Port Manvers on the modern map – reasonable enough, and nothing inconsistent here. But the first stage of his voyage to Greenland, from coming out of the fog and sighting what I believe to have been Nova Scotia, to either northern Newfoundland or southern Labrador is all wrong: the distance cannot be less than some six hundred miles, and the saga records it as two *doegr*, or three hundred miles at the outside. Moreover, the saga accounts of the comparable stages of Leif Eiriksson's voyage and of Karlsefni's voyage are consistent: from Markland to their next 'land' south is given as two *doegr*. Assessing all that can be deduced about all three voyages, this distance *cannot* be right. Landing in a northeaster two *doegr* from southern Labrador or northern Newfoundland would have put Leif ashore with a vengeance: he would almost certainly have been wrecked in southeast Newfoundland. Karlsefni appears to have had a norther. What wind he actually had is unclear, but he is recorded as having had a northerly wind from Helluland, and the implication seems to be that this wind held. It would not have been much more comfortable for a landing on southeast Newfoundland: no seaman in his senses would have attempted such a landing unless driven to it, and there is nothing in the sagas to suggest that any of these landings were desperate expedients. Going again and again over all this, a thought struck me: the error, or what I regarded as the error, was at least consistent – in every case the actual distance was just about twice the *doegr* distance. Then I thought, can this provide an explanation? We know that the *half-doegr* was often used by Norse sailors from Greenland instead of the full *doegr*, no doubt because they had inherited a tradition of coastal sailing in which ships would normally anchor for the night. And we know that even if the *doegr* is regarded non-nautically as a 'day' it is sometimes difficult to tell from the text whether a full day of twenty-four hours or a half day of twelve hours is meant. Suppose that Bjarni had estimated the distance from his first new land to his second correctly as four *doegr*, and that at some time in the centuries before the sagas were written down some saga-teller or commentator, either to air his own knowledge, or with the idea of making things simpler for his audience, had decided to edit the figure with the *half-doegr* unit – that would explain everything. But if so, why should the other *doegr* figures remain apparently the full *doegr*? Going back to the sagas again, it may be significant that while *doegr* distances are given for all three stages of Bjarni's voyage, the *only doegr* distance given for Leif's voyage is for the stage from Markland to Bjarni's first 'land'. Leif's other passages are not described in terms of the *doegr*. Assuming that an editor had decided to reduce *Leif's doegr* to the *half-doegr*, then

Bjarni's would have to be reduced too. *But that would be necessary only for this one stage of Bjarni's voyage.* The other figures could remain as they were, because they would not conflict with anything in Leif's voyage. The arithmetic of Karlsefni's voyage is rather different. The *Graenlendinga Saga* gives no details of Karlsefni's voyage, but says simply:

Karlsefni asked Leif if he could have the houses in Vinland. Leif said that he was willing to lend them, but not to give them away. They put to sea and arrived safe and sound at Leif's houses.

Eirik's Saga gives a more circumstantial account, but describes a voyage which in its early stages may not have attempted to follow Leif exactly. Karlsefni is recorded as having sailed north to the Western Settlement (Godthaab). Leif, too, must have sailed north on leaving Julianehaab to get round the ice, but there is nothing to suggest that he went as far north as Godthaab. So Karlsefni's point of departure from Greenland may have been different from Leif's, which means that his sailing distance from Greenland to Helluland is not necessarily comparable with Leif's, or Bjarni's (in the reverse direction). *Eirik's Saga* gives Karlsefni the same two days (or *doegr*) for the distance from Markland to Bjarni's first 'land', and the fact that all these times or distances are identical almost suggests editing to bring them into line. I think, therefore, that this probably happened at some point in the history of the sagas, and that someone's attempt to 'tidy up' what he regarded as a discrepancy in one of Bjarni's figures has created confusion ever since. Of course one cannot *know* this, and I make no claim to have 'solved' a vexing puzzle. But two things equal to the same thing are equal to one another, and I hope that I have offered at least a reasonable explanation of how confusion may have come about. For that there is confusion in the texts here, I am certain.

In setting out from Greenland in *Griffin* I did not know of Mr Morekin's work on the *doegr*, and I worked then on my 'algebraical' translation of the *doegr*. This enabled me to approach the reconstruction of the Vinland voyages without having to squeeze navigational probabilities into arithmetical terms for time or dis-

M

tance. What I have learned since has strengthened my conviction that we were on the right lines, and that as we sailed from Greenland to get round the ice we were not far astray from the invisible wake of Leif Eiriksson a thousand years before us.

13

Trapped in the Ice

Before leaving Frederikshaab, Tim Lee had obtained the latest ice reports from both our own Met Office in England and from the Danish Meteorological Service that covers Greenland. Our wooden *Griffin* was no icebreaker, nor was she strengthened in any way to withstand ice. Our job was to avoid ice – where ice barred our passage, we could not go. There is no record in the sagas of any of the Vinland ships having had to battle with ice, and I felt sure that Bjarni, Leif, Karlsefni and their companions, as prudent seamen, would have done their best to keep away from ice. We could not escape icebergs and bits of drifting ice – these are hazards that may occur anywhere in the Davis Strait and Labrador Sea at this time of year – but we could guard against them by keeping a sharp lookout. What we had to try to avoid was *pack-ice*, and Tim worked out a course that should have kept us clear of all impacted ice. It didn't, because the ice reports were wrong. The pack extended some ninety miles farther north than any of the Met reports had indicated.

The coastal pack off this part of Greenland in early summer seldom extends to the coast itself; there is a kind of river of clear water (though dotted with drift-ice) between the coast and the pack, and this 'river' may be up to thirty miles wide. As we cleared the mouth of Frederiskhaab fjord we were in this 'river', and trusting to our Met reports, there was nothing to tell us that we were standing into danger as we crossed it. For most of that morning and afternoon we had little or no wind, and at times were all but becalmed. But the old engine consented to go, the flywheel held to its shaft, all seemed well. We were making steady if somewhat slow progress to the west, and it seemed reasonable to hope that we should be clear of most of the off-lying dangers from ice before the last of the long daylight faded. We were soon disillusioned. Our navigation log gives the facts shortly:

1845 Put about and lie 010 degrees because of pack-ice.
1910 Altered course 035 degrees to avoid ice. Watches doubled.
2100 Most concentrated area of drift-ice yet met.
2235 Drift-ice still. Fog bank to the west.
2300 Drifts thickening again.
2330 Pack-ice to port held against current by wind (?). That to starboard closing in.

My journal, scribbled hastily late that night records:

Have just come off a most harrowing watch with my ice-duty mate, Peter Haward. We are doing three hours in pairs. I asked Peter, whose eyes are better than mine and who is better at the helm, to do most of the steering, while I took on his share of the colder job of bow lookout. The engine worked, thank goodness, but ran out of petrol, and being practically windless we had little steerage way. While Peter filled the petrol tank I fended off a couple of bits of ice with the boathook. It was a nasty experience: even those that look about the size of a cushion probably weigh 3–4 cwt. and are as hard as concrete. The icefield is not quiet; there are loud explosions as the floes grind together. It is dangerous, but very beautiful. The floes are in fantastic shapes – aeroplanes, ships, flowers, birds, monsters. The colours are wine-dark, purple, blue and bottle-green. Absolutely lovely – but harrowing. Peter Comber cooked a very good stew for supper tonight, but I could not have any because I was on watch in the bows. When I came off I found my share of the stew in one of the Aladdin flasks, with a slice of bread all buttered for me, and a plate set ready to eat.

Had a radio struggle with Brent today. Our schedule was for 1330 GMT, but we couldn't get through, though we could hear them, and got a (misleading) ice report from Anne, broadcasting 'blind'. They asked for another schedule at 1700 GMT, which was a nuisance, because I wanted to try to get some sleep, and it didn't leave much time. However, I did manage to lie down for just an hour, which was better than nothing. Difficult time again at 1700, heavy interference, and this time we could scarcely hear them at all. But we established contact after a fashion, so they know that we still exist.

A few minutes after midnight, at 0005 on the morning of June 3, Tim, who was on watch, spotted a tiny gap in the pack-ice to the northeast. Peter Haward had not turned in and they made for the gap. It was touch and go, because the gap was not much wider than *Griffin*, and the pack was closing all the time. Had *Griffin* been nipped it would have been all up with us; she would have been crushed at once. But thanks to Peter and Tim, who took a quick and bold decision, we just slipped through. The log notes laconically:

0005 Altered course NE (compass) and sailed through a rather tight gap, then into relatively clear water.

I missed this particular excitement because, having had next to no sleep for forty-eight hours, after I had eaten the stew that Peter Comber had left for me, scribbled my journal, and prepared a message for the next broadcast to the *Guardian*, I fell asleep with the pencil in my hand. When I rejoined Peter Haward on watch at 0400 there was still plenty of drift-ice, but no sign of pack. I said, 'Well done, Peter. You've got us through the worst.' I took the helm feeling cheerful.

I spoke too soon. Within half an hour, a thin white line appeared across what looked like open water ahead of us, and it was apparent that we were *not* clear of the pack. Drifting floes and bergy bits became more frequent, and dodging them became more and more tricky. My eyes are at their worst in trying to focus quickly from an ice floe in the middle distance to the near water at the bows, so I asked Peter to return to our former partnership in which he did the steering while I took over the ice-watch forward – my eyes are more reliable for distant vision. There was no time for shouting directions from the bow to the helm, so we worked on a simple system of arm signals: an arm held vertically meant 'All right. Stand on', and extended right or left meant 'Turn at once'. The partnership worked well. I felt curiously close to Peter, and he seemed to know by instinct, or almost by some flash of telepathy, precisely what signal I wanted to send at the instant that I sent it.

The three hours of that watch were some of the worst hours I have lived through. The sea was a maze of ice, always the promise of open water beyond the line of icebergs and bergy bits ahead, never the fulfilment. We would *seem* to enter a reach where the ice was thinning, but after ten minutes or so what had looked like a clear horizon would show an unmistakable whitish tinge, and there would be another barrier of ice. And all the time there were bits of floating ice to avoid, some showing so little above the surface of the water that they were noticeable only as a faint discoloration until we were almost on top of them. *Griffin* is forty-four feet long, so from the cockpit there was inevitably a 'blind area' dead ahead, which the helmsman could not see. This was the danger area, for some innocent-seeming piece of ice, too small to be seen by the helmsman when far enough away not to be masked by the fore part of the boat, might lurk there, its underwater parts thrusting out spears and daggers of ice, horribly capable of holing *Griffin* if we struck. It was the job of the bow lookout, standing right forward in the nose of the ship, beyond the jib-stay, to watch the danger area, and signal to the helmsman to turn this way or that to avoid any menacing piece of ice. For final defence we had our long boathook, to thrust at any piece of ice which might come on us before there was time to dodge it, or while we were dodging another bit of ice. I did not have much confidence in this final defence, for those bits of drifting ice were surprisingly heavy, and pushing with a boathook was liable to have little effect on them. I did manage to push one or two small bits out of the way, but I doubted if I could do much good against any thing more formidable. Still, the boathook gave a comforting feeling of having *some* weapon in one's hands, of being able at least to try to do something. The real defence was in the lookout, and in the instant response by the helmsman to the lookout man's signals. We also had collision mats, contrived by Tim Lee out of sailcloth. These were designed to be dropped quickly from the bow, to be hauled taut over a hole below the waterline. If a collision mat can be brought into use quickly enough, and is big enough to cover a good area of sound planking round a hole, it can be useful, for the pressure of water trying to enter the hole tends to press the mat against the planking, holding it there, and so protecting the hole. Tim's mats, I hoped, would perhaps give us a little time to launch our rubber life raft and dinghy if we had to abandon ship.

Although our danger from the ice naturally was always in my mind, there was too much to do to be morbid about it. You would see a speck of ice ahead, wonder if it could be cleared without altering course, wait and watch it to decide if it was necessary to give a signal to the helmsman. Sometimes it was possible to have a little shouted conversation. I would call to Peter, 'Have you seen that nasty little b. . . . to port?' If he had, he would raise his hand vertically to acknowledge that he had. We gave names to some of the bergy bits. 'Aeroplane bit coming up almost dead ahead,' I would shout. 'Wonderful Spanish castle well to starboard,' Peter would say.

As we made our way through the maze of ice, dodging this bit and that without finding open water, I was half-interested, half-irritated to see how normal this world of ice was to itself. I could see a seal sleeping on an ice-floe, secure, completely at ease. It was a dangerous alien world to us, but a world with its own inhabitants, as much at home there as we might feel in a sitting room on land. They cared nothing for us. Why should they? If we sank, the ripples would die away quickly, and the ice-world would continue undisturbed. For all its danger to us, it was a beautiful world – a world of marvellous shapes and colours, surgically clean in its purity. We could see the pack-ice being formed. The keystone to a line of pack would be a huge iceberg, bigger than a long street of houses, with a massiveness to dwarf an atomic power station. A berg of this size would have such enormous resistance in its underwater mass that wind would have less effect on it than on the smaller pieces of ice in the line of battle coming up behind it. One floe would hit the iceberg, crashing to a stop against it; then another floe would cannon into that, and so on and on, like some appalling concertina-crash on a motorway, but a crash extending for miles, and with vehicles as big as hotels. So the ice would impact, outriders of smaller floes forming hummocky causeways of ice between the great masses of the keystone bergs. Some of these causeways might run as far as the eye could see.

It became more and more difficult to find a path for *Griffin* through the thickening floes, and about half-way through our watch we came to an impenetrable causeway of ice. It was perhaps not more than two hundred yards across, and beyond it there appeared to be open water, alive with little wavelets, a different quality of water from the millpond stillness of the sea enclosed by the impacted ice. As far as we were concerned it was as unreachable as the moon. All that we could do was to turn and make our way along the barrier of ice, on the wrong side of it, hoping that somewhere we might find a passage through it.

I came off watch after my three hours, privately feeling both frightened and depressed. There seemed to me a real possibility that either we might hit a growler or be nipped in the pack and sink promptly, or that we might remain trapped on the wrong side of the pack for days, perhaps weeks. However, I had to try not to show how frightened I was, so I settled down to do some sewing – buttons on various pairs of trousers that needed replacing. Almost as soon as I started on my sewing, using the domestic kit that Helen had assembled for me, my needle broke. This turned out to be a happy little incident, for I transferred to my sailmaker's kit, and as I sewed I carried on a long dissertation on the superiority of the sailmaker's palm over the domestic thimble. If only women would abandon thimbles and take to palms, I said, what bliss would follow in the homes of England (and America)! Mending would be done in half the time, tempers remain unfrayed, much matrimonial friction be avoided. For a bit this took our minds off ice.

I had just made some coffee when Peter Haward looked in through the companionway. 'I don't want to speak too soon', he said, 'but I *think* we are clear.' The miracle of Tim's watch in the early morning had been granted to us again – unexpectedly we had come upon a tiny gap in the developing pack, and sailed through it.

The navigation log tells the story:

0625 A thick pack, but clear water beyond. Altered course SSE, skirting it, looking for way through.

0750 Have almost doubled back on track, but finally found gap. Drop mainsail to negotiate narrow gap under power. Set main again when through.

A note added by Tim explains:

N W wind Force 2 encountered, and we have sailed into virtually clear water. Apparently this wind has held the drift-ice against the current, causing a strip of ice which was in the process of thickening in area. Now, to windward would appear to be free of drift-ice.

We had escaped, but again we had escaped only into a larger prison, as it were. We had found clear water, but were still to eastward of the ice, in the river or lane of open water between the pack-ice and the coast of Greenland. We wanted to go west, but the ice still barred our way, so all that we could do was to set as northerly a course as the wind permitted, knowing that at some point we *must* get far enough north to have out-distanced the northward-going pack. We could out-distance it, because the pack was moving slowly with the north-going West Greenland Current, but was being 'braked' by the northwesterly wind. We could still make northing by using the wind, and although at first we could not do much better than N N E, at least we were gaining northwards over the ice.

At noon, Reg Garrod on watch reported another line of ice ahead. We had learned our lesson by now, and were determined to keep clear of ice even if it meant closing the land again, or going backwards. We altered course to the east to give this new ice barrier a wide berth. As the afternoon went on, things got better. The ice at last seemed to be trending westwards rather than north. Gradually we were able to head *Griffin* more and more to the north. The wind backed, too, and began going round to the southeast. By evening we were free. The log records:

1855 Clear of ice at last. Rounded top approximately 100 miles north of reported position. Very noticeable swell.

I wrote in my journal:

Doubling up with Reg for watch tonight. *At the moment* it looks as if we have found the northern edge of this blasted ice. *Griffin* is

going at 5–6 knots, running now, with wind about S S E, and there
is a real ocean swell. First time I've ever welcomed a heavy swell!

Rather a slummy day. Tidied up while Peter Haward was on
watch and everybody else asleep. Must do something about this
slumminess, but these things are rather difficult. Washed up cups
full of date-stones. Ugh! A man must be responsible for his own
date-stones.

This rather depressing note probably reflects the tensions of the
day. Our standards of housekeeping on *Griffin* were normally high
– cups washed as they were used, cabin sole constantly gone over
with dustpan and brush to remove the bits of fluff from blankets that
always seem to collect on a small boat, scraps of food, etc. Everyone
was mostly very good about tidiness, and every few days we would
have a general clean-up. Peter Haward had a near-genius for floor
scrubbing. He is the only *man* I have met who can scrub a floor and
leave it looking and feeling as clean as if a woman had done it. I can
scrub out a room or the cabin of a boat and satisfy myself that I have
been all over it, but I can never make a place *feel* as it does after it has
had a woman's touch. People were always good about tackling dirty
work like re-stowing tins in the bilges, or cleaning up in the galley
after cooking in rough weather. But we *were* crowded, and in bad
conditions, when everybody tended to be overtired, small careless-
ness like leaving cups unwashed on the saloon table would creep in.
This had to be guarded against, and it says much for *Griffin's* company that it *was* guarded against, without bickering or ill-humour.

The wind increased as we sailed west beyond the northern rim of
the ice, and by the time that Reg and I went on watch it was a wild
night. We had tried to send our usual Met report to Greenland, giving
our position, but the aerial lead from the backstay to the radio
terminal on the cabin top kept blowing away from its clips, and we
abandoned the attempt. Reg and I had a concert, singing every song
we knew into the wild gale – songs of our youth and Army songs.
We sang 'When you and I were seventeen', 'I'll see you again',
'The Isle of Capri', 'Way down upon the Swanee River', 'There's
a troop ship just leaving Bombay', 'The little harness room across
the square' – everything we could think of. I sang the Charney song,

a private nonsense song composed for the children at home at our
village of Charney Bassett:

> On a misty musty morning
> In a winding Charney Lane,
> *That's* where the soldier wants to be;
> With the sun just dawning –
> Shining through the rain,
> *That's* what the soldier wants to see

And a private version of 'Tipperary':

> It's a long way
> To Charney Bassett,
> It's a long way
> To go;
> It's a long way
> To Charney Bassett,
> To the sweetest girl I know.
> Farewell,
> Frederikshaab,
> Goodbye, Baffin pier –
> It's a long, long way
> To Charney Bassett,
> But my heart's right there.

Our companions were not always polite about Reg's and my
singing. Nevertheless, singing – or what we called singing – gave us
much pleasure, and at bad moments provided a certain emotional
release. We felt that in competition with the gale our singing would
cause offence to none, because nobody would be able to hear it. In
this we were wrong, for one or two of the others observed pointedly
next day that it was bad enough to be kept awake by a gale without
the added torture of caterwauling on deck. The point we took, but
the 'added torture' I did not and do not believe. Some puzzled sea-bird
may have heard our singing, but nobody else could; the gale, and
the crashing seas, saw to that. I wrote next day:

It was a rough night, with *Griffin* right over under double-reefed main and staysail. She was lee gunwhale under, with water pouring along her deck, and practically standing on her head. Looking at her on watch (with Reg) she did look tiny – you could see her being picked up and tossed aside by the sea. But she rose always, gallantly and nobly. I did the first $1\frac{1}{4}$ hours of my watch forward, and got drenched. The yankee, stowed on deck, was torn from its lashings by the wind, and was being carried into the sea, so I had to find a piece of string and tie it inboard. This meant crawling across the deck, and lying full-length to deal with the sail. While lying like this, about a ton of water swept over me, going up my trousers, and up my sleeves. It was bitterly cold, and I had, of course, to work with my hands, so hands were frozen too. Got dry gloves to finish watch – oh, how hands hurt with the cold! Jolly glad to get below when relieved by Peter Haward and Allister. Gloves are now drying over the Tilley lamp – they should be dry fairly soon.

Those gloves were a pair of ancient woollen gloves, knitted for me years before by Helen. I wrote about them:

What a blessing these woollen gloves are, and they were just an afterthought. I found them in a pocket of my black oily coat, which I left in the office the night I went to Dover, because it's a very bulky oily, and I didn't think there would be room for it. Going through the pockets I found the gloves, and thought I might as well bring them. They are now my most treasured possession.

When Tim worked out our position next day, he thought that we might have met a west-going current when we turned west beyond the northern rim of the ice. I noted in my journal:

The question is, *did* we get a west-going current where we turned? Possibly yes. But it was pretty rough, and we were double-reefed, and we may have made a good deal of leeway. But the current *seemed* to give us about 20 miles – too much for leeway, really, one would think. *If* there is a west-going current about here, it would be of considerable interest to the turning point of the Vikings.

The north-going West Greenland Current does curl westwards (or rather, it sends out a west-going stream, for the coastal current continues northerly), anti-clockwise across the Davis Strait, when it reaches roughly the latitude of Godthaab – the area of the Western Settlement of the Greenland Norsemen. We were about fifty miles south of it, more or less in the right part of the sea, though I thought probably still a bit far south to meet a west-going stream properly. *If* a reliable current making towards North America existed hereabouts, it would have added to the value of the Middle Settlement as a port of departure for Vinland. I speculated much on this, but came to no conclusions. By the following day the current had disappeared, or we had sailed out of it. Ocean currents are tricky. The broad sweep of ocean streams goes on for ever, but the precise position of these 'rivers' in the sea is not constant. It was interesting that we had met what appeared to be a west-going stream roughly where I thought that the sailing route from Greenland to Vinland would commonly have turned west; interesting, but no more. We had turned when the northern rim of ice permitted us to turn. Ice was the decisive factor, and that varied from year to year. It looked, though, as if a stream peeling off from the coastal current might have helped to carry a ship westwards. We had done what we did mainly because the conditions of sea and ice had made us do it. The old Norse captains had sailed the same sea. Given roughly similar conditions, they would have done as we had done. I felt that I could reasonably say, 'The Vinland ships must often have turned westward *about here.*' In sum, our experience on this important stretch of the voyage added to my conviction that *Griffin* was following not far astray from the wake of Leif Eiriksson.

Griffin – why, I wondered, do none of the sagas give *names* to any of the Vinland ships? Seaman have not changed much over the centuries: they think of ships by name, love them or hate them by name. Why have no names for the Vinland ships survived? The only reason I could think of was that the sagas, as they have come down to us, have filtered through generations of saga-tellers, editors and scholars who were not themselves seamen. It is sad not to know the name of Bjarni's ship (the ship in which Leif sailed, too, for he bought it from him) as we know the names of *Mayflower*, Columbus's *Santa Maria* and *Pinta* and Drake's *Golden Hind*. But the fact that we are never told the names of Bjarni's, Leif's and Karlsefni's ships strongly suggests landsmen's editing, and adds to the possibility of confusions over seafaring terms like *doegr*.

That day we got into trouble. When Tim got through to Frederik-shaab Radio with his Met report he was asked to stand by for a message for us. It was from the Commander-in-Chief of the Danish Naval Base in Greenland, saying that a cargo ship had reported seeing a yacht 'struggling in drift-ice', and that as no later report of our position had been received from us, aircraft had been alerted to look for us. The C-in-C's signal ended rather tartly with a request that we should comply with the agreed procedure for reporting our position while we remained in Greenland waters.

We had been unable to report our position the night before be-cause our aerial lead kept blowing off in the strong wind, and in fact we had taken the first opportunity of reporting when Tim sent his Met observations. But I felt penitent. We had not asked for any assistance, and although it was true enough that we had been struggling with ice, we had come through on our own – by pro-vidential luck, perhaps, but still, on our own. I sent this signal to the C-in-C:

To: C-in-C, Greenland Command
From: Anderson, leader '*Guardian*' Vinland Expedition
Deeply regret inability communicate our position last night owing trouble wireless aerial in high wind stop Much appreciate your concern for us stop Please convey our thanks to aircrews and others for their help stop Will do our best subject prevailing weather conditions to comply with all your requirements.

I hope that this explained to the Danish naval authorities that we were not light-heartedly ignoring our responsibilities, but that a small sailing boat *cannot* always send radio signals at the right time.

I hated to think of aircrews having to go on duty to look for us, when we had neither asked nor needed help. But it was comforting to know that people on land, with power at least to try to help us, were thinking of us, and ready to do everything they could to come to our rescue.

We reported faithfully to the Danish navy in Greenland every day until we passed out of their sea area and signalled that we were sending our last report, and we heard no more of the incident.

On June 5 I wrote:

Have just had a (hot) seawater shave, and feel much refreshed. Got my trousers (two pairs, outer and inner) dry in the rigging. Going on deck to get them I didn't dress up, but wore just my ordinary below-clothes – that is, trousers, pyjama trousers, long pants, short pants, vest, shirt, three pullovers. I got utterly frozen on the job. It is hard to convey to people how cold it is, and what an Arctic place the deck is. You go on deck to work if you have to, otherwise you stay below.

Goodness, how people sleep! Me too, to some extent, but I can't sleep all the time. The problem, of course, is that there isn't anywhere else *to* go but to your bunk. I had an idiotic thought before we started that I might actually manage to write a book on *Griffin*. It is practically impossible, physically, to write at all, and since we cut our table in half to make a bunk for Allister, there is nowhere *to* write.

We should, some time tonight, pass the latitude of Cape Farewell on our way south. Not my favourite part of the world, though it must be said that Cape Desolation did us proud, giving us one of the loveliest days of the passage, and a very welcome one, too. I feel slightly homeward bound today, or at least, as Peter Comber put it, 'warmward bound'. It is a joy to see some south in the compass course.

(Later) My watch found *Griffin* in a gentle, light wind, sailing beautifully. Reg made me a cup of coffee. Apart from the hellish cold, and natural anxiety about growlers and bergy bits, it was a beautiful watch. Tim cooked spaghetti Bolognaise for supper – real spaghetti, of course, the long sticks, which he and I managed to buy at the grocery in Frederikshaab. I was on watch, and ate mine at the helm. Considerable achievement, I think, to eat spaghetti at the helm of an ocean-racer, running!

The weather held fine over June 6. It was the last fine day we had for some time, but we didn't know what was in store for us, and my journal is full of cheerful jottings:

Last of *Weather Adviser*'s pears found in the bilge. Generously given to me. I cut it into four pieces for all those up – Peter Comber, Reg Garrod, Tim Lee and me – and jolly good it was.

Vinland Saga called us up on the radio. We told them that we had to go to 62°55′N to get round the ice. They are having the same trouble – finding ice much farther N than reported. *Vinland Saga* suggested it might really be better to go northabout the whole of Greenland to get to Copenhagen! First mate asked if I would like to sing to them over radio. I said compliment much appreciated but that I feared trouble with crew. Mate said he understood.

Grand sailing, and thoroughly enjoyed my watches – 0700–0900 and 1800–1900 (dog watch). A soldier's wind from the N, and *Griffin* tramping along doing 7 knots hour after hour. We are about 200 miles off the Labrador coast, and we appear to have met a *warm* southgoing current of about ½ knot. This will be a branch of the *warm* West Greenland Current, which curls over to meet the *cold* Labrador Current, flowing along beside it, without mingling. There is almost a temperature wall between these currents, with maybe a difference of several degrees in seawater temperature over a matter of yards. The Vinland seamen didn't have thermometers, but I'm jolly sure they could tell water temperatures within a degree or so by feel. They would certainly know when they were in warm currents, when in cold. And I suspect that they used this to help in navigating. I think we have misconceptions about Norse sailing because of the idea that they were essentially *coastal* sailors, and liked to cling to a coast. I can't believe that anyone would *want* to cling to the Labrador coast, with the ever-present peril of ice. I think perhaps that the Norse seamen may have liked to feel that they were not far away from *some* coast – to know where they were, which any sailor likes to know at any time. They could do this by using water-temperatures, knowing that they could close the coast by sailing into colder water. They could follow the coast by keeping to the edge of warmer-colder water. This temperature gradient would have been very useful to them, enabling them to follow the coastline without standing into danger to get too near it.

In my morning watch we passed a trawler going north (*Lord Nelson?*). She was too far to read her name, but a little later the British trawler *Lord Nelson* called us up, and had a chat on the radio. She called up another trawler, *Sir Fred Parkes*, to ask about ice for us. Later we were able to call up *Sir Fred Parkes* ourselves for a chat. Tim got in touch with the US weather ship *Bravo* – nice American voice, very friendly. They agreed to take Tim's weather reports. As we were getting over towards North America I had asked Tim to see if he could clock us into the US AMVER system (Automatic Merchant Vessel Emergency Rescue, a valuable help to shipping). They keep track of the movements of ships by computer, so that if anything goes wrong the rescue organisation has an estimated position for any ship at any given time. The weather ship *Bravo* agreed to clock us in. What the computer in New York will make of a *sailing* ship, I don't know. You are supposed to estimate speed to the nearest one-tenth of a knot! What happens if a sailing ship goes backwards?

Cold ham for lunch, and sausages, chips and egg (cooked by Allister) for supper. Allister does chips marvellously.

Peter Comber is better. I'm not at all sure how he is feeling at any given moment, for he is immensely plucky. He spends hours freezing on deck, sitting and reading. Better to freeze than to feel sick, I suppose, but I don't know how he does it. Nobody could be more gallant. He even cooks meals for other people when he must dread the sight of food – and the galley is no place to be in if you are feeling off colour. But Comber manages it.

On watch I sing the Charney song to the wild sea. The sea-gulls listen with interest, but nobody else does. Reg and I know the same songs. He is fifty-two, three years younger than I am, but

N

he grew up in the same period. We agree that the songs of our day were at least singable. I fear that we are not 'with it'.

Have dug out my monocle for wear on watch – found it in my sailmaker's kit. It seems a bit odd to wear a monocle on watch in a sailing boat in the Labrador Sea, but actually it is functionally useful, enabling me to read the thermometer or to have a close look at the compass card without fiddling with glasses. The others greatly admire my monocle. [Alas, *Griffin* soon dealt with the monocle. I wore it on its cord outside my nylon jacket so that I could get at it quickly, but after I had been thrown about the cockpit in the usual way the glass was missing. Miraculously, Peter Haward found the glass, unbroken, in the scuppers. I put it back in its frame, but abandoned trying to wear it.]

Everybody is asleep but Peter Haward, just off watch, Allister, on watch, and me, writing. I like *Griffin* when people are asleep – it is the only time one can move about without getting in someone else's way. I wish it were warmer, though.

Heard Oban Radio calling tonight. Quite like an old friend! Bothered about a distress call to Julianehaab Radio. Julianehaab broadcast to all ships asking the caller to identify himself – an 'alarm message', they called it. We listened, but could hear nothing more. I hope it is not a ship in serious distress. What a sense of *community* you have with all other ships! You can understand how the sea tradition of going to anybody's help grew up. You just feel that you *must* – there can be no question about it.

On at 0500. I suppose I'd better turn in.

14

Off Labrador & Newfoundland

I had now reached a point in the voyage at which I had to commit myself decisively about what to do next. Should we attempt to go to Labrador or Newfoundland? I had no doubt but that the Vinland captains knew Labrador, and thought it probable that, on the early Vinland voyages at least, they took their departure for Vinland from a point somewhere on the south Labrador coast. I should have liked to explore the Labrador coastline but our time was limited and to make any serious attempt to explore Labrador would have required at least another month. Then there was ice. Our experience off Greenland had been chastening, and ice would probably be worse off Labrador. The ice off Greenland was a *necessary* hazard. It had put us in graver danger than I had envisaged because the ice reports were wrong, but we had known that we should have to meet ice off Greenland, and I had planned for this by arranging the voyage so that we should have nearly maximum amount of daylight when we had to deal with ice. This light had helped us greatly – even with minutes more of darkness, our peril in the pack-ice would have been substantially increased. Now we were sailing south, with longer nights and more darkness. None of us would shirk any of the dangers *inherent* in the voyage, and I was confident that if I said that I wanted to put into Labrador no one in *Griffin* would have questioned the decision. But apart from the question of time, which was important to all of us, I saw no real need to go into Labrador. I was not looking for Helluland or Markland, but for Vinland. Helluland and Markland were signposts, as it were, and therefore important in the Vinland story, but their *general* location seemed fairly well established – sailing southwest from Greenland you *must* come to the Labrador coast. The descriptions of Markland in the sagas are sketchy in the extreme, nothing like the good picture that has come down to us of Vinland. It seemed to me that an attempt to close the Labrador coast would be deliberately to stand into unnecessary danger, for no great purpose. I could accept that the Vinland route went to southern Labrador without myself landing on Labrador. I decided *not* to put into Labrador.

Newfoundland raised problems of a different order. There is a Newfoundland school of Vinland studies which holds that Vinland was *in* Newfoundland – either in northeast Newfoundland, in a district of Epaves Bay known as l'Anse aux Meadows (Helge Ingstad), or on the Avalon Peninsula in southeast Newfoundland (Farley Mowat). All my thinking about Vinland, and such studies as I had been able to make in the Faeroes, Iceland and Greenland on the way, had led me to believe that the Newfoundland school was wrong. I did not question that there were early Norse sites in Newfoundland, but I did not believe that Newfoundland was Vinland, or that it was ever more than on the periphery of Vinland in the main period of Norse colonisation in North America. But that was merely my view: if I was looking for Vinland, I could not ignore Newfoundland. Ought I put into Newfoundland, and, if so, where? At this stage I had still an open mind on the subject. I could not accept the views of either of the two main Newfoundland schools of thought, but I accepted that I might well be wrong. I decided not to attempt to put into Labrador, and not to enter the Strait of Belle Isle – wherever the Vinland voyagers may have got to, it seemed certain that they could not have entered the Gulf of St Lawrence without discovering the St Lawrence River, and there is *nothing* anywhere in the sagas to suggest that they knew anything about the St Lawrence. I had to make up my mind about Labrador and the Belle Isle Strait, but I did not yet have to make any final decision about whether or not to land in Newfoundland. I determined to stand on towards the Newfoundland coast and to see what happened.

It may be useful here to sum up briefly the main arguments *against* Newfoundland as the location of Vinland. First, there are the sagas themselves. If these saga records embody real history it seems to me impossible to discount all the topographical descriptions of Vinland that they give. Why should the place be called Vinland –

'Wineland' – at all if Leif Eiriksson and his companions had not found the wild vines and grapes that the sagas tell us they *did* find? Evidence about the vines of Vinland does not derive from the sagas alone: it is corroborated in a most striking manner by the earliest of all historical references to Vinland, in the records of the Archbishopric of Hamburg, in which Greenland and Vinland were then included, compiled by the monk Adam of Bremen at some time before 1075. Adam of Bremen's history of the archbishopric is known to have existed in 1075, so that his knowledge of Vinland must have been acquired at some date before then. He wrote of Vinland by name, and said that it was called Vinland 'because vines grow wild there and yield excellent wine'. He added, again corroborating the sagas, 'self-sown grain grows there in abundance'. Adam of Bremen's work is of the first importance, because it was compiled long before the sagas were put into writing. Even if one takes the latest possible date – 1075 – for Adam's reference to Vinland, it would still be possible, almost probable, for him to have obtained his information directly from someone who had actually been to Vinland, or from some merchant or priest who had met travellers from Vinland. Leif Eiriksson's voyage to Vinland was made about the year 1001, Karlsefni's colonising voyage some years later. Karlsefni himself, with his wife Gudrid and their son Snorri, who was born there, stayed about three years in Vinland, so that there must have been a considerable amount of coming and going between Greenland and Vinland in the first two decades of the eleventh century. If Yale's Vinland map is accepted, the reference on it to Biship Eirik Gnupson's visit to Vinland in 1117-18 not merely suggests but implies continuing settlement throughout the eleventh century and well into the twelfth century. It is hard to see how Adam of Bremen could have obtained his information except from some direct source.

Turn now to the *Graenlendinga Saga*. Having recounted that Leif and his companions had decided to winter in Vinland, it gives this description of the place:

The country seemed to them so kind that no winter fodder would be needed for livestock. There was never any frost all winter, and the grass hardly withered at all.

How can one discount this? I am indebted to Professor Gordon Manley, the climatologist, who has made a study of the climatic factors affecting the Vinland voyages, for the observation that if *anything* in the sagas rings true, this passage does. To men used to the long winters of Greenland and Iceland, and the harsh task of trying to keep cattle alive through the winter, the most noteworthy of all facts about this new land would be that 'no winter fodder was needed', and that the grass in that first winter 'hardly withered at all'. Short of denying *all* historical validity to the sagas, it is *impossible* to doubt the mildness of that first winter at Leif's *budir* or settlement in Vinland.

It could not, then, have been in Newfoundland. The climate may have changed slightly since Leif's day, but we are not concerned here with geological time covering spans of tens of thousands of years, but with the last millennium of human history. The climate is unlikely to have changed all that much, and it is hard to envisage a frost-free winter in Newfoundland at any time in this historical period. There *can* be mild winters, however, in New England. It is equally hard to envisage luxuriant vines and wild grapes as a dominant feature of any part of the Newfoundland landscape. Again, these *are* a dominant feature of Martha's Vineyard and other parts of New England. Topographically, the evidence, from Adam of Bremen onwards, is all against Newfoundland.

I have already stressed the importance of the sun to Norse navigation, and one would expect seamen accustomed to taking observations of the sun to continue the practice in a new land. The *Graenlendinga Saga* bears out this, and records of Leif's *budir*:

In this country night and day were of more even length than in either Greenland or Iceland. On the shortest day of the year the sun was already up by 9 am and did not set until after 3 pm.

That is from the translation of the saga by Magnusson and Palsson, and they observe in a footnote that such times of sunrise and sunset indicate that the location of Vinland must have been south of latitude 50°N, and north of lattiude 40°N. This rules out northern Newfoundland, but could just include the central and southern parts of it, though it could equally well mean New England. Unfortunately, what looks like a precise astronomical observation that ought to put the location of Vinland beyond doubt is far from being precise because the meaning of the old Norse times is uncertain. The words used are *dagmálastad* and *eyktarstad*, which seem to mean 'breakfast time' and 'supper time'. Doubtless these terms had precise meanings to Leif and his companions, but we do not know what they were. Moreover, all we are told is that the sun was up *before* breakfast, and did not set until *after* supper. How much before, and how long after? Scholars have disputed about this for many years. The Norwegian Captain Tornöe has an ingenious theory, based on a study of the medieval Icelandic calendar, that these 'times', although originally real times, had acquired a definitive meaning in relation to sun-angles that would have been understood, and used, by Leif. This theory would put Leif's *budir* comfortably in Massachusetts. All that can be said safely in the present state of knowledge is that Magnusson and Palsson's broad estimate, placing the observation within ten degrees of latitude – from 40°N to 50°N – seems reasonable. Since Newfoundland lies roughly between 46°30′N and 51°40′N, the southern part of it is within the ten-degree limit, though, if the limit itself is right, the balance of statistical probability is again against Newfoundland.

The topographical evidence against Newfoundland is so formidable that alone it seems to me convincing. The astronomical evidence, from one unclear astronomical observation, is dubious. Navigational and historical evidence is more telling. Is it conceivable that seamen as competent as the Norsemen could have settled for years in Newfoundland without discovering the St Lawrence? The Vikings were *experts* in rivers. They had penetrated almost every navigable river in Europe, and if they had discovered the St Lawrence I do not see how the sagas of the Vinland voyages could fail to convey some inkling of it. That is one aspect of what might be termed the *general nature* of Vinland discovery. Another point of *general* importance is an entry in the *Icelandic Annals* that seems to point definitely to the *discovery* of Newfoundland by two priests called Adalbrand and Thorvald in 1285. These two Icelanders appear to have established that Newfoundland was an island, and to have named it Nyaland, or

Nyfundnaland. Moreover, their discovery of Newfoundland was followed by an attempt at settlement, led by one Landa-Rolf, who went there in 1289 and died in Newfoundland in 1295. It may be argued that there is no certainty that the Icelanders' Nyfundnaland *was* Newfoundland, but it is hard to imagine where else it could be. A German historian, Gebhardi, writing as far back as 1778, refers to the Landa-Rolf colonisation, and identifies his 'Nyfundnaland' definitely with the North American coast. The story holds together. If the Icelanders regarded the circumnavigation of Newfoundland as a 'discovery' in 1285, it could scarcely have been discovered by Leif Eiriksson in 1001. Folk memories are long, and the sagas helped to keep memories alive. In a community as closely knit as the Iceland-Greenland Norse, it is unthinkable that a discovery of such importance could have been forgotten between the eleventh and the fourteenth centuries. The historical evidence here is clearly against any attempted settlement of Newfoundland in the early Vinland period. It may well be that the Vinlanders *did* land from time to time on Newfoundland, and even that they established trading stations there. But these would seem to have been of secondary importance to the main settlements in Vinland, and the evidence is against the pioneers Leif Eiriksson and Karlsefni having had anything to do with them.

Still further evidence is in the northeasterly wind which took Leif from Markland to Vinland. Wherever it took him, that wind would not have landed him on Newfoundland, for no seaman of Leif's experience would have hazarded his ship by risking a landing on the Newfoundland coast in a northeaster unless he had to. And Leif did not have to. He was exploring, looking for new land for settlement, and he had no particular reason for landing on New-foundland. Indeed, since he appears to have known nothing of the St Lawrence, and would have taken the Belle Isle Strait (had he been close enough inshore to observe it) for a fjord, he would have regarded the Newfoundland coast merely as an extension to the coast of Labrador, with nothing particularly attractive about it.

Finally, there is the evidence from Bjarni's earlier voyage, which suggests strongly that Leif was making for a destination a good deal farther south than Newfoundland. Apart from the topographical description of Vinland, which cannot possibly be squared with Newfoundland, perhaps each of these arguments, taken by itself, is suggestive rather than conclusive. Taken together, the weight of evidence tells heavily against Newfoundland.

I have set out this reasoning here to explain the fabric of known or deduced fact on which I had to plan as we approached Newfoundland. I was as certain as one can be about anything that happened a thousand years ago that Leif had not entered the Belle Isle Strait, and I did not *think* that he had fetched up anywhere in Newfoundland. But I could not wholly rule out Newfoundland, and if for any reason of wind or weather or set of current in the Labrador Sea it might seem logical to go to Newfoundland, we would go there. I was to learn later how easy, almost how inevitable, it is in the sort of wind that Leif had to slip past Newfoundland altogether.

Our fine weather did not last. I relieved Reg Garrod on watch at 0300 on the morning of June 8 and found *Griffin* hard to hold in a strong northeasterly wind. We were carrying plenty of sail, our full main and big genoa, and she was roaring along at about 8 knots. The wind seemed to be increasing, and I thought that we were carrying too much sail. Reg was still up, pottering after coming off watch, and I asked him to call Peter Haward. Peter came up at once, agreed with me about the sails, and with Reg to help him handed the big genoa and double-reefed the main. I had a fit of private obstinacy here, which did neither me nor anybody else any good:

Did not wear gloves, partly to hold wheel better, partly obstinacy – *would* not wear gloves while Peter and Reg *could* not wear them because of working sails. Result – one of my gloves went in bilges, and is now soaking wet.

The rest of that day was murky with incipient fog. An interesting happening was a sudden fall of six degrees in the temperature of the seawater, indicating that we had entered the cold Labrador Current. With the fog the wind dropped and became variable. The navigation log describes events briefly:

1210 Fog.

1245 Seawater temperature 35·6 (6-degree drop). Probably entered Labrador Current.

1440 Wind shifted N W. Very light. Gybed to 225°. Fog clearing.

1530 Wind veered E N E. Gybed and set course 202°.

1630 Two small bergy bits to starboard. Foggy.

1810 Fog lifted. Iceberg on port bow. Bears 170° at 1820.

2100 Wind of variable strength. Fog at times. One berg in sight.

We were a cheerful company, in spite of the fog, and inevitable anxiety about icebergs and bergy bits. I wrote:

Had a good dinner, cooked by Allister – chicken soup, steak and kidney pudding, mashed potatoes and reconstituted stewed apple. All quite nice, but I do miss *bread*! Managed to dry my wet glove over the Tilley lamp, and it is now wearable again. Did some washing in the *Griffin* washing machine [a line towed astern]. Vest and pants. Nowhere near dry yet, though. It is difficult to get anything dry at any time, and impossible in this clammy fog.

Gulls always interesting. Saw one poor fellow who had a fearful time in trying to get up take-off speed. I suspected that he had had too much dinner.

Interesting theories about navigating by water temperature. I'm pretty sure that the Norse did it. The warm ex-Greenland Current water runs alongside the cold Labrador current without mixing. Difference in temperature about 41°F to 32°F. I'm sure that the Norse would have noticed it, and used it. They would have known that they had only to steer for cold water to get near land.

Noticed that soap lathered a bit better in my shaving water this evening. I think this is an indication of ice nearby. When we were *in* ice, soap lathered quite well – so much fresh water from the ice reduced the salinity of the sea.

Next day the wind returned to the north, strengthened and stayed from north to northeast all day. *Griffin* ran 158 miles this day. I wrote in the evening:

Not a bad day, although a rather heavy one. I was on watch with

Reg (doubled up) from 2300 last night to 0100 this morning. Dirty night – very cold, and bitter rain. Taking off gloves to open thermometer cage to read thermometer left hands utterly frozen, and it took about 15 minutes to thaw out. There was beautiful phosphorescence. Once I saw a phosphorescent something ahead and called to Reg to steer to port. May have been anything or nothing, but better to avoid nothing than to hit *something*!

In berth by about 0130 but left request to be called at 0445 for Brent call at 0600. At that time I thought that I would go to sleep and write something between 0500 and 0600. Instead (as is my usual way, I suppose) I wrote a piece there and then, which took until a bit after 0200. Then slept, and when called at 0445 had a good bit of time in hand. Got up, made myself a cup of coffee, and was all ready when Brent came through. Back to bed about 0700 but had to be up again for watch at 0900–1100. Glorious sailing in a swell, but overcast. The log *said* I did 16 miles in this watch – average 8 knots. I don't altogether believe it, but Peter Haward, who relieved me, checked the log, so it duly went down. It was then a bit puzzling what to do about breakfast. I'd had nothing and was a bit hungry, but it was also getting near time for my GMT drink. Compromised by having a breakfast of corned beef, Ryvita and whisky.

That reference to 'my GMT drink' relates to a private amusement, or indulgence – at any rate it amused the crew, particularly Reg (who sometimes shared the indulgence). I enjoy a drink, but to be enjoyable it has to be at some time that I regard as proper for drinking; preferably from noon to 1300 before lunch, and from 1800 onwards before dinner. At times on *Griffin* there seemed a good case for whisky, although the clock might be against it. I kept my wrist-watch on GMT, whatever our ship's time might be, and one day it occurred to me that if ship's time seemed hostile to a drink, GMT might be favourable. So I allowed myself (and anyone else who wanted it) both a ship's time drink *and* a GMT drink, if we felt like it.

A hurried scribble in my journal late that night describes the worsening weather better than any words I can find now. It says:

We are roaring into the night. Conference with Peter Haward and Tim Lee. Decided to reduce sail around 2300 and potter through the night. I'm sure this is wise.

We were now, by the old Norse notation, about one half-*doegr* off the northeast coast of Newfoundland. The question of whether or not to put into Newfoundland seemed to be answered for me, as I think it was answered for Leif, by the wind. Apart from the undesirability of closing an unknown coast in a strong wind that made that coast a lee shore, for anyone making south this wind was too good to waste. We know that Leif needed to go south to reach Bjarni's first landfall, and we can assume, I think with certainty, that he had obtained from Bjarni the observations of the sun to indicate roughly how far south he had to go. There is also the remote possibility (recorded on the Vinland map) that Bjarni was with Leif on the voyage. In our circumstances, with a wind that seemed much the same as Leif's, everything pointed to the south, skirting the Newfoundland coast, but keeping well clear of it.

A change comes over my journal about this time. I wrote no more in ink, but in pencil only. It became too difficult to fill my pen. The handwriting deteriorates as conditions on *Griffin* grew rougher, but it is still just legible. Between *June* 10–11 I wrote:

An eventful night and day. I went on watch 2100–2300 and at 2200 it seemed time to reduce sail. Peter Haward and Tim Lee did the job, with me at the helm. There was a heavy sea and at times *Griffin* was almost uncontrollable. As the sail came down, the boom, although sheeted in fairly well, came across and hit me a crack on the head, knocking me clean out of the cockpit into the scuppers. My safety harness, shackled to a lifeline, saved me from going overboard. Reg Garrod and Peter Comber, who were washing up in the galley, saw what happened from the companionway, and rushed up. Peter Comber grabbed the wheel, and Reg subdued the boom, while I lay prone in the scuppers. I collected myself and got back to the wheel. Reg offered to take the rest of my watch, but I wouldn't have it. Peter Haward and Tim Lee, forward with the sail, didn't know what had happened. By this time it was about 2215, and it was too dark for anyone aft at the helm to keep a good lookout. So Peter Haward relieved me at the wheel, and I went forward as lookout. It was bitterly cold. I tried the lee side of the deck in the shelter of the (down) trysail. It was quite a good shelter, but I couldn't see under the staysail, our only sail up. So I moved across to the weather side where I could see better, but Lord, it was difficult to hold on. Hands got wretchedly cold. I could get a bit of warmth back by beating them on my knees, but I could only beat one hand at a time, because the other was needed for holding on. So took it in turns to beat one hand at a time. I stayed there until relieved by Allister. Then at last went below, and found that Peter Comber had left me some Irish stew in a vacuum flask. He *is* good, and the stew was good, too.

Turned in (after washing up) about 0015 and wrote *Guardian* piece for next call to Brent. Called 0445 for Brent schedule at 0530. Had some coffee, and on watch again at 0700. More sail work, main and yankee set by Peter Haward and Reg. Running all the time – tricky work at the helm, because had to turn into wind to allow jib to be slack for hoisting, but mustn't gybe. Managed it, but heart in mouth. Huge sea, with *Griffin* rolling all the time; very hard to keep one's feet.

Before the main could be set another tear had to be mended, this time right at the top. Peter Haward did the job with my sail-maker's kit. As soon as the sail was hoisted, there was another tear! It had to come down again to be mended, and Reg did this mend. At last all was well. Came off watch at 0900 and Reg talked about breakfast. I thought he must be frozen after all that work with sails, so I suggested that he should make himself some hot lemonade. 'I want something stronger than that,' he said. I said, 'Put some whisky in it.' He laughed, and said, 'I meant solid.' So he cooked a tin of bacon which he, I and Tim Lee, who decided to get up (he'd been up most of the night), shared. Reg and I washed up. Then heated some seawater for a shave, and felt much better for it, though the bruises on my face from where the boom hit me are a bit awkward for shaving.

During the night we had to pass across a line of shipping leaving Belle Isle Strait. This was not easy under staysail alone, but Peter Haward did it beautifully. Once, to pass astern of a ship, he had to go round more than the staysail would take, and it went back. But he won a bit somehow, and made it on the next try. It was very nice work.

As the day (June 10) went on, the wind moderated and backed, but in the evening we heard a weather forecast for shipping which strengthened my conviction that if Leif Eiriksson had experienced weather similar to ours, he would have kept clear of Newfoundland. The forecast warned us of a gale from the east, saying that after moderating and backing to the N W, the wind would veer to the east, and become an easterly gale. Since the wind *had* backed as forecast, we feared that the gale warning might be equally accurate. It was.

But the gale did not come at once. There was a formidable swell, but the wind stayed at around Force 3, and we carried our mainsail, big yankee and staysail happily enough. I wrote:

Might as well make miles while we can. We are keyed up about the gale, though.

Peter Haward relieved me on watch, and I stayed chatting to him. We discussed the swell, and I asked him what he thought was causing it, since it seemed exceptionally heavy. 'All the remains of all the storms that ever blew,' he said. I relieved my own gale-waiting tension by making up nonsense verse:

> There's endless ice to starboard,
> There's ruddy rocks to port.
> This is a situation
> That gives one food for thought.

I recited this to Peter, who asked, 'What is the next verse?'
I said, 'Perhaps there isn't one.'
'Ah,' said Peter, 'the last entry in the log, I suppose.'
The swell made everything difficult. My journal notes:

This swell is unbelievable, and, I fear, indescribable. All one can say is that it is like living in an earthquake, but few people have lived in earthquakes, so the words don't mean anything. I could never explain how I talked to Anne this morning on the radio – hanging on with one hand and one leg, being hurled across the boat, clinging to the radio telephone receiver. Then, having to find *and pick up* a piece of paper when she started sending weather messages.

Am on double watch with Reg from 0100 to 0300, and must be called again at 0500 for radio call to Brent at 0600. Tonight's watches are:

1700–1900 me
1900–2100 Peter Haward
2100–2300 Allister McIntosh
2300–0100 Tim Lee and Peter Comber
0100–0300 Reg Garrod and me
0300–0500 Peter Haward

We are doubling up for the four darkest hours and keeping to two-hour watches by abandoning dog watches for the moment.

Everybody seems asleep except Peter Haward on watch, and Allister. The ring in our floorboard hatch in the saloon broke, and Allister is boring a hole and putting in a lanyard. How one comes back to bits of string in the end!

It stayed cold, with an air temperature around 37°F, and short of curling up in sleeping bag and blankets there was not much chance of getting warm below, because we kept the forehatch open as much as possible to ventilate the boat. I found it a comfort to wear a woollen cap – if you can keep your head warm, it helps to keep the rest of you warm. Sometimes I wore my woolly hat to sleep. On watch I wore my woolly hat with one of Henri-Lloyd's lined nylon hoods over it. The hood had drawstrings which could be used to leave only eyes and nose exposed. These hoods were invaluable, and we wore them at all times except in fog. At sea in fog you have to live by your ears; the safety of the ship depends on hearing, on picking up the slightest sound which may indicate the beat of another ship's engines, or the approach of rocks or surf. We made a ship's rule that in fog the man on watch was not allowed to wear a hood.

The gale struck fairly suddenly on the night of June 11–12. The weather worsened during the afternoon, bringing a vicious sea, though the wind was no more than about Force 4. As we had been warned to expect a gale, we battened down everything we could. During his afternoon watch, Peter Haward noticed that the canvas cover on the forehatch was split in two or three places, and he thought rightly that it ought to be mended at once, in case it became too rough to work on deck. Had he not been on watch he would have done the job – a cold and beastly job – himself, but he could not leave the helm. Peter Comber volunteered, and as I was still more or less dressed in deck clothes from coming off watch, I went with him. We lay full length across the hatch, sewing as we got a chance to sew in the intervals of being drenched with spray. The lid came off a small needle-box in my sailmaker's kit, and before I could do any-thing about it, all the needles were washed out of the box. This was a serious mishap, for apart from one or two needles of Peter Haward's, these were all the sail-needles that we had on board (or all that we were ever able to find). I peered around the deck trying to spot needles, but spray on my glasses combined with my poor near-sight to make it a hopeless task. Peter Comber saw something glint, crawled to the scuppers, and recovered the needles just before they went overboard.

We toiled away at our sewing, cobbling rents in the hatch cover as we could, until at any rate the worst of them had been repaired in some fashion. We had, of course, to work with bare hands. I forced myself to get some work out of my hands, but when I got below they were so stiff with cold that for a time I wondered if I should ever be able to restore them. After wrapping them in a towel, however, feeling came back in the end.

Between 2000–2100 the wind increased to Force 5. We took in the staysail and double-reefed the mainsail, so that *Griffin* was carrying the double-reefed main alone. When I went on watch with Reg for our doubled night-watch the wind was a good Force 6, and probably nearer Force 7. I was at the helm, with Reg on look-out, when the mainsail suddenly sagged in a queer way. Reg rushed to see if the halliard or topping lift had gone. Both were intact. The sail itself had split right across, and torn along the leech. Reg acted at once to get the sail down, to save what we could of it. Peter Haward was on deck in an instant, followed quickly by all hands. The mainsail this time was beyond any attempt at repair that we could hope to carry out on board, and all that we could do was to lash it securely against further damage. We replaced the main with our little red storm try-sail. Without the mainsail there was a risk, with the strong wind, that we might make too much leeway towards the coast, so we tried to see if *Griffin* could carry the yankee with the trysail. But the wind increased, and the yankee was too much for her. Soon we handed the yankee, and set the smaller staysail. *Griffin* was eased, and rode more comfortably. I was thankful for the reasonable offing from the coast that we still had.

The wind was now a full gale from the northeast, and in spite of the tiny area of sail she carried, and the heavy sea, *Griffin* averaged 5 knots for hour after hour, covering just over ten miles between 0300–0500, eleven miles between 0500–0700, ten miles from 0700–0900 and eleven miles again from 0900–1100. It was exciting sailing, but difficult and sometimes dangerous, for a murk of rain merged with spray whipped off the wave tops to reduce visibility at times to no more than a few yards. In my morning watch, we had a rather alarming encounter with a trawler, which I just saw through the murk, looming ahead of us. She appeared to have nobody on deck at all, at least there was no sign of life on her, though she had steerage way and presumably somebody was at her helm. In the huge seas it was difficult to watch her and to steer *Griffin*, so I called Peter Haward, who came up at once and conned us safely astern of her. At 1720 that afternoon we sighted North America, a stretch of the Avalon Peninsula in SE Newfoundland. In that angry sea it was not an enticing coast. Leif Eiriksson, I thought, would have felt about it as I did.

With evening the gale died out, the wind again backing and moderating. The swell remained heavy. I was determined not to let my journal fall behindhand, but did not write very cheerfully that night:

o

This has been a hellish day – gale and after-gale fatigue, I suppose. Gallant old *Griffin* rose (or sank) as needed in the huge seas, but she took tons of water on board, and rolled beyond belief. Everything is chaos below, and the place littered with wet clothes. My inner (wool) gloves are soaking. Peter Haward tore his nylon trousers on the mast last night, so I've given him mine, and am wearing a pair a size smaller that really belong to Helen. As far as length goes they fit me all right, but the trouble is that I want too many clothes underneath. I'm going to experiment on watch tonight with a rayon pullover for my fourth pullover, instead of a thick wool one. I may get cold, but if I can survive it will be much less bulky, and more convenient.

This rather dismal note is not a fair reflection of our collective state of mind, for my companions were beyond praise – calm, uncomplaining, taking everything as it came, with a joke if there was time to make one, and if one of *Griffin*'s rolls knocked a joke from the lips at least with a grin. Reg Garrod hurt his arm severely by being thrown across the deck when he was working at the sails, and it is typical that he did not mention it until next day. A supper of Horlick's emergency curry went down well, and did us all good.

The loss of our mainsail raised a number of problems. Could we carry on without it? The wind was moderating, and the most sensible course seemed to be to put into St John's, Newfoundland, for repairs. But to do this would destroy much of the meaning of our voyage. I believed more strongly than ever that Leif Eiriksson had sailed, or had been blown, clean past the Newfoundland coast, as we should have been had our northeasterly lasted a few more hours. Leif's northeaster had carried him over two *doegr* at least, and probably, I thought, for a considerably greater distance. Deliberately to put into St John's would mean breaking our voyage at one of its most critical stages. I wanted to carry on if we could. But was it fair to the others to carry on off a dangerous coast with a crippled *Griffin*?

I could not hand over the decision to anybody else. Part of me, the physical part, wanted few things more than to put into St John's.

I was tired after the battering of the gale, and the thought of a night in bed without having to go on watch was tempting. If I was tired, the others must have been equally tired – a few days in port would do us all good. Nobody would blame me for putting into St John's; rather I might reasonably be blamed for standing on in a crippled ship without a mainsail. All the arguments of fatigue and common sense pointed to the wisdom of acknowledging that we could not go on without repairs. But another part of me felt that to put into St John's would be running away from the task I had set myself. The decision was not made easier by the fact that nobody in this extraordinary crew prompted me in any way, or urged the desirability of a rest in port. Everyone was battered and fatigued; no one asked for the respite that we could have had so easily.

Peter Haward came to the rescue, not directly, but in a practical, seamanlike way. We were not talking about St John's, but about sails. 'You know,' he said, 'I don't see why we shouldn't set one of our yankees in the mainsail track. It would give us a bigger area of sail aft of the mast than the trysail. It wouldn't be anything like as good as the mainsail, of course, but it would be better than nothing.'

This seemed a good idea. We were well off for headsails, and both our yankees, No. 1 and No. 2, were new Terylene sails, capable of standing up to any amount of work. Conversion would not be difficult – all that was needed was to replace the hanks on the sail that normally shackled it to the forestay with slides to run up the mainsail track. Peter decided to use the No. 2 yankee, leaving the big No. 1 to its proper job of pulling forward.

I was on watch at the helm when Peter came up the companionway. 'In a few minutes we are going to have a mainsail,' he said. We did. The trysail came down and the No. 2 yankee went up. It looked a bit odd; being cut as a jib the long side of its triangle seemed in the wrong place. But it set well, and *Griffin* felt it, at once becoming more alive. Set high up the mast the sail was more like a topsail than a mainsail, but it was obviously going to earn its keep. I thought no more of St John's. We stood on.

Almost as soon as our improvised jib-topsail was set, Peter and I were struck simultaneously with an idea for improving things still more. 'What would happen,' I said, 'if we set the trysail under our yankee-topsail?'

'I was just thinking of that,' Peter replied. 'It ought to work. The only question is how to arrange the halliards.'

We left it at that for the moment, but the next day Peter and Tim got to work and passed the spinnaker halliard between the spreaders for hoisting the 'topsail'. We had brought a spinnaker from Dover but had left it at Scarborough, feeling that in the latitudes to which we were going we were more likely to want to reef sails than to set spinnakers. Moreover, the spinnaker took up a lot of room in the forepeak, and we had better use for the space. The spinnaker halliard, fortunately, remained in being. So, incidentally, did the fitting on the mast for the spinnaker pole. We kept the pole, and used it often for booming out a headsail when conditions warranted.

Now the halliard proved a godsend. And we had two tracks on the mast, the other being for the trysail, as well as two halliards. When the trysail was set under the yankee-topsail, *Griffin* was again well balanced; so well balanced, indeed, that on certain points of sailing she would all but steer herself. Our improvised rig aft of the mast could not replace the mainsail; it gave us nothing like the area of the full mainsail, and we felt this lack severely when on the wind. But it did give us again a rig that could be balanced, and although *Griffin* lost speed, she sailed happily. We called it 'the Haward rig'.

We held our course southwards along the coast of Newfoundland, and towards midday on Monday, June 13, we sighted Cape Race. That afternoon I wrote:

We are closing Cape Race – a forbidding coast, but lots of little coves, with cliffs, scrub and some woodland. (One of the later Marklands, perhaps?) The wind is pretty well heading us, and we have to beat; and without a mainsail we don't beat very efficiently. Tim is a bit bothered about our charts – they are based on a very old survey of 1860. Peter Haward at the helm is doing very well – in spite of her lack of mainsail he puts *Griffin* about very sweetly, giving her a good run at it.

We have gone in almost to the mouth of one of the coves, within about three cables – Frenchman Cove, I think, on the chart.

Cape Race is the only one of our big capes that we have seen –
Farewell and Desolation were invisible because we stood well
clear of them.

After weathering Cape Race, what would Leif Eiriksson have
done? Did he even sight Cape Race, or did he pass it well out to sea?
We cannot know. I tried to think myself into the mind of a medieval navigator, and found it impossible to forget the configuration
of our charts and of the modern atlas. I *knew* the lie of the land;
Leif did not. I could only guess at what he might have done, but I
tried to base my guesswork on what I thought could reasonably be
deduced about his voyage. Going back to Bjarni's voyage, there was
the probability that his first landfall was well to the south of Newfoundland, and the near certainty that when Leif bought his ship
from him, he would have given Leif some bearings to indicate how
far south he had been. So I thought that if Leif's northeaster had
held, he would have stood on to the south and west; and that if it
had not held past Cape Race, as ours had not, he would have made
such southing as he could, but also going west to follow the trend of
the coast. We spent hours discussing all this, and Peter Haward wrote
an 'appreciation' of what we took to be Leif's position.

At noon on June 13 (*he wrote*) having tacked inshore, we sailed
across the mouth of Chance Cove, six miles northward of Cape
Race, weathered Black Rock, which stands a few feet above sea
level at its entrance, and closed the land a few cables off the spit
dividing this inlet with Frenchman Cove to the south. Now it
was necessary to put about for another seaward tack. Viewed from
the sea, our landfall appeared barren scrub, rather rocky, though
with substantial areas of forest. The two coves would give no
shelter from winds between south and east. Strong squalls came
turbulently from the cliffs. Vikings seeking a good haven with
workable land would hardly have bothered with these two creeks
for long, especially considering the wealth of possibilities which
they would have hoped awaited them. They had crossed 1,000
miles of ocean, and there was a whole new land to explore. If
Bjarni had given Leif a latitude for Vinland, and if Vinland had

been near Cape Cod, there would have been five degrees difference between it and Chance Cove.

Tacking seaward, but managing a southerly course, we noted that Cape Race was a corner, the land bearing away westward thereafter. We weathered the cape, then stood inshore again, N W by W on the port tack. When night fell we were sailing across Trepassey Bay, the first inlet west of Cape Race. We could happily have entered Trepassey Harbour itself; the light-house on Powles Head flashed its welcome every four seconds. But Leif Eiriksson would have been denied this facility. Thus, as a seaman, he would have put about and stood the starboard tack, sailing seaward of all dangers, to await dawn before further investigation. We did what he would have done, even though we were ushered out of the bay by the big light on Cape Pine. Two hours later we were engulfed in dense fog.

This is an example of just the sort of thing that could have happened to Vikings sailing this area 1,000 years ago – one example of practical seafaring that seems persistently overlooked by historians. Once gripped by fog, a sailing ship without a good engine, or modern navigational aids like Radar or Decca, would do just one thing – make a wide offing of any dangerous or unknown coast. Leif Eiriksson would have done that. In spite of our echo sounder, accurate charts, D F set and compass, we also felt little inclination to tack back near the land, even after dawn. Visibility was varying between 50 yards and 200 yards – not without reason did the deadpan voices reading the local coastal radio weather reports talk of visibility diminishing 'to zero in fog'. From our charts we knew that seven miles seaward of Cape St Mary, the next westward headland, was the St Mary's Cays Rocks, awash at high water. Other snares abound in the area for the imprudent mariner.

Bjarni had fog, many days of it we are told, but, generally speaking, we glean little of weather conditions from the sagas. A couple of days of fog, like a brisk day of gale, must have been a common occurrence to seamen like Leif Eiriksson, and to encounter it off Newfoundland would be highly likely, but the saga-writers did not bore their public with such details. Our fog off southern Newfoundland represents one example of the weather the Vikings, whose track we are trying to follow, would have met there. Think of Leif in such a fog in terms of our experience. Some hours after dawn the sun pierced hazily our restricted world, though sea-level visibility remained at 150 yards. The sun would have enabled him to establish that the wind was from the S W. I imagine they must constantly have manned a sand glass, never failing to turn it immediately the hour (or whatever interval they used) was up. The bearing of the sun could have been roughly known. With us, in the afternoon the sun vanished, rain came, and the sky above the fog was overcast. Our compass told us that the wind had backed two points to the S S W. Leif could have guessed that the wind would back as the weather deteriorated, though by how much would have been very much a guess. Holding the starboard tack, close hauled, full and bye, our course now became about S S E. By 1600, considering the sixty miles of the searoom we had gained, and the fact that our none-too-advantageous tack was steadily becoming less so, we put about, and lay first N W by W, and later, more happily, a westerly course. The wind continued to back as the night went on. By dawn, we had some westing, some 40 miles south of Newfoundland. The fog, if anything, was more dense, the breeze freshened, and all thought of closing with the land, had it been possible, would have remained out of the question. Leif Eiriksson, with many more imponderables facing him, would fear blundering into an unknown coast above all else. Making a landfall where offlying dangers extend farther from the coast than the visibility, is hazardous; exploring an uncharted, even merely postulated coast, increases the peril manyfold. Nor could Leif know by this time whether he was sailing W, S W or N W. Later in the day we found the sun again, but our compass told us that with this change, the wind veered. Leif could not have known that, though he would have welcomed knowing his present course again, and knowledge of the way winds veer with clearing skies might have given him a hint. But again the question, 'How much?' would have been ever before him. He would continue close-hauled, but always he must have had a 'hunch' about veering and backing winds that probably reached our conception of a 'sixth sense'. Perhaps, as a navigator with problems we never face today, Leif was also helped by a sense of humour? Often he could not hope for more than a vague idea of his course; on the other hand, as he did not know exactly the lands he was trying to reach, he could face his very real dangers with a stoical philosophy. Though, like us, Leif Eiriksson may have made his landfall from Greenland on Newfoundland, he may have been obliged to give it a very prudent offing. Perhaps our experience will help to show how this could have happened.

So we went first south to get a good offing from the ironbound coast, and then westerly, a course dictated by the prudent seamanship that we believed Leif would have practised in a situation that, as far as we could tell, was probably much like ours. On the night we weathered Cape Pine I had a vivid practical experience of what it is to close an unknown coast in murky weather. I went on watch just as it was getting dark, to find the binnacle light not working. I could see a light on shore, but no sign of the shoreline that I knew was there. With my poor nearsight I could not read the compass, and although I *knew* that it was safe enough, indeed sensible, to steer by the lighthouse rather than the compass I felt indescribably lost. On coming off watch I wrote:

In my imagination we were rushing straight at a horrible shore. Tim Lee said, 'Don't worry, there's a good two miles of sea.' That was rationally all right, but I still see in my mind a coast rushing towards us. I was very glad when we went about. Tried glasses – no good. Threw them off in a rage to Reg, who collected them calmly, and saved them. Then after a bit Reg came up and smoked a pipe in the cockpit – to have a look at the night, he said, but really to keep me company. One of the nicest things he has ever done, for it was *not* a nice night, and I was very grateful.

For a couple of nights we had not been able to work dog watches because there had been so much to do, and lookouts needed, and

my turn had stuck at 2100–2300. This made things rather hard going.
I wrote:

> There never seems time for anything. For the past few nights I've
> been doing 2100–2300. By the time I've come off watch, read
> thermometer and barometer and entered up the log, and got out
> of oilies, it is about 2330. Then I write a piece for the *Guardian* for
> next day – that takes me to, say, 0030. Then a bit of sleep, and
> I'm called at 0430. I have to allow an hour before the Brent radio
> call (at 0530) in case I need to rewrite anything, or write some-
> thing entirely fresh about what may have happened during the
> night. Sometimes I've written a piece three times before it is
> sent. The call takes about half an hour, with waiting, getting
> through, etc. That brings me to 0600. Then I wash and shave
> – say 0700. Then I have about an hour and a half in my bunk,
> getting up in time to dress up in oilies and be ready to go on watch
> again 0900–1100. I don't *need* half an hour to dress up, but if I
> have to do anything at a given time I'm always restless before it,
> and generally allow myself about twenty minutes or half an hour.
> I try to get some sleep in the afternoon – it's the only practicable
> time.

The log for June 14 records, 'Fog all the 24 hours.' We were not
to see much sun again for the next six days.

15

A Week of Fog

From June 14 until the afternoon of June 20, when we were blown suddenly into sunshine and saw the Nova Scotian coastline for the first time, we lived mostly by our ears in a sightless cold world of fog. We were back with Bjarni and his crew, sharing in a strangely intimate way their ordeal of 'many days' in fog. For our task of trying to reconstruct Bjarni's and Leif's voyages, we could not have been granted a more providential physical demonstration of the conditions which brought Europeans to North America for the first time in recorded history. It was the same sea and the same fog. And we knew no more than Bjarni did when the fog would lift.

Of course, in many ways we were better off than Bjarni: we had chronometer and compass, depth-finder and radio, charts and our knowledge of the long-mapped land. We knew more or less where we were. Although the fog shrouded us for almost the whole of six days, it was not always absolute, and occasionally we saw a watery sun which enabled Tim to take some sort of sight. We could rely, too, on Tim's and Peter Haward's dead reckoning, which was astonishingly good. But in one way we were worse off than Bjarni. He was more lost than we were, but he could sail or drift in fog without much fear of being run down, or of colliding with another vessel. To us, this was a real and ever-present danger. *Griffin* was tiny compared with even a small trawler or cargo boat, and the slightest collision would mean immediate disaster. If anything hit us, or if we hit anything, we should be the ones to suffer. Every effort would be made to pick us up, but a man in the sea is hard enough to spot at any time, and in zero visibility we could not rate our chances high.

We took such precautions as we could. Wooden boats do not

show up well on radar screens, but we kept our radar reflector hoisted in the rigging to improve, we hoped, our chances of being observed by radar. We wore lifejackets whenever we had to be on deck, and carried them with us wherever we might be below. Cold as it was, we forbade the wearing of hoods, so that ears were at all times uncovered and alert. We kept our foghorns handy. With our foghorns we had one serious failure. In fitting out at Dover I had equipped *Griffin* with a modern type of foghorn worked by compressed gas. It responded to a touch of a button, and when we tried it out in fine weather, it made a good, deep-throated roar. When we used it in fog it did not work at all – the escaping gas, on meeting cold droplets of fog, apparently condensed again and the horn stayed silent. Fortunately we had two other foghorns on board, a manually operated pump horn, which made a good bellow, and a Dutch mouth-blown brass horn, which I had brought from my own small *Mary Lane*. With the failure of our modern horn, we relied on these. We said bitterly that our fine modern horn ought to have a notice printed on it, explaining, 'This foghorn will not work in fog.'

Psychologically, those days of fog were the most trying of the whole voyage. A gale is a fine, dramatic thing; you may be battered and hard pressed, even in real danger, but the force and fury of wind and sea at least lift the spirit - you are fighting something you can see to fight. Ice had been perilous and often frightening, but it had been beautiful and interesting, too. Fog has the vindictiveness of the secret poisoner – the strongest man cannot fight fog, because he does not know what he has to fight. After twenty-four hours of fog you feel that you have sailed somehow beyond the rim of the human world, to a lightless Hades from which there is no escape. Day after day of fog brings a depression of the soul that cannot be described in words.

Depression had to be fought, and all of us, in our different ways, fought it as well as we could. There were no grumbles, and we contrived to some extent to keep our minds off fog by discussing everything under the sun. I made up reams of nonsense-verse which I recited to the others, and if they did not think it very funny, at least it was funnier than fog.

I made up a 'Griffin song', which we sang to the tune of 'The British Grenadiers'.

> Some talk of Leif and Bjarni
> And some speak Faeroese.
> Some sail around Cape Farewell,
> And some the Iceland seas.
> But of all the world's brave lunatics
> There's none that can compare
> With a tow row, tow row, row, row,
> With the British Griffineer.

And a mathematical song:

> Multiply by seven
> Divide by three
> The answer is
> A cup of tea.

> Look for the square root
> Of minus one,
> And when you've found it
> We shall have fun.

> Better far than the cube of three
> Is a long voyage
> On the sea,
> There, where the gleaming tangents wait
> Fishing with cosines for their bait

> Hard by the ancient harbour wall
> The little logarithms fall . . .

This remained unfinished for some time, because I could think of nothing for the little logarithms to do next. I invited suggestions, but nobody seemed to have any bright ideas. Finally, I finished it like this.

... Meeting a hyperbolic end,
Infinity at last their friend.

Privately, I was rather pleased with this, because it seemed to me to be mathematically exact – the hyperbola meets the axes of its graph only at infinity.

We had been living together now, at exceedingly close quarters, for nearly two months, but in the intimacy of fog we kept on finding new bits and pieces about one another, which helped to keep us interested, and to keep going. We were helped, too, by our diverse backgrounds. Peter Haward, Tim Lee, Peter Comber and I had all been to public schools, and we discussed various experiences of our schooldays. This fascinated Reg and Allister, who had not been to boarding schools at all. Reg told us about his London boyhood, and experiences in business. We discussed life in the Army and Tim's often hilarious adventures in the Navy. The idea that men cooped up alone talk mainly about women is just not true. We spoke little about women, and then only in most general terms. We had one rather philosophical discussion about the relative place of men and women in the modern world, and came to the conclusion that it is becoming more and more a woman's world. Almost all advertisements are designed to appeal to women, who have the spending of much of the community's money. Whether the increasingly dominant position of women in the world makes for a happier life, we did not (and I do not) know.

We continued generally westwards, crossing the mouth of the Cabot Strait, which I was sure that the Vinland voyagers had not entered. I wanted, if I could, to have a look at Scatari Island, off the northeast coast of Nova Scotia, because J. Kr. Tornöe considers that Leif Eiriksson may well have made a landfall, and perhaps landed on, Scatari. For myself, I now think it rather doubtful if Leif ever landed so far north in Nova Scotia, but of course he may have done so. I wanted, if possible, to anchor off Scatari, and go ashore ourselves in the dinghy.

On June 17 – my fifty-fifth birthday – we reached Scatari, and identified the diaphone sounding from its shore. But with visibility almost zero in the fog, we never saw the island. We stood in towards it, hoping that the fog would lift or lighten sufficiently for us to try to find an anchorage, but if anything the fog grew worse as we closed the shore. We were standing into danger, and could not go on closing an unseen island coast. Regretfully I decided that we must abandon the attempt. We put about, and stood towards the south.

Soon after we had put about, we heard the foghorn of another vessel. It seemed fearfully close, and coming nearer. We could hear the beat of engines, but could see nothing. Tim was at the helm, and Peter Haward at the main compass on the cabin top, taking bearings as nearly as he could on the sound. We replied with our pump foghorn, meticulously following the procedure in the International Regulations for the Prevention of Collision at Sea for indicating by the number and intervals of blasts which tack we were on, and what we were doing. The other ship came closer and closer, and still we could see nothing. Peter and Tim were a splendid partnership, Peter continuously giving bearings on the sound of the ship, Tim responding at the helm. It was most tricky helmsmanship, for we had both to check *Griffin*'s speed through the water in case we were heading straight for a collision, and to ensure that we kept steerage way, so that we could act quickly as we might need to.

The other ship also obeyed the rules meticulously. She could obviously hear our foghorn, because she replied to it, and we hoped, though we could not know, that she could see us on her radar screen (if she had radar). She proceeded dead slow, her own foghorn telling us what she was doing. Still we could not see her, and we could not be certain where she was, because sound in fog can do extraordinary things. Suddenly she appeared crossing our bows, no more than a whitish shape or thickening in the fog. We were not more than one and a half cables apart, and we passed just astern of her. We never knew her name. Quickly she vanished into the fog, going off NNE, and we thought probably making for the St Lawrence. She may not even have seen us; a small sailing boat is a grey shape in fog. But she knew that we were there. If her master, or anyone on board her should ever read this, and recall a narrow escape from collision with a sailing boat near the mouth of the Cabot Strait at about 1000 hours on the morning of June 17, 1966, I should like him to know how much we blessed the seamanship and meticulous behaviour in fog that helped to save us.

I cannot pretend that this was a happy birthday.

My birthday continues, and what a day! Fog everlasting, it seems. My afternoon watch, 1500–1700, and fog all the time. I wore Helen's balaclava to try to keep at least the top of my head warm, because no hood – we can't wear hoods in fog because they cover our ears. Result – balaclava soaking wet, now hanging up forlornly to see if it can dry by the Tilley lamp. Reg and Peter Comber are cooking dinner – tinned chicken. We keep up morale well, but how sick we all are of this fog. I suppose fog can't cover the whole world, though it looks as if it does.

Allister made toffee, and I had some because he said it was for my birthday.

I suppose most of us tend to reflect a bit on life on our birthdays, particularly as we get into the later fifties. On watch the night before my birthday, I made up a prayer for men of fifty-five – not perhaps, a very good prayer, but I tried to put into it what I felt I wanted to ask most for the remainder of my life.

Please God, preserve me above all things from envy of other men's good fortune, so that I may enjoy the rest of my life without spoiling things by resentment that I have not been given more. And when my time comes to depart, help me to be able to feel that I have done my share of this world's work as well as I could, that I have paid my debts, and am not leaving any mess for other people to clear up. And when my eyes close in death, help me to regain the faith of a child, that I have only to open them again to find the new home that you have made for me.

Dr Johnson observed, 'When a man knows he is to be hanged in a fortnight, it concentrates the mind wonderfully.' The same sort of mental concentration may occur on the deck of a small sailing boat in dense fog. By obscuring everything else, fog may help to promote clarity of mind.

With some misgivings, because I didn't want to sound pompous or insincere, I sent my prayer in my radio message to the *Guardian* on my birthday. And the *Guardian* loyally printed it, though what people made of it I do not know. All I can say is that in trying to present a true record of my thoughts and feelings on this voyage, my prayer comes into it. And I like to think that the medieval mind of Leif Eiriksson and his companions would not have thought it odd that a man should reflect on the sin of envy. Somehow these reflections made me feel closer to them.

On June 18 we had another birthday – Reg Garrod's fifty-second. Reg saw my birthday out and his in on watch, for he was on from 2300–0100 that night. I relieved him at 0100 with the wish of 'Many happy returns' – and the hope that his birthday would turn out to be less fogbound than mine had been. When I came off my watch at 0300 I wrote:

Reg's 52nd birthday. He spent about three-quarters of an hour of my watch chatting to me – quite splendid of him. Also he made me a cup of hot Ribena. When Peter Haward came up to relieve me, I was frozen, largely because of being unable to wear a hood while listening in the fog. I wore Helen's balaclava, which began wet and ended up wetter – even wet it was quite a comfort, though. Peter made cups of cocoa for both me and him. I'm now sitting wrapped up in a blanket waiting for the 0530 radio call to Brent.

I returned to my journal at mid-day.

Had quite a good sleep from 0700–1000. Then smelled bacon. Asked 'Who is the cook'? It turned out to be Tim. Reg also got up, and Tim did us a super breakfast of bacon, egg and spaghetti. It was the tinned Danish bacon that Tim and I had bought in Greenland, and very good indeed. We then had a discussion on how to get a bit more speed out of a very leisurely *Griffin*. Our improvised rig does its best, but in light airs in fog it is very slow. Looking for a bottle of Vermouth last night, Peter Haward discovered no Vermouth but twelve gallons of petrol we didn't know we had. So

I suggested putting on the engine for six hours in the hope of finding a fetch of wind, or at least of changing our present patch of sea. But suddenly we began to do 3 knots, so decided to leave the engine for a bit. Reg filled it up, however, with the newly-discovered petrol. We then decided to set our big old genoa. Got into oilies to help Peter Haward get it up, then saw a triangular hole in the leech. So down it came again. I got mending kit, and Peter and I sewed it up. Then up jenny again – then no wind! Oh, well.

Visibility at the moment must be nearly a whole mile, foggish, very wet, but we have known it much worse. There were a few stars in my watch last night, but they went away, and I handed over a filthy night to Peter Haward.

The day we left Dover, Mrs Iverson, Bernard Iverson's mother, had given me two boxes of chocolates as a parting present. I put them away with my personal things in a net over my bunk, thinking that as we had plenty to eat and drink at the start of the voyage, I would keep them for a bit. I had never opened them. Now, to celebrate Reg's birthday, I got one of the boxes of chocolates and presented it to the ship's company. It was a great surprise, and everybody was delighted. We decided not to open the box until after lunch. The other box I gave to Tim next day as a 'prize' for navigating us in the fog – of course he shared them around. I had one other surprise which I kept up my sleeve for the moment. Also at Dover, my friend and lawyer Gerald Mendoza had brought on board a mysterious package marked 'Not to be opened before Vinland'. This was a biggish cardboard box, too big to hide, and it stayed unopened on the floor of Reg's and my cabin, between our bunks. We speculated from time to time on its contents, but I would not allow it to be opened.

Reg had rashly promised to stand Tim Lee dinner at a Chinese restaurant in Halifax on his birthday. This was a date that was not going to be kept, because we were still ghosting along in fog at least 160 miles from Halifax. We had a light-hearted argument about whether a promise of a birthday dinner to a navigator was binding if the navigator failed to get the dinner-giver to a restaurant on the

P

due date. My journal describes a scene of cheerful domesticity, in spite of the fog:

> Reg on watch. Tim making a fair copy of the log. Peter Haward pottering. Peter Comber cooking, making coffee. Allister sleeping. Me scribbling in my journal. Tilley lamp alight, giving a faint warmth. My balaclava hopefully drying out above it.

Reg's birthday had turned out to be not much better than mine as far as our ordeal by fog was concerned. That night we comforted ourselves with the reflection that as it was nobody's birthday next day, perhaps the fog would lift.

The morning of June 19, however, was as foggy as ever. My journal records:

> Fog, absolutely thick and horrible. We have just had another bout of foghornery. About 0745 I was in my bunk trying to sleep when I heard our horn. At first the sound was very confused with echoes. Our pump horn makes a small bleat when the handle is withdrawn, then its big bleat as it makes its blast. Then come echoes of both bleats. I couldn't stay in my bunk, so put on lifejacket and went on deck. Two other ships were involved, both apparently astern of us. We gave the regulation bleats to show that we were on the port tack and theoretically we were under way, although we were more or less stationary because there was no wind. We gave our bleats, and tried to identify the other foghorns. As near as we could make out the two ships were crossing *each other*, astern of us. One gave the horn signal to say that he was stopped. We could hear engines, so they could not have been very far away. I downed the genoa which was flapping idly, doing no good, and Peter Haward started the engine. This made it harder to hear the other ships, but gave us about 1½ knots more steerage way. Nice problem – to be able to hear, or to be able to move? At last the louder (nearer?) ship went off to port. I hope I didn't show how darned scared I was. I made a lighthearted remark to Tim about the pleasant note of our foghorn, and suggested that it might be scored for in an orchestra. He laughed politely.

That particular bad moment, however, did not end so badly, because, when we were able to relax, Tim cooked us a good breakfast of bacon, eggs and baked beans. It was the last of our tinned bacon, and went down well. But nerves inevitably were a bit on edge, and I noted this small incident:

Peter Comber was at the helm when we had our foghornery – at the helm of the boat (before we started the engine) almost without steerageway. And when we had a bit of steerageway, the slightest error of judgment by the helmsman at a critical moment might have meant disaster. He was as calm as a rock. When he came off watch about half an hour later and was entering up the log his glasses fell off his nose without his noticing that they had fallen. He was just about to put his foot on them when I leaped across the saloon and rescued them. I think this little incident shows something of our tension. I must try to reduce it somehow, but only God knows how.

We turned to practical calculations about petrol, and the best use to which we could put the bonus of three jerry cans that Peter Haward had discovered when he was hunting in the forepeak. I noted down the arithmetic:

We have twelve gallons of petrol left, about twelve hours' running. We must keep two gallons as an emergency reserve, and for getting into harbour. That gives us about ten hours. The engine is so rocky that we can't get much more than $1\frac{1}{2}$ knots out of it at sea in anything of a swell – in absolutely calm water Tim thinks that we might get $1\frac{3}{4}$ knots. At $1\frac{1}{2}$ knots our ten hours gives us only 15 miles – not much. Even a scrap of wind is vastly better than the engine. Truly we have suffered from this engine, but it has a gallant old heart, for it keeps on chugging away somehow, and $1\frac{1}{2}$ knots is better than a vertical log line.

We decided to use the engine sparingly if we were absolutely becalmed. It could not do much to bring us nearer to Nova Scotia, but I think it did help to keep up people's spirits. Its chugging was a comforting, friendly sound, and it gave us the illusion of getting somewhere.

I concluded my journal that day with some private reflections on leadership:

Leading an expedition of this sort is like going back to being a bombardier in the Army – not an officer. You have to live with everybody, share the chores, and yet somehow maintain a sense of leadership. Not easy, and I don't know that I succeed very well. The greatest blessing is this marvellous ship's company, who have stood by me wonderfully well.

I've had only about four hours' sleep in the past 48 hours, and I could do with some. No chance of any, however, until after my next watch, that is in about 3½ hours' time.

That sleep, to which I was so much looking forward, was interrupted harshly.

Much has happened since I last wrote in this journal, mostly hellish. I went to sleep for a couple of hours, but was awakened by Tim, who said (a) did I want any supper, and (b) that our radio transmitter had packed up. I got up and said No, I didn't want any supper, but would have some orange juice instead – at least, I meant to have some orange juice, and got a tin marked OJ from the bilges, but what it had in it goodness only knows. Then we discussed problems. There was the possibility of using our Marconi life-raft radio – our distress radio – to send a message to Canso Radio in Nova Scotia to be cabled to Brent. We tried this, but it didn't work very well. The trouble was that the earth, a wire with a plummet that should go straight down into the sea, was dragged along by *Griffin* and trailed astern like a log. Using the radio from a life-raft, this wouldn't happen. But the little emergency radio did transmit, and we heard the transmission on the receiver of the Kestrel radio. This showed that something was working. Peter Haward and I tried to get through to Canso on the Kestrel, but got nowhere. Then Tim came and experimented, and found that all our programmes – the frequency-selection switch – were one notch ahead on the dial. This was a brilliant piece of detective work. He checked the frequencies on the BEME loop radio. Then he managed to speak to Canso on one of our frequencies, having heard Canso talking to another ship, and we got a telegram sent through to Brent, saying

Trouble with transmitter. Please try
0830 GMT schedule. If unheard, transmit
messages blind.

This was an important message, because after all our fog I was afraid that if Brent didn't raise us, everybody would fear the worst. It was a great relief to know that this message had gone off. Then Tim took the Kestrel to pieces, and managed to get a bit of sense out of it. A shaft controlling the frequency-selection had slipped, apparently because of a loose coupling, and all the frequencies were haywire. But he made it work a bit.

After this anxiety over the radio I found my night watch rather a relief. The fog seemed to have dispersed a bit, and I had the lights of a distant ship to keep me company. I wondered who and what she was, and thought of her passengers comfortably asleep in their cabins – we shared the same sea, but were experiencing somewhat different aspects of it. Peter Haward relieved me with a cup of cocoa, which was particularly welcome since I had had no supper. I turned in around midnight feeling reasonably hopeful. We ought to make Halifax some time in that coming day or the next. The Marconi people were wonderfully good, and since our message had got through I knew that they would alert somebody in Halifax to repair our radio. A Canadian journal called *Week-end Magazine* had taken an interest in us, and I had asked Anne a couple of days before to ask this magazine to try to get hold of a sailmaker to mend our mainsail. Before our radio broke down I had also sent a signal to the harbourmaster at Halifax, requesting facilities, and we had got back a nice message telling us that a berth had been reserved for us, and that the Royal Nova Scotia Yacht Squadron had generously offered us hospitality and the facilities of their club. My membership of the Admiralty Ferry Crew Association, whose burgee *Griffin* carried at her masthead throughout our voyage, helped here. The Royal Navy has a special relationship with the AFCA, and we found the Royal Canadian Navy no less ready to help.

The AFCA has an interesting history. During the evacuation from Dunkirk in 1940, yachtsmen who were too old for any of the services came forward unofficially to help with the small boats picking up men from the Dunkirk beaches and bringing them back to England. This help proved so useful that a group of yachtsmen co-operated with the Admiralty to establish a permanent body of amateur seamen and retired professional sailors, who undertook to do whatever they were asked by the Navy, in the way of helping with small boats at any time. This body became officially known as the Admiralty Ferry Crew Association, and provided crews as they were needed to deliver small craft from one base or port to another as the Navy wanted them. As the war went on, this service became increasingly valuable to the Navy, hard pressed to find manpower for all its regular duties. Sometimes the average age of AFCA crews on naval delivery jobs was over seventy – but the boats all got delivered. I cannot pretend to any distinction in the AFCA, because at its great period during the war I was in the Army, and I did not join until after the war, when Graham Wilson, of the Marine Wireless Section of the Post Office, whom I had met when we first worked out radio communications for Francis Chichester, introduced me to it. I volunteered as a deck-hand or cook. Humble as my membership was, however, I was immensely proud to belong to the AFCA, flew its burgee on my own small *Mary Lane*, and sent it up proudly on *Griffin* as we left Dover. It is beside me as I write, faded and very tattered, but a treasured possession.

I did not want to be delayed in Halifax, but with the knowledge that we had friends there I turned in that night feeling confident that the help we needed would be forthcoming quickly. I was called by Tim at 0430 to be ready for our Brent radio call at 0530 (0830 GMT). In spite of our radio troubles, we could hear Brent and they could hear us after a fashion, so alarm was avoided. Anne dictated the address and telephone number of the Marconi office in Halifax, and said that a message had been sent there by Marconi in England, requesting that we should be given all possible assistance.

The sea is quick to bring elation down to earth, to sea-level, rather. (It is equally quick to restore hope after despair: neutral in human affairs, the sea is a leveller of emotional perspectives, a leveller and corrector. That, perhaps, is why, though we fear the sea like a stern parent, we continue to love it.) My elation at having achieved a call to Brent with our ailing radio was reduced to nervous anxiety again when I went on watch. The fog, which had seemed to disperse during the night, was back again, as thick as ever. And the little following wind we had had with the dispersal of the fog, had died as the fog returned. We had a small visitor to talk about, a little stormy petrel that had apparently been caught in a fold of the torn mainsail where it was lashed round the boom. The petrel fell out of the mainsail during Tim's watch. He thought it might be hurt, but it wouldn't let him come near it. What happened to it we never knew, for it just disappeared. We hoped that it was all right, that it had recovered itself and flown off. ―

I knew that we were closing the Nova Scotia coast, though we could see nothing; we knew where we were only because of our navigating instruments. I tried to think myself into the mind of Bjarni Herjolfsson in *his* fog a thousand years ago. Was his crew utterly depressed? He must have been worried and anxious, but he must also have been a good leader, for his men continued to follow him; even when, later, they wanted to go ashore and murmured because he would not let them, there was no hint of revolt. However worried and anxious he was, he must have exercised stern self-discipline not to show it. (Did he, too, compose nonsense verse – in Old Norse?)

Did he have an inkling that he was closing land? We assume, I think too readily, that he did not, because he had no instruments, and was sailing an unknown sea. But he may have had aids to navigation that we have lost, instinctive reasoning from fetch and swell as the sea shallowed over banks, instinctive reasoning from the behaviour of sea-birds. One of the puzzles in the saga records of him is *why* he should have sailed west, towards land, when he came out of his fog and saw the sun for the first time after 'many days'. I think it probable that he knew that land lay to the west. How, I do not pretend to know, but I think he knew.

Towards noon conditions for us began to change again. The fog began to thin, and by 1300 hours we estimated visibility at nearly five miles. At 1355 we sighted land, ahead on our starboard bow. It should have been an exciting moment, and I suppose it was – the most important of all our landfalls. As always with me, at what should be climactic moments. I seemed drained of all feeling. My excitement came later. I had never seen the Nova Scotian coast before, and had no idea what it looked like. As the blur of land began to take on shape and feature, my habit of writing began to put it into words: at first a low coast, certainly not cliffs and mountains; then I could see that it was hilly, but with low friendly hills, densely wooded in the chines between them. I thought suddenly, 'I have seen this coast before,' but I knew that I had never in my life been anywhere near it. The puzzle was resolved. The words from the *Graenlendinga Saga* flashed into my mind:

They discussed among themselves what country this might be. Bjarni said he thought it could not be Greenland. The crew asked him if he wanted to land there or not; Bjarni replied, 'I think we should sail in close.' They did so, and soon they could see that the country was not mountainous, but was well wooded, and with low hills.

No better description could be penned today. From seaward, the signs of modern habitation are not disclosed at once, and a coastline appears to seamen closing it much as it has appeared to men in ships throughout the centuries. This *was* Bjarni's landfall. I had, and have, no doubt. The fog that had enveloped us had been *his* fog, and it had cleared for us as it had cleared for him, bringing us to a landfall on the same coast. Trackless the sea might be, and faint the traces in history of this old Viking voyage, but I was sure that the sea, approached as we had approached it, had reproduced for us much of Bjarni's experience and taken us where it had taken him.

It was getting late in the afternoon for a drink by ship's time, so Reg and I stood ourselves a GMT drink. Tim and Peter Haward, who had been poring over charts to work out the entrance to Halifax, joined us. On the chart, there are two entrances to Halifax, the main western entrance, and what looks like a short cut up an arm of water to the east of this. Tim calculated charted depths, and said, 'I think we could save ourselves twenty miles or so by taking the eastern entrance.' This was an important consideration. We had still some way to go to make Halifax, and I wanted very much to get on with the repair jobs that awaited us there. If we could make port that evening, we might save a whole day. We decided on the eastern entrance.

As we made our way into the Eastern Passage I was disturbed to see a seagull apparently *standing* in the water where our channel was supposed to be. The bird had more up-to-date knowledge of the passage than had our cartographers. A moment later we were unmistakably aground. This was at least historically fitting, for Leif and his companions also ran their ship aground, and, we are told, 'were so impatient to land that they could not bear to wait for the rising tide to float the ship', and ran ashore. We were impatient to land, but running ashore was scarcely practicable. Instead, we ran from side to side across the deck and jumped in unison in the bows, so contriving to 'shake' *Griffin* off the mudbank on which she had grounded, into water where she was just able to float. We breathed again, but it was hard to know what to do next. The chart certainly showed a channel with eleven feet of water in it, but the seagull indicated in a manner that could not be ignored that whatever may have been the case when our chart was drawn, this particular channel was now silted up. We thought that we might just be able to scrape round the edge of the bank on which the gull was standing, and set off gingerly. In a few minutes we were aground again. This time help was at hand. A fishing boat with one man handling her put off from the shore and came alongside. She was called the *Wayne P.*, and her owner, Mr Philip Purdy, asked if he could help us. As delicately as I could I asked if he was thinking of salvage – you can get into a lot of trouble by accepting help if these things are not understood beforehand – but Mr Purdy at once made it clear that he had come out as a friend, and scorned the thought of salvage. He came on board and explained that there *was* a channel through the Eastern Passage, but it changed after every storm. It twisted and turned so much that he doubted if we could find it, and offered us a tow. We accepted thankfully. The *Wayne P.*'s powerful engine soon pulled us off the mudbank, and with Mr Purdy's skilful pilotage we got through the narrows into safe water leading on to Halifax Harbour. Here Mr Purdy left us, after explaining how to get to the Royal Nova Scotia Yacht Squadron's moorings and clubhouse.

Entering Halifax was no problem now, and soon we made out the Yacht Squadron's quay. Peter Haward brought us alongside and friendly hands took our lines.

It was then 2000 (local time) and getting late in the evening. Members of the Yacht Squadron, one of the oldest yacht clubs in the New World, were immensely hospitable and invited us to come ashore for drinks and food, but we were a foreign ship, not yet cleared by Customs. This is often a serious problem for yachts. One arrives at a yacht club in a foreign port, everyone is friendly, and it seems the most natural thing in the world to go ashore. But to do so without a proper clearance may be to commit all sorts of offences, to the later embarrassment of oneself, and worse, of one's hosts. I was determined not to blot our copybook in this way, so I asked my mates to stay with *Griffin* while I went with officials of the club to telephone the port authorities. Halifax, being a naval port, has a Queen's Harbourmaster (Commander Petley-Jones). He was, of course, well known to the club, and I was given his home telephone number. Conscious that I was being a nuisance, I rang this number. The commander himself was out, but his wife gave me an office number which was manned at night. I telephoned there, and was answered by an officer of the Canadian WRNS. My signal of two days before, saying that we were making for Halifax (no more than a matter of common courtesy, but yachtsmen sometimes neglect these things) turned out useful here, for the Queen's Harbourmaster's office knew about us, and were expecting us. We were given temporary permission to go ashore, and I was asked to telephone again in the morning.

The people of the Yacht Squadron were kindness itself. The Royal Canadian Navy came and collected Tim, and he disappeared to naval hospitality. The rest of us were taken care of by members of the club. Reg and I were whisked off by Mr L. A. Kitz, a former Mayor of Halifax, who took us to his house where his wife, who was playing bridge with friends, at once interrupted her bridge party to look after us. We were invited to have baths – beautiful lie-down baths. We had had showers in the Faeroes, Iceland and Greenland, but this was the first lie-down bath I had been in since leaving England. It was sheer luxury – never before has Rupert Brooke's line about 'the benison of hot water' seemed so full of meaning.

We could not, however, afford a holiday. I was up at 0600 next morning, and as soon as I had shaved and breakfasted went ashore to start telephoning – too eagerly, as it turned out, for offices were not yet open. But it was a lovely morning, and I sat on the quay, feeling clear sunshine like a benediction after our days of fog, and enjoying the superb view across the harbour. The first priority when offices opened was Customs and clearance. The Queen's Harbour-master had arranged for all this to be done at a quay in the old Naval Victualling Depot in the heart of the town, where he had provided a berth for us. Still more thoughtfully, he said that he would send over a pilot to take us there from the yacht club. Mr Stewart Mac-Leod, of the Canadian *Weekend Magazine*, had come down to the club the night before and came again early this morning, to tell me that a sailmaker was standing by to get to work on our mainsail, and to offer any other help he could. Mr MacLeod later wrote a sensitive and understanding article about us for his magazine.

Next came Marconi. The Yacht Club is a bit outside the town, and it seemed better to arrange for the sailmaker and radio engineers to meet us at our new berth in the Victualling Depot, since this was handy to the town. So I did this, and as the pilot sent over by the Queen's Harbourmaster had come, we got ready to move. While I had been telephoning and seeing people, Peter Haward had got the mainsail off the boom, and spread out in the sun to dry. This saved much time later, for it enabled the sailmaker to get down to the job of repair as soon as he collected the sail.

Everyone in Halifax was as good as his word. Our berth in the Victualling Depot was convenient and comfortable. Commander Petley-Jones was waiting on the quay to greet us, and with him were the Port Health Officer and other officials to give us clearance. I was asked to take my ship's papers to the Customs office in a building in another part of the town, but was politely told to do this at my convenience. What can be an ordeal was made almost a social occasion. But there was still a great deal of work to do. Halifax was interested in us, and with the officials on the quay was a little crowd of reporters, television and broadcasting people.

Again, we had to allot tasks, and again *Griffin*'s company responded gamely. I went off to deal with the inescapable demands of the land – bank, cable office, Customs office – knowing that work on our sail and radio was in hand, and that with luck we ought to be able to sail again next day. We did, clearing from our berth in the Victualling Depot in the late afternoon of June 22 to call at the Yacht Club quay to take on water and replenish our jerry cans with fuel. We took our departure from the club after a farewell drink soon after 1900.

At Halifax, Allister left us. He had friends in Canada whom he wanted to visit, and he wanted to see as much as he could of Canada before going on to the United States. We were sad to see him go, but, unlike the rest of us, he was not tied to commitments in Britain, and we wanted him to make the most of this opportunity of seeing Canada. Our friends of *Weekend Magazine* had arranged for him to travel to Montreal by lorry, which was a trip worth making in itself. Like the ancestors of so many Scots families in the New World, he had worked his passage in a sailing boat, and by an exceptionally hard and difficult route.

Allister's departure meant that there were now only five of us to share watchkeeping, but it also meant that we had a bit more room on *Griffin*. We stuck to the same rota of watches, except that with one fewer on the list they came round rather more frequently.

We had now to weather Cape Sable at the southern tip of Nova Scotia and make our way across the Gulf of Maine.

Why? The reconstruction of this final part of Leif Eiriksson's voyage presented many difficulties. The saga records are tantalisingly brusque and brief. We know that Leif set out to explore the land that Bjarni had discovered, and we know that the prime object of his navigation was to re-sail Bjarni's voyage more or less on a reciprocal course. We know that he reached a fine new country which he called Vinland, but we are not told precisely where it was, or that it was precisely where Bjarni had made his first landfall on coming out of his fog. The experience of our own voyage convinced me that Bjarni's landfall was on the coast of Nova Scotia, but since he did not go ashore one must look elsewhere for descriptions of the land as *land*, and not merely as a coast seen from the sea. Here one must turn to the accounts of Leif's Vinland, and to the records of Thorfinn Karlsefni's later voyage to Leif's Vinland. We know that Karlsefni and Leif went to the same place, because Karlsefni set out to occupy the houses that Leif had built at his *budir* or settlement, and the *Graenlendinga Saga* tells us specifically that Karlsefni 'arrived safe and sound at Leif's Houses'. It is interesting to note here that although Leif's own responsibilities on succeeding his father Eirik the Red as head of the Norse Greenland community took him back to Greenland, he never surrendered what he regarded as his property rights in Vinland. Karlsefni asked Leif if he could have the houses he had built in Vinland, but Leif replied that while he was willing to lend them, he would not give them away. Leif gave exactly the same answer to his sister Freydis when she took an expedition to Vinland – he would lend his houses, but not transfer them to anyone else. This indicates, or rather, it does more than indicate, for I think it tells us definitely, two things. First, that Leif regarded Vinland as a *permanent* colony of the Greenland community and, secondly, that neither he nor other people in Greenland had any doubts about their ability to return to Vinland when they wanted to. However obscure the sailing directions for Vinland may be to us, to Leif and his contemporaries they were clear and precise.

The description of the Vinland landscape in the sagas – beautiful grassland, good trees, mild winter, and, above all, the masses of wild grapes – fits New England better than it does Nova Scotia. And the description in *Eirik's Saga* of the *Furdustrandir* or 'wonder sands', past which Karlsefni sailed to get to Vinland does not match the indented Nova Scotian coast at all. But it *does* match – and astonishingly well – the immense beaches stretching from Cape Cod to Nantucket Sound. Indeed, I think there is nowhere else on the northern part of the eastern seaboard of the American continent where 'wonder sands' can be considered quite such a dominant feature of the seascape. Clearly, these sands were an important item in the sailing directions for Vinland, and they were obviously considered so unmistakable that they located Vinland for later navigators beyond a doubt. The prominent headland which the Vinland voyagers called 'Keelness' (Kjalarnes) can reasonably be identified as Cape Cod.

Everything else fits the Cape Cod – Nantucket – Martha's Vineyard area; taken as a whole, the topographical descriptions of Vinland match this locality more exactly than anywhere else in North America. Every *positive* statement in the sagas can be related to this part of Massachusetts without straining the sense in any way. There are no *negative* considerations against it. And the *positive* evidence is strong – the sands, the shoals, the fish in the rivers, the occasional whale washed up on the beach, the grapes, the wild grain, the climate. This is not merely my own reconstruction of the Vinland voyages. Captain Tornöe, in his *Norsemen Before Columbus*, has argued the case in detail, and others have been struck by the remarkable way in which the Cape Cod sands answer to the description of the *Furdustrandir*.

The task I had set myself was to go over all the evidence, and to discover if I could the *practical navigational probabilities* of the route from Greenland, and so, I hoped, to help to determine the *probability* of where Vinland lay. Luck, or choosing the right time of year, or a correct assessment of probabilities in the earlier stages of our voyage, or a combination of all these things, had enabled me to feel that from Greenland to Nova Scotia we had followed more or less Leif's course, and this feeling was borne out by what seemed the reproduction in our own experience of Bjarni's experience in fog, and on coming out of his fog. I was sure that Leif had seen or touched on Nova Scotia, but all the evidence pointed to his having sailed on farther south. He was exploring, looking for new land for settlement by his people, land that would provide what they lacked in Greenland, wood for ships and houses, year-round or almost year-round pasturage for cattle, as many of the comforts of life as were to be had. The piratical period of the Vikings was over – in the eleventh century they were looking for a homeland to absorb their growing population, not merely for other people's settlements to raid and plunder. They wanted settlements for themselves.

I do not think that the economic reasons behind the Vinland voyages have yet been sufficiently stressed, but they seem to me of the first importance in trying to determine where Leif went. He was exploring with the aim of *settlement and colonisation*, and one would expect him to want to see for himself as much of this new country as he could. He may have coasted Nova Scotia, but on rounding Cape Sable I do not think that he would have turned north; he had no reason for going north here, and all his instincts in looking for good settling land would have led him south. We do not know what winds he had. If his northeaster had been part of a prolonged spell of northeasterlies, and the fact that he apparently met no fog himself rather suggests that he had a spell of brisk winds, it would have been not only easy but obvious for him to stand on across the Gulf of Maine towards Cape Cod. It is a logical continuation of his voyage. From the south of Nova Scotia to Cape Cod is well under three hundred miles, so he would not have waited long for his next landfall. The evidence suggests strongly, I think overwhelmingly, that this is what he did.

So we stood on across the Gulf of Maine. Our printed log book, *Reed's Log Book for Yachts*, heads each page of the daily summary, 'From........ To........'. Boldly, we headed this last stage of our voyage 'From Halifax to Vinland'. On leaving Halifax we had to give a new destination to the AMVER organisation. I asked Tim to give our destination as 'Vinland'. I don't know what the computer made of it; at least it was never queried.

16

To Vinland

We had a gentle sail across the Gulf of Maine, and it began to get warm. I shed first one pullover, then two, and one pair of socks. The sailmaker in Halifax had done an excellent job on our sail. Although it seemed now to have more patches than original sail, it set well, and it was a joy to have a mainsail again. I felt that we could not risk it in a wind of any strength, but this was a rather theoretical consideration, for we had nothing much above Force 4, and for most of the time the wind was light. Once we took it down because the wind seemed gusting to Force 5 or so, but it soon went up again. For what use it was, we felt free to use our engine, for we had stocked up with fuel at Halifax, and we were now within easy reach of plenty of places where we could put in for more if we had any need of it. We were not lavish with fresh water – the habits of the voyage were too strong, and so, perhaps, was the discipline of the sea. But there was no longer any need for the strictest rationing, and we allowed ourselves a wash or shave in fresh water as we felt inclined.

In pleasant weather there was no longer such desperate eagerness to get below on coming off watch. Reg, whom I relieved, and Peter Haward, who relieved me, talked long under the afternoon sun, or the night stars. Reg and I recalled an old song that we had recited to each other at bad times off Newfoundland:

> A full nor'easter's blowing up,
> Just listen to it roar now;
> Lord help them, how I pities them,
> Unhappy folk on shore now.

When you and I, Bill, on the deck
Are comfortably lying,
Just think what tiles and chimneypots
About *their* heads are flying!

The idea of 'comfortably lying' on *Griffin*'s deck in a full gale, with tons of water cascading on board, had at bad times helped to make us laugh. Now we felt that the pictures in yachting magazines might even be true sometimes, and might even apply to us. Peter Comber had shopped well for us in Halifax, and we had fresh food and green vegetables again. One thing we did not have was what we regarded as edible bread. True, Peter had bought bread, but it was bread of the New World, chalk-white, and of about the consistency of cotton wool. We called it 'non-bread', or sometimes 'anti-bread'. We longed for the crisp, crunchy bread that you get in France, and that you can still get sometimes (though rarely) in England.

A fairly typical entry in my journal at this time is for June 24, when we were about a day and a half out from Halifax:

0700 (ship's time). Writing in my bunk just before having some kip. Came off watch 0500, Brent radio call at 0530 – not a bad call, with a nice message from the Mayor of Scarborough congratulating us on having reached Nova Scotia. Helped re-set mainsail – we'd taken it down for a bit and replaced it with trysail and our old yankee 'topsail' because of a forecast Force 5. I say 'helped' but I did no more than take the helm while Reg and Peter Haward did the work. Then washed, shaved and tidied up. Now bed, much needed, for I am considerably short of sleep. Didn't get much in Halifax – too much to do, and too many things to worry about. Have just sharpened a pencil lying down – no mean feat. The secret of pencil sharpening, like that of running a successful restaurant, is to have sharp knives. I am a knife-snob. I like sharp knives.

All things are relative. Although the Gulf of Maine was gentle compared with the Labrador Sea or the Atlantic approaching Greenland, and this part of our voyage stays in my memory as a fairly halcyon

Q

period, it was not all that gentle *all* the time. We had the worst thunderstorm of the voyage: it did not last long, but it was frightening while it lasted, with the whole sky ripped across by lightning. We hurriedly disconnected the lead from our radio aerial to the set. And patches of fog came back, not as bad as we had known it, but our fog-experience was still so recent that any return of fog was hateful. Later that same day (June 24) I wrote:

Am on watch next, 1300–1500, and not looking forward to it, for fog has come back. In fog, the man on watch has to wear his lifejacket. Nobody said anything, but it was gloomy to see Reg going up with his lifejacket on. We have about 240 miles to go – not much after coming 4,400, but, I suppose just because we are so near the end of this long voyage, I am the more terrified of some disaster. But God has brought us through so much that I pray to Him with, I hope, a proper kind of faith. That is, I don't know what His will may be, but I try to say with the right sort of humility, 'Not as I will, but as Thou wilt. Thy will be done.'

That fog, however, was not serious (though fog had not done with us yet). The next entry in my journal is more domestic:

Kitchen paper is the most valuable thing on board this boat. I don't know *what* we'd do without it. Of course, we have never had enough. We brought a derisory quantity with us from Dover, and got some more at Scarborough, but nothing like enough. The thirty shillings in Greenland kröner that I invested in kitchen paper at Frederikshaab was about the best investment I've ever made. It is poorish quality paper, but vastly better than nothing, and we shall have used the lot before we are through. In a way, kitchen paper is more useful at sea than on land – it can go straight into the ocean as it is used, the sea soon deals with it, and it creates no problems of litter. What a mess civilisation makes of things. The problem of litter, already enormous and unsolvable, grows worse every day. I say 'unsolvable', but what I mean is that no one is prepared to solve it. There *need* be no problem of litter, if (a) individuals would be decently tidy and if (b) the community would spend the necessary money on providing receptacles for litter *and on taking them away and emptying them*. But I can't see anybody doing this, so litter, particularly in the rich countries like Britain and the United States, gets worse and worse. The Latin races, popularly supposed to be dirtier than we are, in reality, I think, are *much* cleaner. They make nothing like such a mess of their surroundings. They have the sun, which helps, but I don't think they are so *beastly* about leaving litter everywhere. Perhaps as they get richer they will get worse. I don't know. I think that the filth of so much of Britain is a national shame. Partly, I suppose, it is being rich enough to be able to afford waste – in India an empty lemonade bottle is real wealth to somebody, so empty bottles just don't get thrown into hedges or gutters. I don't know what proportion of the weight of stores we carry on *Griffin* is sheer waste, needless packing, etc., but I'm sure that quite a high proportion is unnecessary and waste. Leif had thirty to forty people with him on his voyage. We have been six, are now five. Yet I reckon that we throw overboard in one day as much litter as he had to dispose of on his whole voyage. Civilisation can almost be measured in terms of the mess that man makes of his surroundings.

We were not making much progress in the light winds, and all of us, I think, were getting a bit on edge with the approach of real life again. We had not exactly dodged life for the past two months, but had contrived to alter the normal time-scale of living. Our problems were those of one thousand years ago. Now we were returning to the twentieth century.

I decided that the time had come to open Gerald Mendoza's mysterious parcel. We were in Vinland waters, anyway.

We opened the parcel with ceremony, in the saloon. It disclosed not a bottle, but a magnum of champagne! No present could have been better for giving us a needed lift to our spirits. Plastic is not exactly in keeping with champagne, but it bubbled richly into our familiar mugs, and we all felt that this was An Occasion. I wrote:

It has had a good effect on the crew, because they are singing happily while doing the washing up. 'Bound for the Rio Grande', and 'Clementine'. Fair enough, because I cooked the dinner, and washed an appalling frying pan. We had veal cutlets, mashed potato, cauliflower, fried apples – why don't people fry apples more with meat? – and gravy. Although I say it, a good dinner. Followed (but not by me) with ginger cake and plum jam.

Reg offered to take the champagne bottle back to England, bore a hole in it, and make a lamp for me. I thought it more fitting that it should be buried at sea, so Reg cast it formally into the Gulf of Maine, and soon it sank. I reflected in my journal:

Glass is pretty permanent. Some marine archaeologist of about the year 3000 may wonder what this curious bottle is doing on the sea bed of the Gulf of Maine. It may promote all sorts of theories about Vinland!

Celebrating the approaching end to our voyage with champagne was all very well, but I had a weight of things to do in these last days. I needed to enter Vinland by Nantucket Sound, for I was convinced that this was the way that Leif had sailed. But I had also to get the crew ashore, and make arrangements for getting them back to England. We were running very short of time. Peter Haward's need was the most urgent. He had a job to do in England at the beginning of July, and it was now June 25, and we were still at sea. Thanks to the constant help of the *Guardian* office at home, and to our Marconi radio, I was able to make arrangements while at sea, and we had booked a flight to London for Peter Haward from Boston on the night of June 28. Tim was the next most urgent case, for he had to report back to the Navy in the first week of July. We booked a flight for him from New York on July 1. These things were made additionally difficult by the British seamen's strike, which had thrown a heavy extra load on the air services, so it was a question of getting flights when we could. It had to be done at short notice, because right to the last I could not be sure of exactly when we should be arriving anywhere. We could, of course, have navigated for convenience. The easiest thing would have been to go to Boston to make sure of landing Peter Haward in time for his flight, and then to have made our way at ease to the waters around Martha's Vineyard via the Cape Cod Canal. But I didn't want to do any of this. Just as I had felt that putting into St John's, Newfoundland, for a rest would have been to break away from Leif's route, I wanted to come upon Martha's Vineyard by the way in which I thought that Leif had come upon it. Leif was an explorer, and he could go where he pleased, needing to ask leave of no one. I had to consider such things as making a legal entry to the United States. In the days of the whaling fleets ships came and went from Martha's Vineyard as a matter of course, but I was not at all sure whether Martha's Vineyard nowadays was officially a port of entry for the United States. (It isn't.) So I was afraid that I might be told that we couldn't land on Martha's Vineyard.

I turned to our radio. With Tim's help I sent a signal to the US Coastguard at Boston, explaining my position, and asking permission to land on Martha's Vineyard. We said that we would listen for a reply at 1800 GMT on June 25. We did, and we got a most helpful reply, instructing me to telephone the US Customs at New Bedford via the Boston Marine operator (another radio station). We got through to Boston Marine, and put through our call to New Bedford – to be told that the number was engaged! This seemed absurd at sea, somehow, but there it was. However, the Boston Marine operator, a woman with a particularly nice voice, did not desert us: she told us to stand by, and said that she would put us through to New Bedford as soon as the line was free. She kept her word, and in about ten minutes came through again, saying that New Bedford was on the line. It was a good call, as clear as any telephone call on land, and I explained things to a friendly American voice at the other end. The voice, a man's this time, took in all that I was trying to say, and told me to go to Martha's Vineyard and to telephone the New Bedford Customs from there when we arrived. That was an immense relief.

There remained the need to determine just where to go on Martha's Vineyard. Again, Leif could land on any beach he liked the look of: we, alas, needed telephones and transport for getting Peter Haward quickly to Boston. In Halifax I had asked Stewart MacLeod of the *Weekend Magazine* if he could find out what yacht clubs there were around Martha's Vineyard, and whether any club would welcome us. He went off to do a lot of telephoning, and came back to tell me that there was a yacht club at Edgartown on Martha's Vineyard, that he had telephoned this club, and had been told that they would be happy to see us, and would give us all the help they could. So again we called up the Boston Marine operator, and asked if we could be put through to the Edgartown Yacht Club. This American marine telephone service is near-miraculous, for we got through to the yacht club more quickly than I should have expected to make the call on land – and I did not even know the telephone number of the yacht club. I spoke to the club secretary, Mr Richards, who said that they were looking forward to meeting us, and would look after us in every way they could.

Leif, I reflected, had no radio telephone. But then he had had no need to clear Customs or catch aeroplanes. He was prepared, if necessary, to fight his way ashore. I considered *Griffin*'s crew, tough, reliable and loyal. We could muster a marlin spike or two, and a Very pistol – not exactly formidable armament. Perhaps the telephone was better.

On this day, June 25, Tim caught his first fish. We had trailed his fishing line across thousands of miles of the richest fishing grounds of the world, without a bite. At last, with great excitement, there was a fish on the line. Tim hauled it in, and we saw that he had caught a small shark, or dogfish, about four feet long. But we did not succeed in getting it on board. It could not have been hooked very well, for as it was hauled in it fell off the hook and went back into the sea. I was not sorry. We had no need of food, and the fish was as much entitled to live as we were.

At 2145 on the night of June 26 we raised Cape Cod light, and when I went on watch at 0100 on June 27, we were quite close inshore, making our way along the Cape Cod coast. My journal, scribbled later that day, describes our last adventure:

Well, it can't be said that our voyage is ending 'not with a bang but a whimper'. It very nearly ended with a hellish bang. We made our landfall on the Cape Cod coast all right, and when I went on watch to relieve Reg we were in the middle of going

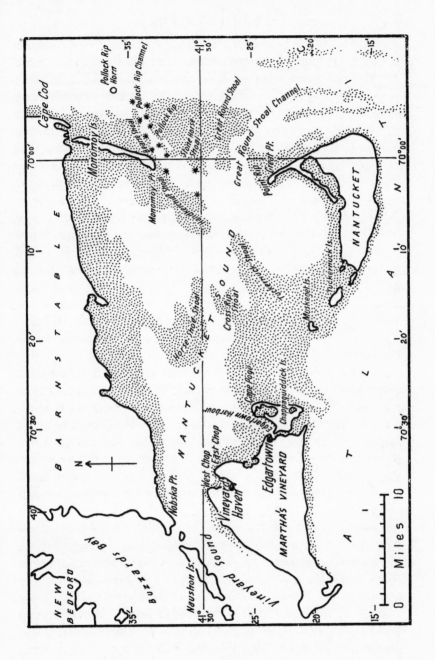

about. There seemed to be shore lights everywhere; houses, cars, a
bright neon sign. My wretched eyes were hard put to it to keep
track of lights and compass. It was a lovely night, clear and soft,
and I was longing for dawn to see the 'wonder sands'. Peter
Haward relieved me at 0300, and in about half an hour all the
lights went out, and it was dense fog. I didn't turn in again, but
stayed around, shutting my eyes when I could in the saloon, and
feeling very much on edge. Tim Lee did identify a whistle buoy
near the Pollock Rip Light-vessel, so we knew (then) where we
were. But there were frightful shoals to get through ahead.
Really, there wasn't much alternative, except (a) to stand out to
sea, wait for the fog to lift and lose another day, which we
couldn't afford without missing Peter Haward's flight, or (b) to
anchor. I discussed anchoring, but Peter is much against anchoring
in fog except in direst need – you don't know where you are, you
don't know what will be the situation when the tide turns, you
may be in a mess if it comes on to blow. So we went ahead, heard
one whistle buoy, but didn't hear any of the gongs or bells that the
buoys on the chart are supposed to have. We navigated by guess
and by God. Reg Garrod, Peter Haward and Peter Comber were
in the cockpit, at the helm, and endlessly going about. Tim Lee
stayed at the chart table for hour after hour, every nerve strained,
like a good gun dog, pointing. I had my job at the echo sounder,
beside Tim, keeping up a running commentary of depths, which
helped him to guess roughly where we were, from the soundings
on the chart. But this is a rough guide at best, because in shoal
water soundings are always liable to vary as sandbanks change
shape. Suddenly Peter Haward called out that we were approaching overfalls, a bar of some sort. We couldn't wholly avoid the
overfalls. I was sick with apprehension when the depths went
$2\frac{1}{2}$ fathoms, 2 fathoms, $1\frac{1}{2}$ fathoms, 1 fathom. Theoretically we
should have been wrecked at 1 fathom for *Griffin* draws nearly
seven feet, but the transducer for the echo-sounder is below the
keel, so there is a bit of 'borrowed water' – like living on
'borrowed time'. It must have been a very near thing. Peter
Haward and Tim Lee tried to work back the way we had come,
but also making a bit to the north, because it looked from the

chart as if there might be a way through to the north. But the fog was so dense that it was impossible to see anything. Gradually we did get into deeper water, but we were afraid that it might be a trap, because there are several 'holes' in these sands, all surrounded by shallows.

At last the fog lifted a scrap momentarily, and Peter Haward called out that he could see a buoy. It had 'No. 9' on it, and that enabled Tim to identify it on the chart, so at last we knew where we were. So we went on from buoy to buoy, for although the fog was still pretty thick we could *just* see them, and we knew from the chart where they ought to be.

The fog never cleared completely for us, but it did lighten from time to time. Suddenly Tim called out, 'John, there are your sands.' And there they were, or at least a little stretch of them, gleaming palely through the fog. And I thought, 'All I want to do now is to keep off them!' But I have no doubt that the great beaches of Cape Cod *were* the 'wonder sands' of the Vikings. We had met them in bad conditions, in another peril of the sea, and suddenly it seemed to me that this, too, was an essential part of the Vinland story. The Vinland colonies could be supplied and reinforced *only* by sea. How often all those centuries ago must European men and women have stood on the Vinland shore, looking out to sea for ships that did not come? For ships that had been wrecked in fog? The fogs off Newfoundland and Nova Scotia, off the Vinland coast itself, must have been a constant hazard to the ships from Greenland. It is a fog-prone route almost all the way. Those fogs may have played a critical part in the ultimate failure of the Vinland colonies.

When we were able to relax after that appalling morning, I made another radio-telephone call to the Edgartown Yacht Club to allay anxiety about us, and to give them a course in case press representatives and photographers might be thinking of coming out in a launch to meet us. There *were* press and television people at Edgartown, and we fixed a rendezvous at a buoy called the Rip Shoal Light Buoy. This seemed all right at the time, but the fog came down thick again. Finally, I saw what I thought was a buoy and pointed it out to Peter Haward, who said that it was a boat. It *was* a boat; and it was the launch that had come out to greet us. It came nearer, and was full of friendly waving people. Among them I was delighted to see Jim Markwick, of the New York office of the *Guardian*, who had not only come to welcome us, but had brought his mother with him. This seemed to make our arrival in Vinland not merely the end of an adventure, but almost a homecoming.

My journal has given a sketch rather than a navigational account of our entrance to Nantucket Sound. Threading our way in through that dense fog was such a brilliant feat of navigation by Tim and Peter Haward that the entries in our ship's log are repeated in Appendix III.

I cannot now write of that first night at Martha's Vineyard: it was a confusion of press and television interviews, kindness by people at the Edgartown Yacht Club, and weariness. I am sorry to say that I behaved rather badly to the U.S. Customs and Immigration Authorities. There was a letter from the Customs at New Bedford waiting for us at the Yacht Club – a very nice letter, and if I had had time to read it properly, everything would have been all right. But I was so tired, and there were so many people wanting to talk to me that I did no more than glance at it. In fact, it asked me to get in touch with the writer by telephone *to arrange* our clearance. I took it to mean that our clearance *had been arranged* by telephone. So I did nothing about it until next day, when a very angry message came from New Bedford pointing out icily that I was breaking all sorts of laws by entering the United States at a place that was not a port of entry, and instructing me to report to the Customs at New Bedford forthwith, with all my crew. I could not take Peter Haward because he had already gone to Boston for his flight to England. (He had some trouble with the Immigration people there, because he was leaving the United States without having officially arrived, but they let him leave for London.) The rest of us went over to New Bedford by air – it is only a short flight from Martha's Vineyard – and the U.S. Customs were much nicer to me than I deserved, giving me clearance for *Griffin* and ourselves, without invoking any of the fearsome penalties I had laid myself open to. I could make excuses for myself, but I was angry with myself, too. I had done exactly what yachtsmen should never do in taking it for granted that official regulations would be tempered for me. They *were* tempered for me, and generously, but I should not have taken anything for granted, and tired as I was, I should have read the Customs' letter properly. I can but repeat my gratitude to the U.S. authorities for treating me much better thzn I deserved.

A sad event on our arrival at Edgartown was a cablegram for Peter Comber asking him to try to get back to England at once because his daughter was ill. With the help of our friends at the yacht club we were able to get a flight for him from New York on June 29. That left Tim, Reg and me to deal with all that had to be done for making ready *Griffin* for laying up after her long voyage, and on July 1 Tim had to depart. So Reg and I were alone together. Our thoughts went back to the village inn at Charney Bassett, thousands of miles away. The adventure had started over a drink between us. On saying goodbye to Tim, we went and stood ourselves a drink in the yacht club bar.

We too had to get back to England, and as soon as we had tidied up and made arrangements for *Griffin* to be looked after, we went to New York and came home on the *Queen Elizabeth*. We should both have liked to sail *Griffin* home, but it was impossible. We did discuss whether the two of us could handle her, but my eyes bother me so much that I could not regard myself as a reliable fifty per cent of *Griffin*'s crew. And her gear was heavy for a crew of two, who would soon be fatigued in any case from having to stand watch and watch. And there was no time, for *Griffin* would need some refitting after her long voyage before recrossing the Atlantic. So this could not be. After our last night on board in the anchorage off Edgartown, we said goodbye to her sadly, but proudly, too. We were leaving her in the good hands of American friends who had offered to look after her. As we rowed across in the dinghy to go ashore to start our journey to New York it was foggy again, and we had to navigate the anchorage watchfully to avoid losing our way. I quoted one of our *Griffin* rhymes:

There's ruddy rocks to starboard
There's endless ice to port.
This is a situation
That gives one food for thought.

Reg said, 'I wonder, what was the next verse?'

17

A Footnote in History

What did we achieve? I do not claim to have 'discovered' or 'proved' anything. The objectives of our expedition were limited, and I kept strictly to the brief that I had given myself. This was to make a *navigational investigation* of the Vinland voyage – we started and finished with the sea. We were not explorers in the ordinary sense, the seas we sailed are known, the coasts charted. We had no goal that could be reached decisively – the North Pole, say, or a northwest passage from the Atlantic to the Pacific. We were making an experiment in time as well as an experiment in geography, sailing into the past as well as crossing a known ocean. All the time we were concerned with what the lawyers call 'circumstantial evidence', that is evidence to explain some human action built up from all the circumstances surrounding that action, and not drawn directly from witnesses who can say, 'I saw that man do this.' Circumstantial evidence can be very strong evidence, but there is always something a little unsatisfactory about it, a residuum of doubt.

But the whole of history is the assembly of circumstantial evidence, the patient reconstruction of the actions and thoughts of men now dead, who cannot be put in the witness box and cross-examined. If you deal fairly with the evidence, careful not to strain it, or to make inferences which the known facts do not fit, then you can, I think, achieve something of historical value by attempting to reconstruct a pattern of events which the known facts *do* fit. This we did, and I have tried to set out fairly in this book, with reservations on my views or judgments when they seem called for, the pattern of the Norse Vinland voyages which seems most likely to be true. I cannot say that Bjarni *did* sight the coast of Nova Scotia, or that Leif Eiriksson *did* go ashore on Martha's Vineyard. But after the practical experience of our voyage I can say that I think it *almost certain* that these things happened.

It may be felt that we were helped by luck, or accident. We were. It was no part of my original plan to call at the Faeroes, but the accident that took us there enabled me to study at first hand something of the economic background to Norse expansion in the North Atlantic in the generations before the expansion from Iceland to Greenland, and on to North America. I could not plan to be trapped in fog – but the accident of our fog gave us first-hand experience of the same kind of fog as that which had entrapped Bjarni, and from this experience enabled us to draw reasonable conclusions about Bjarni's emergence from the fog. Certainly these things are luck or accident, but I think we *used* our luck, ill-luck as well as good luck (it was good luck to meet a northeasterly gale where I think it almost certain that Leif had met one). And you cannot discount luck in human affairs – Newton's apple, for instance. The thing is to try to exploit it.

I cannot say that I have *proved* that Newfoundland was *not* Vinland, but I do say that this location for Vinland is so improbable that it ought now to be ruled out. I think that there were Norse settlements in Newfoundland, and that they will well repay investigation. But I am sure that they were trading settlements established after Leif's and Karlsefni's colonisation farther south, and that they were never regarded as forming part of Vinland proper. The Landa-Rolf settlement of Newfoundland in the late thirteenth century also requires more study, for there must surely be traces of this still to be found. Newfoundland is an important area in the history of Norse activities in America before Columbus – and Cabot – but it must be seen in its proper historical perspective.

It could not have been Vinland. Perhaps it is always rather tempting to ignore the obvious, to devise highly individual theories to depict historical events. Most of us read detective stories in which the obvious is just what did *not* happen. But this is not the normal pattern of life; if you are looking for an explanation of something that has happened at home or in the office, the obvious explanation is nearly always the correct one. Every description of Vinland in the sagas fits Nantucket Sound and the Massachusetts seaboard, fits well, and fits this area better than anywhere else. There is substantial evidence in the sagas pointing to Cape Cod and Massachusetts in the accounts of various other expeditions *to* and *in* Vinland. There is Karlsefni's exploring *in* Vinland; there is the expedition in which Thorvald Eiriksson, Leif's brother, was killed by an Indian arrow; there is the joint expedition by Freydis, Leif's sister, and two partners – a horrible story this, in which Freydis tricked her partners and murdered them and their wives to try to obtain Vinland for herself. The description of landscape and events in all these stories, all fit Massachusetts and New England.

I think I have shown not only that it was *practical* for Leif to have got to Nantucket Sound and Martha's Vineyard, but that this was the most *logical* and *probable* route for him to have sailed. That is on navigational evidence alone. Although I must not stray far from the sea, a voyage must have an end and the mariners go ashore. Reg Garrod and I had the good fortune to be taken round Martha's Vineyard by Dr and Mrs Sidney N. Riggs, who know the island intimately – Mrs Riggs (Dionis Coffin Riggs) is a descendant of some of the earliest post-Columbus European settlers there. They showed us the woods and the wild vines – even today, acres and acres of wild vines, a most beautiful natural feature of the island, and one that must strike anybody with a sense of rich and luscious bounty. Perhaps it is not exactly evidence, but if you are looking for a place called *Vinland* and come upon a place called *Vineyard* precisely where you think it was, the coincidence is at least interesting. Man does not change all that much. Martha's Vineyard is an old name, going back to 1602, when the island was given its name, because of its wild vines, by Captain Bartholomew Gosnold (Martha was his daughter). If the vines so struck his imagination that he called the island after them, may they not have struck earlier explorers in exactly the same way? And there may be more than coincidence. To me it is inconceivable that *all* memories of the Norse colonies were lost by the early seventeenth century. The settlements must finally have succumbed to the Indians, but folk-memories are not destroyed; nor, in such victories, is *everybody* likely to be killed. Some women and young children, at any rate, were probably carried off as captives, to merge ultimately into the community of their captors. It is at least possible that when Gosnold got to the island in 1602 some remnant of an Indian tribe with Norse blood told him as nearly as their tongues could get that he had come to Vinland.

I feel the same about the name Newfoundland. It is a fairly obvious, though not particularly enterprising, name for any new country, and Cabot may have hit upon the name himself in 1497. But if Newfoundland was circumnavigated by Icelanders in 1285, and called Nyaland or Nyfundnaland, it is stretching coincidence rather far to accept that Cabot hit by chance upon precisely the same name two hundred years later. Cabot sailed from Bristol, and Bristol merchants of his period had many links with Iceland, notably in the valuable trade in dried fish – 'stockfish' – which was the staple food of the poor over much of Western Europe from the end of the Middle Ages onwards. Cabot may very well have known from Icelandic sources just where he was going – to a known and named land. Or he may have come upon some remnant of the thirteenth-century Norse settlement who spoke of 'Nyfundnaland'. The history of the North Atlantic from the eleventh to the fifteenth centuries has much to be unravelled, but already enough is known about the reality of the Norse discoveries for the history of this period to need considerable re-assessment and re-writing. This is not to denigrate Christopher Columbus, or to belittle the achievement of his great voyage of 1492, but it needs placing more accurately in its true historical perspective. Did Columbus know, at least roughly, where he was going?

I think it probable that he did. His own writings, at least those that have so far come to light, make no reference to Iceland, but his son's biography of him records that he spent some time in Iceland in his earlier years. If so, it is hard to think that a man of his vivid and inquiring mind would not have picked up scraps of knowledge and information of new land to the west. In 1959 Moscow Radio broadcast a report that a Russian historian had found correspondence between Columbus and Queen Isabella of Spain showing that Columbus knew of the existence of the West Indies before he sailed, and assessed clearly their value to Spain. There is nothing improbable about such correspondence coming to light in Moscow. The medieval Dukes of Moscow were closely related to the ruling families in Scandinavia, for they were themselves an offshoot of

Viking expansion. In the fifteenth century there were close links between Denmark and Portugal; Danish sea-captains gave information to Prince Henry the Navigator, and served in some of the Portuguese expeditions to the east that Prince Henry sent out. Any navigational knowledge of new land to the west, and of a possible new route to the east, would have been of absorbing interest to Prince Henry, who may reasonably be supposed to have learned something of the Vinland voyages. Later, about the years 1470–3, at least twenty years before Columbus sailed, a joint Portuguese-Danish expedition was dispatched to discover 'new lands in the North'. This expedition, under the Danish captains Pining and Pothorst, certainly got to Iceland and Greenland, probably to Labrador and Newfoundland, and perhaps much farther south. The Portuguese captain Joas Vaz Corte-Real, with help from the Danes, also explored in this area a generation before Columbus, and there were other expeditions mounted from Scandinavia with Portuguese help and finance around these middle years of the fifteenth century. The Dukes of Moscow were almost certainly also concerned in financing at least some of these expeditions, with, of course, a share in the profits of any trade that might ensue. So it is highly probable that records of voyages and discoveries of this period exist somewhere in the archives of Russia.

The trouble is that all navigational information of this period was regarded by those who possessed it as a trade secret of the highest value; not only was information guarded, it might also be deliberately falsified to put trade rivals off the track. Moscow, Copenhagen and Lisbon all had reason to be interested in what Columbus was doing and saying, and spies no doubt tried to get hold of letters and information as eagerly as military secrets are sought today.

At least up to the eighteenth century, Denmark never formally abandoned what the Scandinavians, at any rate, regarded as their 'rights' in North America. As late as 1705 an Icelandic historian urged the King of Denmark, then combined with Norway, to claim sovereignty over North America on the ground that Norse settlers from Greenland had got there long before anybody else. On the principle of first come, first served, by which the European Powers were then beginning to carve up the rest of the world, a

R

Danish-Norwegian claim to North America would have been sound. But whatever the *de jure* position, the *de facto* situation was that Britain, France and the Netherlands, with Spain entrenched in the southwest, were grabbing every yard of American soil they could get: and Denmark was scarcely capable of taking on all the major Powers of Europe. So the Danish claim went by default, and has since been overwritten by the later history of the New World. Columbus has so dominated school history books, that the idea of European colonisation in America long before him has scarcely been considered.

I hope that our voyage and this book may add a little to knowledge of the reality of the Vinland colonies. They came too early in history to succeed, but they were among the most gallant of human failures. And as we learn more about them, we may learn much of importance to the history of both Europe and America and, perhaps, to our knowledge of ourselves. One of the elements of tragedy in Vinland was that the attempt to create a nation there outstripped the administrative capacity (then) of the Catholic Church. The early Norse settlers were devout Christians – Leif's mother, Thjodhild, built the first Christian church in Greenland. Karlsefni's wife, Gudrid, the mother of Snorri who was born in Vinland, the first named American of European stock, made a pilgrimage to Rome. On leaving Vinland, she and Karlsefni went back to Iceland, where they bought land, no doubt with the proceeds of the furs, timber and other products of Vinland trade. Gudrid made her pilgrimage after her husband had died and her son, Snorri, had married. She returned to Iceland from Rome, built a church, and became a nun. The Vinland settlers looked to the Church for much of the administration of their community, for law and learning as well as religious affairs. The Church tried to look after them – Bishop Eirik Gnupson's visit as Papal Legate early in the twelfth century is evidence of this. But they were too distant, communications too slow and too uncertain. A priest might die, and it might be years before he could be replaced. In such circumstances an isolated small community, rough, but deeply religious, might tend first to despair, and then to disintegrate.

Bishop Eirik's visit to Vinland was in 1117–8. In 1160, Pope Alexander III wrote a curious letter to the Archbishop of Trondheim, in Norway, conveying a dispensation from the normal ecclesiastical laws of marriage for the inhabitants of an island situated 'twelve days' journey or more from Norway', and 'twelve days' journey from all other lands'. (In the context, 'all other lands' seems to mean 'all other Christian lands'.) The people on this 'island' were said to be so nearly related in consanguinity 'that they can hardly contract marriage legally in accordance with Canon Law'. This gives a vivid picture of a small, isolated community of a few closely related families, which the Church found it next to impossible to visit. Some authorities have held that the 'island' was Greenland, but this hardly seems possible, for in 1160 Greenland was not remote and unknown, there was regular traffic with Iceland and Norway, and an established Church. Tornöe suggests that the 'island' was in Vinland, and that the community was a settlement on Martha's Vineyard. This seems highly plausible. The Vinland colonies certainly looked to Greenland and to Europe – ultimately to Rome – for their Church administration. There is no evidence of a separate Vinland bishopric; at least, none that has come to light.

Whatever may be the complex of reasons, the Vinland colonies failed. By how much they failed, or how nearly they succeeded, we do not yet know. I believe that they endured into the fifteenth century as fortified settlements and trading posts, and that a final effort at consolidation was made with a general emigration from Greenland towards the close of the fourteenth century. When this effort failed to advance against Red Indian power, the colonies were doomed, although pockets may have lingered here and there for generations later. It is another element of tragedy in American history that the early European settlers who came after Columbus were seldom much interested in local Indian customs and folklore, being more concerned to drive Indians away from the lands they themselves wanted to settle. Much evidence relating to the Vinland colonies is irretrievably lost. But it cannot all be lost.

For at least two centuries, from A.D. 1000 to A.D. 1200, there was vigorous Norse activity on the North American coast, centred, I believe, on what is now Massachusetts, but with permanent or semi-permanent trading posts and logging camps from as far south as New York and Long Island to Nova Scotia, and perhaps in Newfoundland, too. Vinland was the country that tried to become a nation – New Norway or New Iceland long before it was New England.

All human history is a jigsaw puzzle; one man may find a small piece that fits here, but the pattern cannot emerge until many men have found and fitted many pieces. If *Griffin's* voyage has a final place as a footnote to this brave, sad chapter of human history, we who sailed in her will feel that we did our job.

APPENDICES

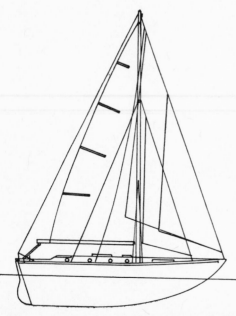

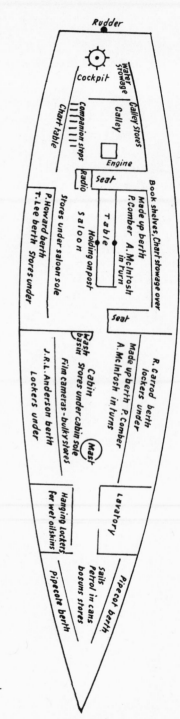

Rudder

Water stowage

Cockpit

Galley Stores

Galley

Companion steps

Chart table

Engine

Book shelves, Chart stowage over

Made up berth
P. Comber   A. McIntosh
in turn

Radio

Seat

Table

Holding on post

S a l o o n

Stores under saloon sole

P. Howard berth
T. Lee berth   Stores under

Seat

R. Garrod berth
lockers under

Made up berth   P. Comber
A. McIntosh in turns

Wash basin

Cabin
Stores under cabin sole

Film cameras - bulky stores

Mast

J.R.L. Anderson berth
Lockers under

Lavatory

Hanging lockers
for wet oilskins

Sails
Petrol in cans
bosuns stores

Pipecot berth

Pipecot berth

APPENDIX I

Griffin

Griffin, designed as a gaff cutter, by W. E. Forster, was built by H. King and Sons at Pin Mill in 1938. She is 44 ft overall, with a maximum beam of 11·7 ft and a draught of 5 ft 7 in. In practice, we reckoned her draught at 6 ft. Her net registered tonnage is 7·71 (24 tons Thames Measurement). The sail plan shows her conversion from gaff rig to Bermudan. We used her old mainsail recut to provide a Bermudan mainsail of 420 sq ft. This was an unfortunate economy, because the old sail was not up to the conditions we met. She had new Terylene headsails – No. 1 yankee of 408 sq ft, No. 2 yankee of 198 sq ft, and staysail of 150 sq ft. We also carried her old genoa, a grand sail of 620 sq ft, and it proved very useful. Towards the end of the voyage, however, it needed constant repair. Her working rig was main, yankee and staysail. For running, we used either the genoa or No. 1 yankee boomed out on the spinnaker pole (we took no spinnaker). For heavy weather we had our storm trysail, a small sail of exceptionally thick canvas.

APPENDIX II

Time and distance run

(A table extracted from *Griffin*'s log by T. R. Lee)

Dover to Scarborough

Date	Distance naut. miles	Time hours	mins	Average speed knots
27 April	26·0	5	20	
28 ,,	117·4	24	00	
29 ,,	90·1	17	50	
	233·5	47	10	4·95

Scarborough to Vaag

Date	Distance naut. miles	Time hours	mins	Average speed knots
2 May	31·3	9	00	
3 ,,	88·2	24	00	
4 ,,	149·0	24	00	
5 ,,	66·0	24	00	
6 ,,	131·4	24	00	
7 ,,	64·6	24	00	
8 ,,	54·8	11	30	
	585·3	140	30	4·17

Vaag to Reykjavik

Date	Distance naut. miles	Time hours	mins	Average speed knots
12 May	30·4	8	50	
13 ,,	144·4	24	00	
14 ,,	111·2	24	00	
15 ,,	99·0	24	00	
16 ,,	159·5	24	00	
17 ,,	106·5	17	30	
	651·0	122	20	5·32

Reykjavik to Frederikshaab

Date	Distance naut. miles	Time hours	mins	Average speed knots	Remarks
20 May	47·5	6	50		
21 ,,	126·7	24	00		
22 ,,	108·2	25	00		Time changed at sea. (Apart from this occasion we always changed clocks in port.)
23 ,,	90·8	19	25		4 h. 35 m. at Weather Ship *Alpha.*
24 ,,	176·7	24	00		
25 ,,	133·1	24	00		
26 ,,	177·0	24	00		
27 ,,	141·0	24	00		
28 ,,	43·0	24	00		
29 ,,	74·4	24	00		
30 ,,	9·4	3	00		
	1,127·8	222	15	5·07	

Frederikshaab to Halifax

Date	Distance naut. miles	Time hours	mins	Average speed knots
2 June	70·4	15	35	
3 ,,	102·4	24	00	
4 ,,	94·2	24	00	
5 ,,	53·0	24	00	
6 ,,	149·7	24	00	

S

Date	Distance naut. miles	Time hours	mins	Average speed knots
7 June	115·8	24	00	
8 ,,	90·5	24	00	
9 ;,	158·0	24	00	
10 ,,	123·0	24	00	
11 ,,	73·0	24	00	
12 ,,	107·7	24	00	
13 ,,	91·3	24	00	
14 ,,	90·5	24	00	
15 ,,	107·7	24	00	
16 ,,	110·3	24	00	
17 ,,	89·5	24	00	
18 ,,	71·0	24	00	
19 ,,	71·2	24	00	
20 ,,	70·8	19	55	
	1840·0	443	30	4·15

Halifax to Edgartown, Martha's Vineyard

Date	Distance naut. miles	Time hours	mins	Average speed knots
22 June	22·2	4	50	
23 ,,	116·0	24	00	
24 ,,	83·4	24	00	
25 ,,	74·3	24	00	
26 ,,	106·4	24	00	
27 ,,	100·8	18	30	
	504·0	119	20	4·22
Voyage Total	4941·6	1095	05	4·51

APPENDIX III

Entrance to Nantucket Sound – extract from log

0340 No. 6 Fl. buoy abeam 2'. Log 419·5. Co. 175. Vis. closing. Pollock Rip Lt. sighted at 0300 but now obscured. Hoist radar reflector.

0350 Vis. under 2'.

0355 Fog.

0450 Put about to 280°. Log 425·6.

0505 Pollock Rip LV Nautophone 2 points on port bow.

0553 Fix 010°. 2' from Pollock Rip LV.

0600 Headed. Co. 290°.

0610 Put about 190°. Log 431·5.

0645 Buoy (Morse 'A') heard on port bow.

0658 Buoy (Morse 'A') abeam to starboard. Log 435·4.

0718 Put about to 292°. Log 436·8. Feeling way into Pollock Rip Channel. Dense fog. Sounding with care. No buoys seen.

0715–0900 Steering by soundings, usually going about when soundings reduced to 18 ft. At 0845 estimated position on N edge of Stone Horse Shoal in $3\frac{1}{2}$ fathoms.

0900 Unexpected shoal sounding and heavy overfalls. Altered course SE then NE at 0908 to stem tide. Probably Stone Horse Shoal.

0935 Vis. cleared to $\frac{1}{2}$'.

0950 Sight two buoys and Monomoy Beach.

1000 Identified No. 9 buoy and passed $\frac{1}{2}$ cable S of it. Wind WSW Force 3.

1007 No. 10 bell buoy abeam to starboard, 2 cables. Course 195°. Log 450.5.

1125 Log 457·3. Put about to 310°.

1157 Log 459·6. No. 15 buoy abeam to starboard $\frac{1}{2}$ mile.

1255 Put about to 185°. Log 465·2.

1325 No. 17 buoy abeam to port 20 yards. Log 467·6. Vis. 400 yards.

1345 Put about to 305°. Log 469·7.

1444 Sighted No. 20 buoy and launch with photographers $\frac{1}{2}$' to west of it.

1442 Posn. 180°. No. 20 buoy 50 yards.

1500 Vis. cleared to 1'.

1527 Put about to 175°. Log 479·0.

1545 Put about to 270°. Log 481·0.

1545–1600 Steered uncertain course, photometer alongside compass.
(A wicked hazard, this. Who was responsible? I don't know
– it can happen all too easily. It was a dangerous quarter of
an hour. – JRLA.)

1708 Posn. 1 cable N of No. 22 buoy.

1754 Shoal sounding. Land 300 yards ahead. Posn. N of Cape Poge. Put
about to NW, and then 290°. Completely missed Squash Meadow
Banks.

1802 Put about by No. 2 buoy to 185° to lay Edgartown Harbour.
Courses various for beating up harbour, going about on soundings.
Visibility 50–400 yards.

1840 Handed Log reading 500.

1850 Secured alongside Edgartown Yacht Club.

APPENDIX IV

Radio

Griffin's call-sign is MMSR – 'Mike Mike Sierra Romeo' in the international notation. During the voyage we were in direct contact with the
following radio stations: North Foreland, Humber, Cullercoats, Stone-
haven, Wick, Oban, Thorshavn, Reykjavik, Ocean Station Alpha,
Prinz Christianssund, Julianehaab, Frederikshaab, Foeringerhavnen,
Gronne Dal, Ocean Station Bravo, Belle Isle, St John's, St Lawrence,
Sydney, Prince Edward Island, Halifax, Canso, Boston Marine, US
Coastguard, London – GCN 2, GCN 3, GCN 4. We called coastal
stations principally for sending weather reports. In the North Sea I sent
my daily messages to the *Guardian* on link-calls via British coastal radio
stations on 2 megacycles, Later, I sent all *Guardian* messages directly to
London, first on 8 megacycles, then on 12 megacycles. For those tech-
nically interested in radio, I asked William Maconachie, of Marconi
International Marine, for a technical description of the Kestrel. He writes:

Kestrel is a generic name adopted by Marconi Marine for a series of
radiotelephone transmitter/receivers of which at the time of writing
(October 1966) there are two – Kestrel I and Kestrel II. Two new and
even more powerful Kestrels (III and IV), the latter with additional frequency coverage, are now being developed and should be in production

when this book is in print early in 1967. Kestrel I and Kestrel II are basically identical in design, the former working only in the intermediate frequencies between 1·6 and 4 megacycles and suitable for comparatively short-distance communication: and the latter covering both the intermediate and high frequencies up to 12 Mc/s., and thus being suitable for working over much greater distances. Throughout his book Mr Anderson speaks of the equipment with which he is now so familiar merely as the Kestrel, but, as readers will appreciate, he is referring to the Kestrel II, the first model of which was fitted in Francis Chichester's *Gipsy Moth III* in 1962.

Commercially designed for voluntarily-equipped vessels such as the small fishing boat, coaster or yacht, the equipment comprises three units, each contained in a metal cabinet. The transmitter and receiver units are separate, have identical dimensions (each 14 in. by 9¼ in. by 12¼ in.) and can be fitted side by side, or one above the other. The third unit, the transistorised power pack (9 in. by 9½ in. by 14 in.) can be installed in any convenient position nearby. Editions of both Kestrel I and Kestrel II are available for working from 24 volts d.c., 12 volts d.c. or 115/230 volts 50/60 cycles a.c. With a rotating loop aerial, or with a small goniometer and fixed loop aerial, any Kestrel installation can be used for direction-finding as well as for communication. A two-tone alarm generator can also be fitted.

Frequency Coverages

Kestrel I – *Transmitter*, 1·6 to 3·8 Mc/s., with eleven crystal-controlled spot frequencies. Frequency stability ± 0·02%. The range can be extended to 4·13 Mc/s with a suitable aerial.
Receiver, three bands 190 to 525, 620 to 1650 and 1600 to 4500 kc/s.

Kestrel II – *Transmitter* has five bands, with seventeen spot frequencies distributed as follows –
1·6 to 3·8 Mc/s – seven spot frequencies
4·063 to 4·13 Mc/s – three spot frequencies
6·204 Mc/s – one spot frequency
8·198 to 8·27 Mc/s – three spot frequencies
12·333 to 12·404 Mc/s – three spot frequencies
Frequency stability ± 0·02% for 1·6 to 3·8 Mc/s., ± 0·005% all other ranges.
Receiver has six bands 190 to 525, 620 to 1650, 1600 to 4500,

6204, 8748 to 8812, and 13133 to 13197 kc/s. All HF ranges have bandspread tuning using a 4750 kc/s crystal-controlled converter. This provides a high degree of frequency stability combined with easy selection of the required transmission.

With both Kestrel I and Kestrel II, power into the aerial circuit is 75 watts; output is 36 to 50 watts on IF and 70 watts on HF. Receiver current consumption is 1 amp., and that of the transmitter from 13·5 to 18·5 amps., naturally minimum in 'no speech' condition.

Both Kestrels can be fitted for either simplex or duplex operation. If duplex is required a unit is incorporated in the receiver for automatic rejection of the transmitter frequency. The calling and distress frequency of 2182 kc/s is emphasised on the controls of both transmitter and receiver.

Kestrels III and IV

Although production of these new models has not yet begun at the time of going to print, development is almost complete and the broad outline of specification has been defined. Again, both the new Kestrels will be identical in outward dimensions and basic design, but both transmitter and receiver will be contained in one cabinet 23¾ in. high by 15 in. wide by 14½ in. deep. The power pack will be separate as before. The transmitters are to be transistorised throughout except for the final RF stage and modulators, while the receivers will be fully transistorised with an audio output of 1½ watts. Crystal-controlled spot selection of 23 frequencies as well as manual tuning is provided in both receivers.

The new Kestrels will operate from 12 or 24/32 volts d.c. or from 115/230 volts a.c. supplies, with power outputs appreciably higher than those of Kestrels I and II. Kestrel III, for IF working, is designed to cover the frequency bands 1600 to 3800 kc/s on transmission, with 21 crystal-controlled spot frequencies, and 190 to 4500 kc/s on reception. Kestrel IV is to have full transmit coverage of 1600 to 4130 kc/s and also the HF bands 6, 8, 12 and 16 Mc/s, with 41 crystal-controlled spot frequencies 20 of which are in the HF bands. Reception will also cover the same HF bands as well as 190 to 4500 kc/s and excepting 22 Mc/s, will therefore cover all the marine frequencies (other than VHF) used for both ship/shore and ship/ship communication. Both Kestrel III and Kestrel IV will meet the requirements for vessels compulsorily or voluntarily equipped for radio-telephone communication on intermediate frequencies, and Kestrel IV will meet those for voluntary fitting for HF working. When they come into production they will supersede Kestrel I and Kestrel II respectively and although John Anderson, Francis Chichester, and others may view the passing of their faithful Kestrels with a pang, the second generation bids fair to serve them even better. Francis Chichester, in fact, is already well on the way to acquaintance with Kestrel IV since the basic Kestrel II he is using on his round-the-world solo voyage (1966–67) has been modified to incorporate a number of Kestrel IV features.

APPENDIX V

Medical Supplies

Medical and first-aid equipment for the voyage called for a great deal of thought. *Griffin* carried no doctor, but (as with other small boats on long voyages) there was always the possibility that we might have to deal as best we could with some grave illness or injury. We could have obtained medical advice by radio, but it would still have been necessary for us to carry out any advice that we might be given from our own resources. Our final selection of medical stores was based on a list prescribed by Dr G. F. C. Hawkins, Medical Officer at Wellington College, who generously gave much time to thinking of our problems. Two other doctors helped greatly with suggestions – Dr J. R. Bowker, Company Medical Officer of the *Guardian*, and Dr R. C. Squires of Wantage. We were presented by Smith, Son and Nephew with an excellent first-aid box of dressings and bandages. Our medical stores included:

100 tablets Alum Hydrox
100 tablets Aspirin
100 tablets Paracetamol
100 tablets Codeine
Amp. Omnopon – 30 mgm
Calamine Lotion – 500 ml
Mycil Powder – 1 tin
Crem. Zinc – 100 gm
Hibitane Lozenges – 60
Sulphacetamide eye drops 10%
Framycetin eye drops – 2 tubes
Cocaine eye drops – 1 fl oz

100 tablets Piriton
100 tablets Marzine
100 tablets Soneryl
100 tablets Senokot
100 tablets Penicillin – 250 mg
100 tablets Tetracyline – 250 mgm
Mist. Kaolin and Morph. – 500 ml
200 tablets Orastrep
100 tablets Dexedrine – 5 mgm
Carbol Resin
Tulle Gras – 3 boxes
One bottle of Dettol – 500 ml

Cetrimide 1% – 500 ml

Bethnovate 1 x 15 gm. 1 x 30 gm

Sofra Tulle Gauze 2 x 10

12 x 1 Megga Intra-Muscular
  Penicillin injection

Two pairs scissors

Two dressing basins

Two medicine glasses

Three clinical thermometers

Owing to the excellent state of health enjoyed by the crew throughout the voyage, we drew little on our medical supplies. The Sofra Tulle Gauze dressing was particularly valuable. It would have been wise to take dark glasses for wear against dazzle from ice. Fortunately (or, perhaps, unfortunately) we had so little sunshine when we were in the ice that the lack of dark glasses did not matter much: but on the few occasions when there was bright sunshine on ice I felt the need of eye protection badly.

APPENDIX VI

Stores

Catering for the voyage was based on the possibility that *Griffin* might have to spend thirty days at sea, without any chance of replenishing stores. Virtually all the work of organising food supplies was done by Peter Comber, who based his calculations about stores by working backwards from a series of ideal menus for each day, multiplied by thirty days. This was his basic list:

3 lb back bacon

Eighteen tins bacon

Whole ready-cooked ham

Six 2 lb tins ham

Two whole liver sausages

Eighteen tins Irish stew

Eight tins steak and kidney

Eighteen tins sausages

Two 4 lb tins brisket

Four tins kidneys

Twelve tins lambs' tongues

Twelve 12 oz Dana pork/ham

Ten tins stewed steak

Eight tins minced beef and onion

Sixteen 12 oz tins corned beef

Eight tins whole chicken

Twelve tins pink salmon

Eight tins herring roes

Twelve tins sardines in oil

Eighteen dozen farm eggs

One dozen large sliced loaves

Three dozen large tins evaporated
  milk

One dozen tins Marvel milk

20 lb granulated sugar
6 lb Demerara sugar
6 lb lump sugar
1 cwt potatoes
Twenty packets Quip
14 lb fresh carrots
Three packets dried onions
Two ½ lb packets lentils
Six tins garden peas
Six tins spinnach
Eight tins tomatoes
Four tins butter beans
Eight tins mixed vegetables
Crate of grapefruit
Crate of oranges
Crate of hard eating apples
Six tins loganberries
Twelve tins mixed fruit salad
Four tins sliced peaches
Four tins pineapple rings
Eight tins grapefruit juice
Sixteen tins orange juice
Six packets apple flakes
Six packets prunes
Twenty packets apricots
Twenty packets dates
12 lb sultanas
12 lb raisins
Six small packets 'Flying Start'
One small packet 'Familia'
Ten packets 'Fruitifort'
Ten large tins Heinz beans
Ten tins Ambrosia rice
Eight tins sweet corn
Eight large tins spaghetti
Four large tins ravioli
Six tins braised beef and onion
Six tins sliced pork
Two mixed fruit puddings
Six treacle puddings

Four ginger puddings
Two sultana puddings
Two fig puddings
Six large tins Heinz tomato soup
Six tins chicken soup
Six tins lentil soup
Six tins mulligatawny soup
Six tins mushroom soup
Twelve chicken cubes
Four tins country vegetable soup
Four tins oxtail soup
Four packets dried green pea soup
Four packets celery soup
Four packets Florida vegetable soup
Nine 2 lb tins marmalade
Six 1 lb jars honey
Four 1 lb jars strawberry jam
Four 1 lb jars raspberry jam
Four 1 lb jars plum jam
Four 1 lb jars apricot jam
Six 2 lb tins golden syrup
Four tins Tetley teabags
One dozen 2s 8d tins Nescafé
Two 10½ lb slabs H.P. cake
Six 2s 6d H.P. Madeira cakes
Five packets digestive biscuits
Five packets ginger biscuits
Five packets Garibaldi biscuits
Five packets Bath Oliver biscuits
Five packets Petit Beurre biscuits
Eight packets cream crackers
Two tins custard
Four tins Green Label curry paste
Four jars pickled onions
Six large bottles Heinz tomato
  ketchup
Eight tins sauerkraut
Twenty tins butter
10 lb fresh butter
Four quarts Saladin corn oil

Three 2½-lb. Edam cheeses
15 lb New Zealand Cheddar
    cheese
One whole Gouda cheese
    (10 lb 9 oz)
Four dozen Cadbury's fruit and
    nut chocolate
Four dozen Cadbury's milk
    chocolate
Four dozen Cadbury's Bournville
    chocolate
Twelve packets Uncle Ben's Rice
Three medium tins Ovaltine
Three tins drinking chocolate
Two ½ lb tins cocoa
Two tins Cerebos salt
Four large tubes mustard
2 oz pepper
Three 4s 6d jars Green Label
    chutney
Eight 4 oz jars Marmite
One 16 oz jar Marmite
Four dozen Oxo cubes
Six bottles Rose's lime juice
One gross matches
Eight Jeyes pads

Three cans Jeyes fluid
Two rolls of foil
Three kitchen rolls
One air freshener
Two large containers Fairy Liquid
Two dozen packets Ryvita
Four dozen packets Ryebread
Six packets chocolate Oliver
    biscuits
One dozen ginger cakes
One dozen tins Lyons pure coffee
One dozen bottles Ribena
One 4s Oteg (for preserving eggs)
4 lb whole almonds
4 lb halved walnuts
Catering milk granules
Twelve tins potatoes
Six tins runner beans
2 lb pearl barley
Six small bottles pure lemon juice
3 lb pork sausages
Two cucumbers
4 lb fresh tomatoes
Six fillet steaks
Two Magnum Lux Flakes
7 lb slab cake

We added little to these supplies in the Faeroes or Iceland, except for bread. In Greenland, we were able to buy various Danish canned products, particularly bacon and ham, which came in very useful. For the short passage from Nova Scotia to Martha's Vineyard, we lived mainly on fresh food obtained at Halifax, Nova Scotia. The stores listed above provided our basic supplies throughout the voyage.

On the whole, our forecasting was good. Our most serious underestimate was of soft drinks – lime juice, Ribena, etc. These were in demand by everybody throughout the voyage, and we could have used twice the quantity we took. Hot lemonade and hot Ribena proved extremely comforting on coming off watch in severe weather – this was a use that we did not foresee. Chutney was popular, and we suffered from the breaking of two of our bottles of chutney in one storm quite early in the voyage. We should have done better to take no glass bottles or glass jars of anything, but it is not easy to obtain some things except in glass. Biscuits were a constant standby, and we had about enough, although as things turned out, it would have been better to have cut down on some of the other varieties, and to have doubled or trebled our supplies of Garibaldi biscuits. We underestimated our consumption of coffee, and over-estimated our consumption of tea: we were able to make up our supply of coffee when we reached the weather ship on which we called in mid-ocean. As I have made clear in the text, we grossly under-estimated our need for kitchen paper.

APPENDIX VII

Bibliography

The best bibliography I know of books and articles relating to the Norse discovery and settlement of North America is that compiled by Captain J. Kr. Tornöe and published in his *Columbus in the Arctic? And the Vineland Literature* (Bokcentralen, Oslo 1, Norway). Some of the works he lists, however, go back beyond the eighteenth century, and others may be out of print and hard to obtain; it is a scholar's bibliography rather than a list of books for the general reader. But it is a notable compilation, and anyone embarking seriously on Vinland studies must certainly consult it. The following brief bibliography may be helpful as a starting point to more detailed studies:

The Vinland Map and the Tartar Relation, R. A. Skelton, Thomas E. Marston and George D. Painter (Yale University Press).
The Vinland Sagas: the Norse Discovery of America, Magnus Magnusson and Herman Palsson (Penguin Classics).
The Norse Atlantic Saga. Being the Norse Voyages of Discovery and Settlement to Iceland, Greenland, America, Professor Gwyn Jones (Oxford).
Norsemen before Columbus, J. Kr. Tornöe (Allen and Unwin).
Columbus in the Arctic? And the Vineland Literature, J. Kr. Tornöe (Oslo).
Lodestone and Evening Star, Ian Cameron (Hodder and Stoughton).
Northwest to Fortune, Vilhjalmar Stefansson (Allen and Unwin).
The Norse Discoveries of America. The Wineland Sagas translated and discussed, G. M. Gathorne-Hardy (Oxford).

West Viking, Farley Mowat (Little, Brown and Co.).

The Ship, Björn Landström (Allen and Unwin).

Faeroerne I Farver, Carlo Andersen (E. Wangels Forlag, Copenhagen).

The Atlantic Islands, Kenneth Williamson (Collins).

These Fragile Outposts, Barbara Blau Chamberlain (published for the American Museum of Natural History by the Natural History Press, New York).

Cape Cod, Martha's Vineyard and Nantucket, Frances Blake (Doubleday and Co.).

The following are the references for statements of fact made in my own book:

CHAPTER 1

Announcement of the Vinland map, the *Guardian*, October 11, 1965.

CHAPTER 2

Bjarni Herjolfsson's voyage, Magnusson and Palsson, *The Vinland Sagas*, Tornöe, *Norsemen before Columbus*.

History of Eirik the Red, Magnusson and Palsson, *The Vinland Sagas*.

Visit of Bishop Eirik Gnupson, Papal Legate, to Vinland in 1117. *The Vinland Map and Tartar Relation*.

CHAPTER 3

Navigation from Greenland to North America. *The Arctic Pilot* (British Admiralty), British Admiralty Charts, Danish Charts.

Singlehanded Transatlantic Race. Francis Chichester, *The Lonely Sea and the Sky*, J. R. L. Anderson, *The Greatest Race in the World*.

Transmission of pictures by radio from *Rehu Moana*, the *Guardian*, June 6, 1963. Official statement by the Post Office, London, June 6, 1963. Pictures from a ship at sea were transmitted by the Australian Post Office from the Press launch *Koolania*, during the visit of the Queen and the Duke of Edinburgh to Australia in March 1963, but conditions were not strictly comparable.

CHAPTER 4

Departure of *Griffin* from Dover, arrival at Scarborough, departure from Scarborough, the *Guardian*, April 28, April 30, May 3, 1966.

CHAPTER 6

The Faeroes. *North Sea Pilot*, Vol. I. Kenneth Williamson, *The Atlantic Islands*. C. Anderson, *Faeroerne I Furver*.

CHAPTER 11
Frederikshaab. *Arctic Pilot*, Vol. III.
Greenland generally. Personal conversations. Martin Lindsay, *Those Greenland Days*, *Arctic Pilot*, Vols. II and III.

CHAPTER 12
Evidence for navigational reconstruction. *Graenlendinga Saga, Eirik's Saga* (Magnusson and Palsson translation). Ian Cameron, *Lodestone and Evening Star*. Theories of J. Kr. Tornöe in works already mentioned. *Icelandic Annals* referred to by several writers. 'No reference to Greenland in the Icelandic Annals after 1410.' *The Vinland Sagas*, p. 22.
The *doegr*. Personal communication from A. N. Ryan, Liverpool University to the author, R. Morekin in *Bergens Sjofartsmuseum Arshefte* (1964).

CHAPTER 14
Theories of Norse settlement in Newfoundland. Helge Ingstad, *National Geographic Magazine*, and *Landet under Leidarstjernen*; Farley Mowat, *West Viking*.
Adam of Bremen. *Gesta Hamnaburgensis ecclesiae pontificum*, 1075.
Theories of 'dagmalastad' and 'eÿktarstad'. Magnusson and Palsson, Tornöe, op. cit.
Discovery of Newfoundland by Adalbrand and Thorvald in 1285, and Landa-Rolf settlement, *Icelandic Annals*, *Columbus in the Arctic*, Tornöe, L. A. Gebhardi, *Kongeret Norges historie*, Odense 1777–78 (Tornöe's bibliography).
Appreciation of Leif Eiriksson's navigational problems on weathering Cape Race. Peter Haward, personal communication to the author.

CHAPTER 15
Stewart MacLeod's article in 'Weekend Magazine'. *Weekend Magazine* (Canada), August 27, 1966.

CHAPTER 16
Report of *Griffin*'s arrival at Edgartown, Martha's Vineyard, *Vineyard Gazette*, June 29, 1966.

CHAPTER 17
Naming of Martha's Vineyard in 1602 by Bartholomew Gosnold. *Encyclopaedia Britannica*, and various works of local history.
Moscow Radio broadcast and finding of new correspondence between Columbus and Queen Isabella of Spain. *Aftenposten*, Oslo, October 12, 1959, *New York Herald Tribune*, October 2, 1959 (Tornöe's bibliography).

Corte-Real expedition and other Portugese-Danish voyages in the North Atlantic. Ian Cameron, *Lodestone and Evening Star*, Tornöe, op. cit.

Eighteenth-century Danish claim to sovereignty over North America. Tormod Torfaeus, *History of Denmark and Norway*, 1695–1705 (Tornöe's bibliography).

Pope Alexander III's letter conveying dispensation for requirements of legal marriage in Vinland (Martha's Vineyard?). *Latinske dokument til Norske historie fram til ar 1204*. Eriik Vandrik (Tornöe's bibliography).